S0-BFA-403

DUTCH FOR TRAVELLERS

Hans Hoogendoorn

Brigitte Kristel

Bob Ordish

© Royal Dutch Touring Club ANWB, The Hague

All rights reserved.
This book has been written with the utmost care. The ANWB cannot be held responsible, though, for the results of any inaccuracies or faults this book may contain.

ISBN 90-18-00267-4

First edition 1993

English text: Brigitte Kristel and Bob Ordish (S. Brouwer Vertalingen, Amsterdam)
Grammar and background information: RomText, The Hague
Cover design: Studio ANWB
Cartography: DigiKart, The Hague
Illustrations: Hilbert Bolland
Pictographs: Arie Hogendoorn
Desktop Publishing: PS Holland, Amsterdam
Lithography: De Vries, Eefde
Printed by: Habo Da Costa, Vianen

CONTENTS

INTRODUCTION

How to use this phrase book

The various sections of this book each describe particular,
standard situations that will offer you the opportunity to try out
your Dutch or require you to do so: arrival in the Netherlands or
Belgium, at your hotel, travelling around, eating out, shopping,
seeing the sights, filling up with petrol, possibly visiting a doctor.
The sections - each marked by a small pictogram - then go on to
give a large number of phrases and sentences. These are
grouped in blocks of three lines: the first line supplies the English
sentence (**bold**), the second the Dutch equivalent (blue) and
the third gives as accurate a rendering as possible of the Dutch
pronunciation. In some of the examples the English sentence is
preceded by the symbol (◄), indicating that this is the reply or
question you can expect to receive from the Dutch person you
are talking to. The sections also provide a brief English-Dutch
vocabulary relating to the specific situation they describe.
Very often you can take different words from the vocabulary and
slot them into the sentences shown above. You will find a more
extensive vocabulary at the back.
We wish you every success in your attempts to master the Dutch
pronunciation. And don't be put off by the widespread Dutch
habit of immediately responding to a foreign accent by replying
in English. This is well meant but can seriously hinder your
progress in the language. If you insist on continuing in Dutch,
though, people are sure to respect your efforts. After all, actually
speaking a language is the only way of learning it.

Holland or the Netherlands?

Although foreigners often refer to the country as 'Holland' its
official name is 'the Netherlands' - rather in the way that people
say 'England' when they mean 'Britain'. It's only comparatively
recently that the Dutch themselves started to make the distinction

in everyday speech, and this even concerns the name of the language itself. For English speakers there is no problem - we just use the term 'Dutch'. The Dutch themselves, however, have two terms: the now generally accepted *Nederlands*, and *Hollands*. The latter is somewhat dated but still heard. For a closer understanding of the distinction we need to go back in history. As early as the Middle Ages the seventeen earldoms (*graafschappen*), duchies (*hertogdommen*) and bishoprics (*bisdommen*) located in the delta formed by the three great rivers - the Rhine (*Rijn*), Meuse (*Maas*) and Scheldt (*Schelde*) - were known as 'the Netherlands' (*de Nederlanden*, meaning 'the low lands'). Although self-governing, politically these territories were strongly influenced by one or other of their powerful neighbours, the German Empire and France. The existence of these two spheres of influence gave rise to marked cultural and later also religious differences between the northern and southern Netherlands (with the Rhine marking the boundary).

Around 1500 the Netherlands came under the administration of the German Habsburg dynasty, which ruled much of medieval Europe for centuries. After the death of the great emperor, Charles V - 'Charles the Wise' - the Netherlands devolved to his son, the king of Spain. By now, however, Protestantism had gained a firm hold in the northern Netherlands and the chasm with Catholic Spain was unbridgeable. This, along with conflicts of commercial interest, triggered the eighty-year war of independence (1568-1648) against the Spaniards. The struggle was waged mainly by the northern Netherlands, with only part of the south making common cause. Following recognition of the independence of the north and their southern partners, the Republic of the United Netherlands (*Republiek der Verenigde Nederlanden*) was set up. The Dutch themselves quickly started to refer to the new state as *Nederland*, using the singular form rather than the plural *Nederlanden* that is the basis of the English term 'Netherlands'. The earldom of *Holland* (now consisting of the provinces of North and South Holland) played a leading economic and military role in all this, partly because of the many refugees who fled there from the south. When Holland then went on to become a major trading and naval power, for most foreigners its name became synonymous with 'the Netherlands' (*Nederland*). When Napoleon reunited that part of the southern Netherlands which had remained loyal to the Habsburgs - the lion's share - with the north in 1806, he therefore decreed the name 'Holland' for the new kingdom that was to be proclaimed. However, following the Congress of Vienna in 1815 (held after Napoleon's defeat at Waterloo), the plural term 'Kingdom of the Netherlands' (*Koninkrijk der Nederlanden*) was opted for again although the country's borders were left virtually unchanged. The southern Netherlands, separated from the north for too long to feel comfortable within the union, broke away in 1831 to form the new state of 'Belgium' (*België*). The north retained its name, with the Dutch continuing to refer to *Nederland* and almost all foreigners to the familiar-sounding *Holland*. Nor do the Dutch themselves generally have any objection to this - interestingly, they also use the term when they are abroad. In the English edition of this book, we use 'Holland' and 'the Netherlands' interchangeably.

Introduction to the Dutch language

Dutch is the official language of *the Netherlands*. It is also one of the two official languages of *Belgium* where, very roughly, it is spoken north of an east-to-west line going through Brussels (French is spoken elsewhere - see map). Frisian (*Fries*) is officially recognised as a second language in the Dutch province of *Friesland* (and it really is a language in its own right, not just a dialect of Dutch!); German also enjoys this status in the extreme east of Belgium. The Brussels region is officially bilingual (Dutch and French); in the environs of the Belgian capital, and in individual towns and villages along the 'linguistic frontier', the official language is determined by the local authority. This is a situation that has often given rise to discord between the rival language communities.

Main languages
- Dutch
- German
- French
- bilingual : Dutch and French
- Luxemburgish (French widely used)

Mixed usage of languages
- Dutch in France
- Dutch in French-speaking Belgium
- French in Dutch-speaking Belgium
- Friesian and Dutch
- German-speaking Belgium
- German in French-speaking Belgium
- French, Dutch and German

Groningen

Saxon dialects

Haarlem
Amsterdam

Den Haag
(The Hague)
Utrecht

Holland dialects

Rotterdam

NETHERLANDS

*Brabant and
East-Flemish
dialects*

GERMANY

Middelburg

Brugge
(Bruges)

Antwerpen
(Antwerp)

*Zeeland and
West-Flemish
dialects*

Gent
(Ghent)

*Limburg
dialects*

Brussel
(Brussels)

BELGIUM

Liège

LUXEMBURG

*Lëtzeburg
(Luxemburg)*

F R A N C E

Dutch speaking regions

Dutch is the language of administration and frequently of education in Surinam (*Suriname*) the former colony of Dutch Guiana in South America (other languages, including English, are also widely spoken there). The same applies to the self-governing overseas territories of *Aruba* and the Netherlands Antilles (*Nederlandse Antillen*), in the Caribbean. Finally, there is also a tiny Dutch-speaking minority in French Flanders, in the extreme northwest corner of France. All told, Dutch is used by about twenty-five million people as their everyday language of communication.

The Dutch spoken in Belgium is frequently referred to as Flemish (*Vlaams*). This gives a somewhat misleading impression.

The language of government, the media and literature is Dutch, hardly differing from the Dutch spoken in the Netherlands. There are innumerable dialects in Belgium, though, including Western Flemish (*Westvlaams*) and Eastern Flemish (*Oostvlaams*). However, the state border between the Netherlands and Belgium does not mark a rigid border between dialects, which merge into one another gradually. 'Flemish' therefore has more validity as a cultural and historical concept than as a linguistic term.

Like English, Dutch is a Germanic language. In other words, it stems from what linguists refer to as 'Proto-Germanic', the prehistoric unrecorded language that is the ancestor of all the languages in this group. The Middle Ages gradually saw the development of three distinct branches: North Germanic (consisting of the Scandinavian languages and their dialects), East Germanic (now completely extinct) and West Germanic. The latter gradually divided into two subbranches: the North Sea group, comprising English and Friesian, and the Continental group with Dutch and German. The standard German spoken today crystallised largely out of the 'High German' dialects of southern Germany and the Alpine region. The Low German dialects of northern Germany, which are closely related to Dutch and share the same medieval origins, were gradually displaced and do not have official status.

Dutch emigrants and traders spread the use of their language throughout the colonies. The Dutch spoken by colonists in South Africa gave rise to today's *Afrikaans*, which Dutch people find fairly easy to understand.

If you've ever tackled German you'll be pleasantly surprised by Dutch grammar, which is considerably less complicated. Although there are many exceptions to the rules these tend to crop up frequently, so if you make the effort you do get the hang of the exceptions after a while. The greatest obstacle is probably the pronunciation, and some Dutch sounds (g, ch, sch, ui) have no real equivalent in English (Scots will probably have the least trouble, with the likes of 'loch', etc). Dutch spelling can also be rather tricky. One thing that will strike you about written Dutch is the profusion of double vowels - aa, ee, oo, uu. These always indicate a 'long' sound; single vowels are short, except when at the end of a syllable.

	singular	plural	
(short)	kap	kap-pen	(hood)
(long)	kaap	ka-pen	(cape)
(short)	zon	zon-nen	(sun)
(long)	zoon	zo-nen	(son)

We provide more such examples in our look at Dutch grammar. For the sentences and vocabularies shown in this book we mark the syllable that has to be stressed in **bold** (condensed) type since there is no single rule on this.

BASIC GRAMMAR

Gender and articles

There are three genders in the Dutch language: masculine, feminine and neuter. In actual practice hardly a distinction is made between masculine and feminine words. The same definite article applies to both: **de** (both singular and plural). Singular neuter words carry the definite article **het**, plural neuter words carry **de**. The indefinite article (singular only) is always **een** (in spoken language usually shortened to **'n**):

	definite article	*indefinite article*
mscl.:	**de** man - the man	**een** man - a man
fem.:	**de** vrouw - the woman	**een** vrouw - a woman
neut.:	**het** kind - the child	**een** kind - a child

The Dutch article is never inflected, with the exception of a limited number of traditional, archaic expressions. In the genitive case the preposition van (of) is added, in the dative case the preposition aan (to) or voor (for) may be added:
Het huis **van de** man - The man's house
Het huis **van de** vrouw - The woman's house
Het huis **van het** kind - The child's house

De man geeft een boek **aan het** kind (more commonly used: geeft **het** kind een boek) - The man gives a book to the child

De vrouw koopt **voor het** kind een boek (less commonly used: De vrouw koopt **het** kind een boek) - The woman buys the child a book

In the case of proper names and a number of nouns the relation of association or ownership can be indicated by adding -s (words ending in a vowel get 's, except words ending in -e).
Monica's fiets - Monica's bicycle
Nederlands hoofdstad - the capital of Holland
Vaders huis - father's house

Diminutives

The diminutive of a noun can be formed by adding the affix **-tje**; diminutives are **always neuter**:
(het) wiel   (het) wiel**tje**   (the small) wheel

Sometimes the last consonant is doubled and followed by -e:

| (de) kar | (het) kar**retje** | (the small) cart |
| (de) bal | (het) bal**letje** | (the small) ball |

or the **t** is left out:
(de) fiets - (het) fiets**je** - (the small) bicycle

Diminutives of words ending in **-m** are often formed by adding **-pje** (de boom - het boom**pje** - the (small) tree, but: de kam - het kam**metje** - the (small) comb).

Plural

There are three plural noun forms. We start with the most commonly used and work our way down:

1 *plural -en*
| (de) vrouw | (de) vrouw**en** | | (the) woman | (the) women |

Because of the pronunciation rules the final consonant may be doubled or a double vowel can be reduced to a single one:
| (de) man | (de) ma**nnen** (not: manen) | (the) man | (the) men |
| (de) straat | (de) stra**ten** (not: straaten) | (the) street(s) |

There are various plural forms for words ending in **-s**: mens - mens**en** (human being - people), huis - hui**zen** (house - houses), bus - bu**ssen** (bus - busses).

Some words have an irregular plural ending (het kind - de kind**eren** - the child(ren); het ei - de ei**eren** - the egg(s)) or an entirely irregular plural form (de stad - de steden - the city - the cities; het schip - de sch**epen** - the ship(s)).

2 plural *-s*
The plural form of the following word groups is made by adding **-s** instead of **-en**:
a. words ending in an unstressed **-el**, **-em** or **-er**
b. diminutives
c. foreign words ending in a vowel.

(de) lepel	(de) lepel**s**	(the) spoon(s)
(de) bodem	(de) bodem**s**	(the) bottom(s)
(de) meester	(de) meester**s**	(the) master(s)
(het) fietsje	(de) fietsje**s**	(the) small bicycle(s)
(de) auto	(de) auto**'s***	(the) car(s)

* as a result of pronunciation rules the letter **-s** is preceded by an apostrophe if the word ends in a vowel (camera's, ski's, foto's, menu's) unless the final vowel is an **e** (dames ladies).

3. other irregular endings

There are many words of Greek or Latin origin in the Dutch language; these have their own plural endings, usually taken from the original language:

(het) museum	(de) musea	(the) museum(s)
(het) centrum	(de) centra	(the) centre(s)
(de) basis	(de) bases	(the) base(s)

The adjective

The adjective takes the ending -e except when the noun is singular neuter and preceded by the indefinite article;

de oude man	een oude man	de oude mannen
the old man	an old man	the old men
het kleine kind	een klein kind	de kleine kinderen
the small child	a small child	the small children

A double vowel is reduced to a single one (groot: de grote vrouw - large: the large woman), and, again, the final consonant may be doubled (vol: de volle maan - full: the full moon).

The degrees of comparison are formed by adding the affixes -er and -st:

oud	ouder	oudst:
de oude man	de oudere man	de oudste man
the old man	the elder/older man	the eldest/oldest man
klein	kleiner	kleinst:
het kleine kind	het kleinere kind	het kleinste kind
the small child	the smaller child	the smallest child

The final consonant is often doubled in the comparative: fel - feller - felst (bright), krom - krommer - kromst (crooked). Words ending in -r receive an additional d: zwaar - zwaarder - zwaarst (heavy). The -s at the end of a word is often changed to a z: wijs - wijzer - wijst (wise). A number of adjectives, in particular long ones, do not take affixes. In those case the comparative and superlative cases are formed by adding the words meer and meest: gebruikelijk - **meer** gebruikelijk - **meest** gebruikelijk (usual).

Important adjectives which have irregular degrees of comparison are:

veel - meer - meest	(many - more - most)
goed - beter - best	(good - better - best)
weinig - minder - minst	(little - less - least)

The comparative degree is followed by the word dan (than). When both parts are equal the construction even/net zo ... als (just as ... as) is used:

De man is groter **dan** de vrouw   (The man is taller than his wife)
De man is **even** groot (**net zo** groot) **als** de vrouw   (The man is just as tall as his wife)

The adverb

Adverbs are not inflected but also have degrees of comparison:
De auto rijdt snel - The car rides fast
De auto rijdt snel**ler** (dan ...)
De auto rijdt **het** snel**st**

Het kind tekent mooi - The child is drawing beautifully
Het kind tekent mooi**er** (dan ...)
Het kind tekent **het** mooi**st**

The personal pronoun

Many personal pronouns have two versions: one (a) is used in written language and in stressed positions, whereas the other (b) is used in colloquial, everyday speech and in unstressed positions.

	nom.		gen.		dat.		acc.	
	a	b	a	b	a	b	a	b
singular								
1	ik	'k	mijn	m'n	mij	me	mij	me
2	jij	je	jouw	je	jou	je	jou	je
	u	-	uw	-	u	-	u	-
3	hij	-	zijn	z'n	hem	'm	hem	'm
	zij	ze	haar	d'r	haar	'r	haar	'r
	het	't	zijn	z'n	het	't	het	't
plural								
1	wij	we	ons	-	ons	-	ons	-
2	jullie	-	jullie	-	jullie	-	jullie	-
	u	-	uw	-	u	-	u	-
3	zij	ze	hun	-	hun/hen	ze	hun	ze

U is a polite form of address, that can be used both in the 2nd person singular and plural. Whether you have to use the polite **u** or the more informal **jij** depends on your relationship with the person you speak to. When you are not sure which form to use, use **u** and wait for the other person to induce you to say **jij** (sg.) or **jullie** (pl.). The possessive pronoun

haar (her) has an unstressed form (d'r in the genitive case, 'r in the dative and accusative cases), but these forms are restricted to colloquial speech only. Hun en hen (them) can also apply to women (plural); the formal form **haar** is slightly outdated: De vrouwen eisen **haar** rechten op (The women demand their rights).

There are three ways in which personal pronouns can be made into possessive pronouns (both singular and plural):

a.   You may use the above mentioned genitive form.
b.   You can use the dative form, preceded by van.
c.   (less common) You can use the personal pronoun in a substantive way, adding -e.

a.   Dit is **mijn jouw/uw zijn ons jullie hun** huis
      This is my/your/his/our/your/their house
b.   Dit huis is **van mij jou/u hem ons jullie hen**
      This house is mine/yours/his/ours/yours/theirs
c.   Dit huis is **het mijne jouwe/uwe zijne onze hunne**

Except in the case of c. the possessive pronoun is never inflected. Ons (our) is an exception: it is almost always inflected to onze (except when a singular neuter word is used or when it is preceded by van).

Dit is **onze** auto   Dit zijn **onze** auto's
This is our car   These are our cars
Dit is **ons** kind   Dit zijn **onze** kinderen
This is our child   These are our children
Dit huis is **van ons**   Deze huizen zijn van ons
This house is ours   These houses are ours

As in all Germanic languages the possessive pronoun is guided by the gender of the owner and never of the objects owned. When the gender of a person or animal is known, a clear distinction is made between zijn (his) and haar (her):
De man rijdt in **zijn** auto - The man drives his car (the owner is male)
De vrouw pakt **haar** fiets - The woman takes her bicycle (the owner is female)
De man neemt de vrouw **haar** fiets af - The man deprives the woman of her bicycle (the subject is male, but the owner of the bike is female)
Het paard loopt naast **haar** veulen - The horse is walking next to her filly (it may be assumed that the horse is female)

As hardly a distinction can be made between masculine and feminine objects one almost always uses zijn (his): Het land en **zijn** inwoners (the country and its inhabitants). Occasionally a 'possessive' inanimate object is regarded as feminine: De stad en **haar** monumenten (the city and its - lit. her - monuments).

The demonstrative pronoun

There are different demonstrative pronouns for persons and things, depending on the distance to the speaker:

	masculine/feminine:	*neuter:*
close by:	**deze** man (this man)	**dit** huis (this house)
	deze mannen (these)	**deze** huizen (these)
further away:	**die** man (that)	**dat** huis (that)
	die mannen (those)	**die** huizen (those)

The relative pronoun

There are different relative pronouns for persons (and animals) and inanimate objects:
persons

Nom.:	De boer **die** daar werkt (msc./fem.) - The farmer who works there
	Het meisje **dat** hier woont (neut.) - The girl who lives here
Gen.:	De slager **van wie** ik dit vlees kocht* - The butcher I bought the meat from
Dat.:	De man **aan wie**** ik geld gaf - The man I gave money to
Acc.:	De hond **die** hij sloeg (msc./fem.) - The dog he beat
	Het kind **dat** zij meebracht (neut.) - The child she brought with her

inanimate objects

Nom.:	De auto **die** hier staat (msc./fem.) - The car which stands here
	Het huis **dat** aan zee ligt (neut.) - The house which is situated near the sea
Gen.:	De fiets **waarvan** het licht kapot is - The bicycle of which the lamp is broken
Dat.:	De straat **waarin***** ik loop - The street I walk in
Acc.:	De stad **die** ik heb bezocht - The city I visited
	Het land **dat** ik binnenkom - The country which I enter

* there is also an older, less commonly used genetive form:
De slager **wiens** vlees ik kocht - The butcher whose meat I bought (masc.)
De vrouw **wier** dochter ik trouwde - The woman whose daughter I married (fem.)
** also: van wie, voor wie, in wie, op wie, etc.
*** also: waarvan, waarvoor, waarop, waaraan, etc.

The interrogative pronoun

Again there are different pronouns for persons and inanimate objects:
persons

Nom.:	**Wie** heeft dit gedaan? - Who did this?
Gen.:	**Van wie** is deze jas? (archaic: **Wiens** jas is dit?) - Whose coat is this?
Dat.:	**Aan wie** is die brief geschreven? - Whom did you write this letter to?
Acc.:	**Wie** hebt u daar gezien? - Who did you see there?

inanimate objects

Nom.: **Wat** is er gebeurd? - What happened?
Gen.: **Waarvan** is dit alles betaald? - What did you pay this with? (lit.: of which)
Dat.: **Waaraan** moeten we nog denken? - What do we have to think of?
Acc.: **Wat** hebt u gekocht? - What did you buy?

In everyday speech the forms waarvan, waaraan, waarop, waarin etc. are often divided in two:
Waar is dit alles **van** betaald?
Waar moeten we nog **aan** denken?

The verb

In Dutch there are:
a. weak verbs (the past tense is formed by conjugation);
b. strong verbs (the past tense is formed by a change of vowels);
c. irregular verbs.

The **present tense** consists of the stem of the verb, (usually) followed by an ending:

present tense - stem

rijden	rijd	(to drive - drive)
zingen	zing	(to sing - sing)
maken	m**aa**k (!)	(to make - make)
leven	**lee**f *	(to live - live)

ik	rijd	zing	maak	leef
jij/u	rij**dt****	zing**t**	maak**t**	lee**ft**
hij/zij/het	rij**dt**	zing**t**	maak**t**	lee**ft**
wij	rij**den**	zing**en**	maken	le**ven**
jullie***	rij**den**	zing**en**	maken	le**ven**
zij	rij**den**	zing**en**	maken	le**ven**

* The stem of a verb can never end in **v** or **z**: leven - lee**f** (to live), verhuizen - verhui**s** (to move).
** When the 2nd person singular is the subject of an interrogative sentence, the ending disappears: rijd jij? (do you drive?) zing jij? (do you sing?)
*** A verb following **u** is conjugated the same way both in singular and plural: u rijdt.
The simplification of vowels (aa-a, ee-e, oo-o, uu-u) and the doubling of consonants again occur in accordance with the rules of pronunciation.

When the stem already ends in -t, no extra t is added in the 2nd and 3rd person singular; in plural the ending -ten is added:
ik zit - jij zit - hij zit - wij zit**ten** - jullie zit**ten** - zij zit**ten** (I sit, etc.)

The **past tense** and the **past perfect** are conjugated in various ways, depending on the type of verb (weak, strong or irregular).

Weak verbs take the ending -te(n) when the verb stem ends in -**ch**, -**f**, -**k**, -**p** or -**s**; in all other cases the ending -**de(n)** is used:

infinitive	*stem*				
la**ch**en	la**ch** (to laugh)				
bo**ff**en	bo**f** (to be lucky)				
pa**kk**en.	pa**k** (to take)				
ho**p**en	hoo**p** (!) (to hope)				
vi**ss**en	vi**s** (to fish)				

ik/jij/u/hij/zij/het(I/you/he/she/it)
lach**te**	bof**te**	pak**te**	hoop**te**	vis**te**	leer**de**

wij/jullie/zij (we/you/they)
lach**ten**	bof**ten**	pak**ten**	hoop**ten**	vis**ten**	leer**den**

Although a **z** or **v** in the infinitive changes into **s** or **f** in the verb stem, the ending will still be **de**: verhuizen - verhui**s** - verhui**sde** (to move); leven - lee**f** - lee**fde** (to live).
The past participle is formed by putting **ge**- in front of the verb stem and, according to the same rules mentioned above, -**t** or -**d** at the end: **ge**bof**t**, **ge**pak**t**, **ge**hoop**t**, **ge**vis**t**, **ge**leer**d**, **ge**leef**d**. Verbs prefixed by **be**-, **er**-, **her**-, **ont**- and **ver**- do not take **ge**- in the past participle: verhuis**d**.

In the case of strong verbs a vowel change takes place (and the -**t** or -**d** ending is omitted); the past participle is formed by adding **ge**- to the verb stem (in which the vowel may change) and putting -**en** at the end. For example:

pres. tense	*past tense*	*past part.*
(to drive, ride)		
ik ri**j**d	reed	**ge**red**en**
hij ri**j**dt	reed	
wij ri**j**den	reden	

(to walk)

ik **loop**	liep	**gelopen**
hij **loopt**	liep	
wij **lopen**	liepen	

(to find)

ik **vind**	vond	**gevonden**
hij **vindt**	vond	
wij **vinden**	vonden	

(to sit)

ik **zit**	zat	**gezeten**
hij **zit**	zat	
wij **zitten**	zaten	

In many dictionaries you will find a list of the most important strong verbs. Which vowel change may take place is not dictated by clear rules (verbs which have an **ij** in the stem are often strong; in those cases the **ij** is replaced by **e(e)**: rijden - reed - gereden (to drive, ride), blijven - bleef - gebleven (to stay), prijzen - prees - geprezen (to praise), etc.

Irregular verbs are often characterised by a vowel change in the past tense; sometimes the conjugation is totally deviant. The past participle may end both in **-t** and **-en**. We will give a few examples.

The auxiliaries are always irregular (as in most other languages):

	zijn	**hebben**	**mogen**	**kunnen**	**zullen**
	to be	to have	may	can	shall/will
present tense					
ik	ben	heb	mag	kan	zal
jij	bent	hebt	mag	kan	zal
hij	is	heeft	mag	kan	zal
wij	zijn	hebben	mogen	kunnen	zullen
past tense					
ik	was	had	mocht	kon	zou
jij	was	had	mocht	kon	zou
hij	was	had	mocht	kon	zou
wij	waren	hadden	mochten	konden	zouden

Th **present perfect** and the **past perfect** are formed by using either zijn (to be) or hebben (to have):

Ik **heb** een boek **gelezen**   I have read a book
Jij **bent** naar Amsterdam **gereisd**   You have traveled to Amsterdam

The **future tense** is formed by using the auxiliary **zullen** (shall/will):
Ik **zal**/Wij **zullen** morgen komen   I/we shall come tomorrow
Ik **zou**/Wij **zouden** morgen komen   I/we would have come tomorrow

RULES OF PRONUNCIATION

Vowels

a, aa	short a, transcribed as **a**, is pronounced like **a** in father; long a (before the end of a syllable) and aa are pronounced and transcribed like English **ah**
au	is pronounced very much like **ou** in loud and transcribed as such
e, ee	e, when short, is pronounced like **e** in bet and transcribed as **eh**; e, when long, and **ee**, like **ay** in say and transcribed as such; in unstressed syllables e is pronounced like **er** in other and transcribed as **e**
eeu(w)	this combination of vowels is pronounced, very approximately, like **ay** in say, followed by **oo** in moon, so Dutch leeuw (lion) is transcribed as la**yoo**
ei	ei in Dutch represents the same sound as Dutch ij and is a cross between **eye** and **ee** in sheep; the sound is transcribed as **aiy**, so Dutch trein (train) is pronounced as tr**aiy**n
eu	as in French 'peu' and represented by the symbol **ø**: Dutch leuk (nice) is pronounced lø k
i	when short, like English **i** in hit; when long (before the end of a syllable), like **ee** in bee
ie	like long **i** (see above)
ieu(w)	like **ee** in bee, followed by **oo** in moon, so nieuw is pronounced n**eeoo**
ij	represents the same sound as Dutch ei (see above); this letter may have a separate status in dictionaries and be found between x and z, but is usually seen as a combination of i and j and therefore to be found under i
o, oo	when short, like **o** in drop; when long, like **oa** in road
oe	like **oo** in moon, so Dutch koe (cow) is pronounced k**oo**
ou	pronounced like **ou** in loud
u, uu	short **u**: midway between **ew** in new and **u** in bus, and transcribed as **u**; long **u** (at the end of a syllable) and **uu** as Scottish **ui** in Muir or **u** in cure, and transcribed as **ew** (as in new), so Dutch muur (wall) is pronounced as m**ew**r
ui	approximates to **ow** in Scottish now, transcribed as **œ**, so Dutch huis (house) is pronounced as h**œ**s

Consonants

b   as in English, but at the end of a word pronounced like **p** in hel**p**

c   before a consonant and a, o, u, like **k** in **k**eep; before e and i like **s** in **s**torm

ch   approximates to Scottish **ch** in Lo**ch** and transcribed as **gh**, so Dutch school (school) is transcribed as s**gh**oal

g   pronounced like Dutch and Scottish **ch** (see above), except in a few words of French origin like rage (mania), when g is pronounced like **zh**; in Belgium and the southern parts of the Netherlands the pronunciation of g is softer and less guttural than in Standard Dutch

ng   pronounced like English **ng** in si**ng**

j   like **y** in **y**ear and transcribed as such; in words of French origin like **zh**, for example lits-jumeaux (twin bed): lee-**zh**ewmoa

n   as in English, although in everyday speech the n in verbs ending in -en (i.e. almost all verbs) is often not pronounced at all

r   should be trilled

sch   pronounced like the **s** followed by Dutch **g** or **ch** (see above) except at word ends (usually -isch), when this sound is simply pronounced like **s**, for example fantastisch (fantastic) is pronounced fantastee**s**

t   as in English, but in words ending in -tie pronounced as **ts**, for example politie (police) is transcribed as poalee**ts**ee

th   Dutch **th** is pronounced like English **t**, for example thee (tea) is transcribed as t**a**y

tj   this combination, which mostly occurs in diminutives, is pronounced as English **t** followed by **y**, for example kaartje (ticket) is pronounced kahr**ty**e

v   basically as in English, but often pronounced unvoiced, which means it sounds much like **f**

w   pronounced with the lips less rounded than in English, but essentially like English **v** as in **v**ery.

The syllable that has been printed in **bold** (condensed) type should be stressed. If no syllable has been printed that way, it doesn't matter which syllable is stressed.
If an English word is commonly used in Dutch, we have given no phonetic rendering, but put the English word between inverted commas instead.

SOME BASIC EXPRESSIONS

EVERYDAY WORDS AND PHRASES

yes	ja	yah
no	nee	nay
maybe	misschien	mi**sgheen**
please	alstublieft	alstew**bleeft**
here you are	alstublieft	alstew**bleeft**
thank you	dank u wel*	dank ew wehl
thank you very much	hartelijk dank	**har**telek dank
you're welcome	graag gedaan	ghrahgh ghe**dahn**
excuse me	neemt u mij niet kwalijk	naymt ew maiy neet **kwah**lek
I'm so sorry	het spijt me*	heht spaiyt me

where?	waar?	wahr?
where is/are ....?	waar is/zijn ....?	wahr is/zaiyn ....?
when?	wanneer?	wa**nayr**?
what?	wat?	wat?
how?	hoe?	hoo?
how much?	hoeveel?	hoo**vayl**?
which?	welk(e)?	**wehlk**(e)?
who?	wie?	wee?
why?	waarom?	wahr**om**?
what do you call this?	hoe heet dit?	hoo hayt dit?
what does this mean?	wat betekent dit?	wat be**tay**kent dit?
it's	het is	heht is ....
it's not	het is niet	heht is neet ....
there is/are	er is/zijn	ehr is/zaiyn ....
there is/are no	er is/zijn geen	ehr is/zaiyn ghayn ....
is/are there any ....?	is/zijn er ....?	is/zaiyn ehr ....?
is/are there no ....?	is/zijn er geen ....?	is/zaiyn ehr ghayn ....?

* You will be surprised to hear many people say 'merci' (the French word) for 'dank u' en 'sorry' to express some regret.

PREPOSITIONS, INTERJECTIONS, ETC.

across	over	**oa**ver
after	na	nah
already	al	al
always	altijd	altaiyt
and	en	ehn
anyone	iemand	**ee**mant
at once	dadelijk	**dah**delek
behind	achter	**agh**ter
beneath	onder	**on**der
between	tussen	**tus**sen
down	beneden	be**nay**den
downstairs	omlaag	om**lahgh**
during	tijdens	**taiy**dens
for	voor	voar
from	van	van
here	hier	heer
home	thuis	tœs
in	in	in
(to the) left	links(af)	links(af)
near	dichtbij	dight**baiy**
never	nooit	noayt
next to	naast	nahst
no one, nobody	niemand	**nee**mant
not	niet	neet
on top of ...	op	op
of	van	van
or	of	of
outside	buiten	**bœ**ten
overthere	daar	dahr
(to the) right	rechts(af)	rehghts(af)
since	sinds	sints
somebody	iemand	**ee**mant
soon	spoedig	**spoo**degh
then	dan	dan
through	door	doar
to	naar	nahr
until	tot	tot
up	boven	**boa**ven
upstairs	omhoog	om**hoagh**
with	met	meht

| without | zonder | **zon**der |
| with pleasure | graag | ghrahgh |

A FEW ADJECTIVES

bad	slecht	slehght
beautiful	mooi	moay
better	beter	**bay**ter
cheap	goedkoop	ghoot**koap**
close by	dichtbij	dight**baiy**
closed	dicht	dight
cold	koud	kout
delicious	heerlijk	**hayr**lek
difficult	moeilijk	**mooy**lek
easy	gemakkelijk	ghe**ma**kelek
empty	leeg	laygh
expensive	duur	dewr
far	ver	vehr
free	vrij	vraiy
full	vol	vol
good	goed	ghoot
heavy	zwaar	zwahr
hot	warm	warm
light	licht	light
new	nieuw	neeoo
occupied	bezet	be**zeht**
old	oud	out
open	open	**oa**pen
quick	snel	snehl
right	juist	yœst
slow	langzaam	**lang**zahm
ugly	lelijk	**lay**lek
warm	warm	warm
wrong	verkeerd	ver**kayrt**
worse	slechter	**slehgh**ter
young	jong	yong

LANGUAGE PROBLEMS

I don't speak Dutch
Ik spreek geen Nederlands
ik sprayk ghayn **nay**derlants

I don't understand you
Ik versta u niet
ik ver**stah** ew neet

Could you repeat that for me?
Kunt u dat nog even herhalen?
kunt ew dat nogh **ay**ven hehr**hah**len?

Does anyone here speak English?
Spreekt hier iemand Engels?
spraykt heer **ee**mant **ehng**els?

I'm English
Ik ben Engels
ik behn **ehng**els

I'm Irish
Ik ben Iers
ik behn eers

Dutch is a difficult language
Nederlands is een moeilijke taal
nayderlants is en **mooy**leke tahl

I can't read this
Dit kan ik niet lezen
dit kan ik neet **lay**zen

Could you spell it for me/write it down?
Kunt u het spellen/opschrijven?
kunt ew heht **speh**len/**op**sghraiyven?

I speak only a little Dutch
Ik spreek maar een beetje Nederlands
ik sprayk mahr en **bay**tye **nay**derlants

Could you speak more slowly?
Kunt u wat langzamer praten?
kunt ew wat **lang**zahmer **prah**ten?

Do you speak English?
Spreekt u Engels?
spraykt ew **ehng**els?

I'm foreign (m/f)
Ik ben buitenlander/buitenlandse
ik behn **bœ**tenlander/**bœ**tenlantse

How do you say this in Dutch?
Hoe zeg je dit in het Nederlands?
hoo zehgh ye dit in heht **nay**derlants?

How do you pronounce this?
Hoe spreek je dit uit?
hoo sprayk ye dit œt?

It's going too fast for me
Het gaat mij te snel
heht ghaht maiy te snehl

Could you translate this for me?
Kunt u dit voor mij vertalen?
kunt ew dit voar maiy ver**tah**len?

GREETINGS

Good morning	Goedemorgen	ghoode**mor**ghen
Good afternoon	Goedemiddag	ghoode**mi**dagh
Good evening	Goedenavond	ghooden**ah**vont
Good night/sleep well	Goedenacht/welterusten	ghoode**naght**/wehlte**rus**ten
Welcome	Welkom	**wehl**kom

Good bye	Tot ziens	tot zeens
See you later	Tot straks	tot straks
See you tomorrow	Tot morgen	tot **mor**ghen
Have a pleasant journey	Goede reis	**ghoo**de raiys
This is Mr/Mrs ...	Dit is de heer/mevrouw	dit is de hayr/mie**vrou** ....

How do you do?
Hoe maakt u het?
hoo mahkt ew heht?

◀ **Fine, thank you**
Uitstekend, dank u
œt**stay**kent, dank ew

Nice to meet you
Aangenaam (kennis te maken)
ahnghenahm (**keh**nis te **mah**ken)

Hi! How are things going? (pop.)
Hallo! Hoe gaat het ermee?
ha**loa**! hoo ghaht heht ehr**may**?

◀ **What's your name?**
Hoe is uw naam?
hoo is ew nahm?

My name is ....
Mijn naam is ....
maiyn nahm is ....

This is my ....
Dit is mijn ....
dit is maiyn ....

husband	man	man
wife	vrouw	vrou
son	zoon	zoan
daughter	dochter	**dogh**ter
father	vader	**vah**der
mother	moeder	**moo**der
(boy-)friend/(girl-)friend	vriend/vriendin	vreent/vreen**din**

◀ **Where do you come from?**
Waar komt u vandaan?
wahr komt ew van**dahn**?

I'm from England
Ik kom uit Engeland
ik kom œt **ehng**elant

◀ **Did you have a pleasant journey?**
Hebt u een goede reis gehad?
hehpt ew en **ghoo**de raiys ghe**hat**?

◀ **Give my regards to ....**
Doet u de groeten aan ...
doot ew de **ghroo**te ahn ...

MAKING FRIENDS/DATING

◀ **Shall I show you around town?**
Zal ik u de stad laten zien?
zal ik ew de stat **lah**ten zeen?

◀ **Shall we go out tonight?**
Zullen we vanavond uitgaan?
zulen we van**ah**vont œtgahn?

Yes, I'd like that/No, thank you
Ja, dat is leuk/Nee, dank je
yah, dat is løk/nay, dank ye

◀ **Shall I pick you up?**
Zal ik je afhalen?
zal ik ye **af**hahlen?

◄ **Shall we meet in front of the hotel/at the camp site?**

Zullen we voor het hotel/bij de camping afspreken?

zu**len** we voar heht hoa**tehl**/baiy de **kehm**ping **af**sprayken?

Okay, at .... o'clock

Ja/Goed, om ... uur

jah/ghoot, om ... ewr

Leave me alone!

Laat me met rust!

laht me meht rust!

I don't want/like this!

Daar ben ik niet van gediend!

dahr behn ik neet van ghe**deent**!

◄ **May I see you to your hotel/camp site?**

Mag ik je naar het hotel/de camping brengen?

magh ik ye nahr heht hoa**tehl**/de **kehm**ping **brehng**en?

Dutch etiquette

Good manners are appreciated everywhere and the Netherlands
are no exception. And, although this is generally a very relaxed
country, the Dutch can still be surprisingly formal on some
occasions. For a start, it's far less common to drop in on
someone without notice - people appreciate it far more if you
phone and arrange things beforehand. If you're visiting
someone for the first time you usually bring a small gift. Flowers
are a good idea (naturally enough!). The Dutch shake hands
more than do, say, the British or Americans, and good friends
will embrace and kiss each other three times on the cheeks
(i.e. a man and woman or two women but, unlike the Russians,
two men much less so).

Although no particular ritual is attached to the evening meal
(*avondeten*) it's certainly advisable not to turn up in the middle
of it - unless, of course, you've been specifically invited. Bear in
mind that most Dutch people sit down to their evening meal
rather earlier than the British do - usually between 6 and 7 p.m.
Afternoon visitors are offered tea or coffee (the Dutch greatly
prefer 'real' coffee to the instant variety) along with a small cake
or pastry (*koekje, gebakje*). However, since the Dutch regard
restraint as a virtue, hospitality is less lavish than it tends to be
in more southerly climes. 'South' in this sense already starts in
Belgium - including its Dutch-speaking areas - where the people
have a certain flamboyance (it's the French influence).

VISITING

Does .... live here?
Woont ..... hier?
woant ..... heer?

◀ **Yes, please come in**
Ja, komt u binnen
yah, komt ew **bi**nen

◀ **He/She is not home right now**
Hij/Zij is momenteel niet thuis
haiy/zaiy is moamehn**tayl** neet tœs

Can I leave a message?
Kan ik een boodschap achterlaten?
kan ik en **boat**sghap **agh**terlahten?

May I smoke in here?
Mag ik hier roken?
magh ik heer **roa**ken?

◀ **Would you like anything to drink?**
Wilt u iets drinken?
wilt ew eets **drin**ken?

◀ **Will you stay for dinner?**
Blijft u eten?
blaiyft ew **ay**ten?

I/We should be going
Het is tijd om te gaan
heht is taiyt om te ghahn

◀ **No, he moved out**
Nee, die is verhuisd
nay, dee is ver**hœst**

Do you know his new address?
Weet u zijn nieuwe adres?
wayt ew zaiyn **neeoo**-e ah**drehs**?

When will he/she be back?
Wanneer komt hij/zij terug?
wa**nayr** komt haiy/zaiy te**rugh**?

◀ **Please sit down**
Gaat u zitten
ghaht ew **zi**ten

◀ **Of course, go right ahead/I'd rather you wouldn't**
Natuurlijk/Liever niet
nah**tewr**lek/**lee**ver neet

Here's to your health!
Op uw gezondheid!
op eww ghe**zont**haiyt!

And to yours!
Op de uwe!
op de **eww**we!

Enjoy your meal!
Eet smakelijk!
ayt **smah**kelek!

Thank you for your hospitality/a lovely meal
Bedankt voor de gastvrijheid/het lekkere eten
be**dankt** voar de ghast**vraiy**haiyt/heht **leh**kere **ay**ten

CONGRATULATIONS

See also the section on 'Dates, seasons, months' for special holiday greetings

Happy birthday	Gefeliciteerd met uw verjaardag	ghe**fay**leeseetayrt meht eww ver**yahr**dagh
Happy anniversary	Gefeliciteerd met uw trouwdag	ghe**fay**leeseetayrt meht eww **trou**dagh

29

Congratulations	Gefeliciteerd	ghe**fay**leeseetayrt ....
on your marriage	met uw huwelijk	meht eww **heww**lek
on the birth of	met de geboorte van	meht de ghe**boar**te van ....
All the best!	Het allerbeste!	heht **a**lerbehste!
Good luck!	Succes!/Veel geluk!	sew**xehs**/vayl ghe**luk**!
Take care!	Sterkte!	**stehrk**te!
Have fun!	Veel plezier!	vayl ple**zeer**!
Get well soon	Van harte beterschap	van **har**te **bay**tersghap

NUMBERS AND ARITHMETIC

0	nul	nul
1	een	ayn
2	twee	tway
3	drie	dree
4	vier	veer
5	vijf	vaiyf
6	zes	zehs
7	zeven	**zay**ven
8	acht	aght
9	negen	**nay**ghen
10	tien	teen
11	elf	ehlf
12	twaalf	twahlf
13	dertien	**dehr**teen
14	veertien	**vayr**teen
15	vijftien	**vaiyf**teen
16	zestien	**zehs**teen
17	zeventien	**zay**venteen
18	achttien	**aght**teen
19	negentien	**nay**ghenteen
20	twintig	**twin**tegh
21	eenentwintig	**ayn**-en-twintegh
22	tweeëntwintig	**tway**-en-twintegh
30	dertig	**dehr**tegh
40	veertig	**vayr**tegh
50	vijftig	**vaiyf**tegh
60	zestig	**zehs**tegh
70	zeventig	**zay**ventegh
80	tachtig	**tagh**tegh
90	negentig	**nay**ghentegh
100	honderd	**hon**dert

101	honderd een	**hon**dert ayn
123	honderd drieëntwintig	**hon**dert **dree**-en-twintegh
200	tweehonderd	**tway**hondert
500	vijfhonderd	**vaiyf**hondert
1000	duizend	**dœ**zent
1500	vijftienhonderd	**vaiyf**teenhondert
2000	tweeduizend	**tway**dœzent
10.000	tienduizend	**teen**dœzent
100.000	honderdduizend	**hon**dert-dœzent
1.000.000	(een) miljoen	(ayn) mil**yoon**

Note 1: The Dutch put a comma where the English put a decimal point and the other way around. So Dutch 1.824 = English 1,824 and English 4.56 = Dutch 4,56!
Note 2: An English billion corresponds to a Dutch **miljard** and not to a Dutch **biljoen** (= 1,000,000,000,000).

1/2	een half	en half
1/3	een derde	en **dehr**de
1/4	een kwart/vierde	en kwart/**veer**de
3/4	driekwart	dreekwart
5%	vijf procent	vaiyf proa**sehnt**

first (1st)	eerste (1e, 1ste)	**ayr**ste
second (2nd)	tweede (2e, 2de)	**tway**de
third (3rd)	derde (3e, 3de)	**dehr**de
tenth(10th)	tiende (10e, 10de)	**teen**de
one hundredth (100th)	honderdste (100e, 100ste)	**hon**dertste

2 x 4 = 8	twee keer/maal vier is acht	tway kayr/mahl veer is aght
6 : 2 = 3	zes gedeeld door twee is drie	zehs ghe**daylt** doar tway is dree
4 + 6 = 10	vier plus/en zes is tien	veer plus/ehn zehs is teen
8 - 3 = 5	acht min drie is vijf	aght min dree is vaiyf

I am twenty-five years old
Ik ben 25 (jaar)
ik behn **vaiyf**-en-twintegh (yahr)

There are four of us
We zijn met zijn vieren
we zaiyn meht zen **vee**ren

TIME

What time is it?
Hoe laat is het?
hoo laht is heht?

◀ **It's ....**
Het is ....
heht is ....

three o'clock
drie uur
dree ewr

a quarter past two
kwart over twee
kwart **oa**ver tway

half past three
half vier
half veer

a quarter to four
kwart voor vier
kwart voar veer

five past three
vijf over drie
vaiyf **oa**ver dree

five to three
vijf voor drie
vaiyf voar dree

twenty past three
tien voor half vier
teen voar half veer

twenty to five
tien over half vier
teen **oa**ver half veer

15.23 hr.
vijftien uur drieëntwintig
vaiyfteen ewr **dree**-en-twintegh

tomorrow	morgen	**mor**ghen
the day after tomorrow	overmorgen	**oa**vermorghen
yesterday	gisteren	**ghis**teren
the day before yesterday	eergisteren	ayrghisteren

during the day	overdag	oaver**dagh**
at night	's nachts	snaghts
in the morning	's morgens	**smor**ghens
in the afternoon	's middags	**smi**daghs
in the evening	's avonds	**sah**vonts
this morning	vanmorgen	van**mor**ghen
this afternoon	vanmiddag	van**mi**dagh
tonight, this evening	vanavond	van**ah**vont
last night	gisterenavond	**ghis**teren-ahvont
summer time	zomertijd	**zoa**mertaiyt
local time	plaatselijke tijd	**plaht**seleke taiyt
at what time ....?	(om) hoe laat ....?	(om) hoo laht ....?
at .... o'clock	om .... uur	om .... ewr
midnight	middernacht	mider**naght**

The clock/This watch is fast/slow
De klok/Dit horloge loopt voor/achter
de klok/dit hor**loa**zhe loapt voar/**agh**ter

DATES, SEASONS, MONTHS, ETC.

1994	negentien (honderd) vierennegentig	**nay**ghenteen (**hon**dert) **veer**-en-nayghentegh
last year	vorig jaar	**voa**regh yahr
next year	volgend jaar	**vol**ghent yahr
spring	voorjaar, lente	**voar**yahr, **lehn**te
summer	zomer	**zoa**mer
autumn	najaar, herfst	**nah**yahr, hehrfst
winter	winter	**win**ter
January	januari	yanewa**wah**ree
February	februari	faybrewa**wah**ree
March	maart	mahrt
April	april	ah**pril**
May	mei	maiy
June	juni	**yew**nee
July	juli	**yew**lee
August	augustus	ou**ghus**tes
September	september	sehp**tehm**ber
October	oktober	ok**toa**ber
November	november	noa**vehm**ber
December	december	day**sehm**ber

What's the date today?
Welke datum is het vandaag?
wehlke **dah**tem is heht van**dahgh**?

The Hague, the 25th of May 1994	Den Haag, 25 mei 1994	dehn hahgh, 25 maiy 1994
on next May 25th/ on May 25th last	op 25 mei aanstaande/ jongstleden	op 25 maiy ahn**stahn**de/ yongst**lay**den
a year and a half	anderhalf jaar	**an**derhalf yahr
half a year	(een) half jaar	(en) half yahr
a month	een maand	en mahnt
two weeks (a fortnight)	twee weken (veertien dagen)	tway **way**ken (**vayr**teen **dah**ghen)
a week	een week	en wayk

New Year	Nieuwjaar	neeoo-yahr
Twelfth Day	Driekoningen	dree**koa**ningen
Maundy Thursday	Witte Donderdag	**wi**te **don**derdagh
Good Friday	Goede Vrijdag	**ghoo**de **vraiy**dagh
Easter	Pasen	**pah**sen
Labour Day, May Day	Dag van de Arbeid	dagh van de **ar**baiyt
Ascension Day	Hemelvaartsdag	**hay**melvahrtsdagh
Whitsuntide	Pinksteren	**pink**steren
Corpus Christi	Sacramentsdag	**sah**krahmehntsdagh
Assumption	Maria Hemelvaart	mah**ree**yah **hay**melvahrt
All Saints Day	Allerheiligen	aler**haiy**leghen
Christmas	Kerstmis	**kehrst**mis
New Year's Eve	Oudejaarsavond	oude-yahrs-**ah**vont

Merry Christmas and a happy New Year!
Prettige Kerstdagen en een gelukkig Nieuwjaar!
prehteghe **kehrst**dahgen ehn en ghe**lu**kegh neeoo-**yahr**!

Sunday	zondag	**zon**dagh
Monday	maandag	**mahn**dagh
Tuesday	dinsdag	**dins**dagh
Wednesday	woensdag	**woons**dagh
Thursday	donderdag	**don**derdagh
Friday	vrijdag	**vraiy**dagh
Saturday	zaterdag	**zah**terdagh
Sundays and public holidays	zon- en feestdagen	zon ehn **fayst**dahghen
weekdays	werkdagen	**wehrk**-dah-ghen
daily	dagelijks	**dah**gheleks

Official holidays

Besides a number of religious holidays and the New Year, the Dutch have the following public holidays:

Koninginnedag (30 April) (the Queen's official birthday): 30 April is actually the natural birthday of the Queen Mother, Juliana, but the present queen, Beatrix (whose own birthday is on 31 January) retains the traditional date. This is a full public holiday with children's parties, fairs and markets.

Bevrijdingsdag (5 May): this commemorates the end of the Second World War and the Allied liberation of the Netherlands from Nazi German occupation (1945). The festivities resemble those of 'Koninginnedag', but the shops are open,

Sinterklaas (5 December) (Saint Nicholas' Eve): this is a more important festival than Christmas, although the latter is catching on under Anglo-Saxon influence. Sint Nikolaas (or Sinterklaas) arrives from Spain with his helpers, who all bear the name *Zwarte Piet* (Black Pete). Together, 'they' distribute presents to all the family (especially the children, of course). The adults write poems to each other (the fiction is that Sinterklaas has written them), and everyone gets a chocolate letter representing their initial. There are also delicious sweetmeats such as *pepernoten* (small ginger nuts), *speculaas* (spiced almond biscuits) and *taai-taai* (gingerbread).

Oudejaarsavond (31 December) (New Year's Eve): a family occasion lasting till just before midnight. Traditionally, you eat *oliebollen* (rather greasy doughnut balls) and then people flood into the streets to let off fireworks.

There are two additional historical anniversaries in Belgium:
Nationale Feestdag (21 July) (National Holiday)
Wapenstilstandsdag 1918 (11 November)
(Armistice/Remembrance Day)

The following are also recognised public holidays in Belgium:
De Dag van de Arbeid (1 May) (Labour Day)
Maria Hemelvaart (15 August) (Assumption)
Allerheiligen (1 November) (All Saints' Day)

THE WEATHER

What will the weather be like today?
Wat voor weer krijgen we vandaag?
wat voar wayr **kraiy**ghen we van**dahgh**?

◀ The weather will stay fine/poor
Het blijft mooi/slecht weer
heht blaiyft moay/slehght wayr

◀ The weather will be better/worse
Het wordt beter/slechter weer
heht wort **bay**ter/**slehgh**ter wayr

◀ A temperature of 15 degrees (below zero)*
Een temperatuur van 15 graden (onder nul)
en tehmpayrah**tewr** van **vaif**teen **ghrah**den (**on**der nul)

◀ I haven't heard the weather forecast
Ik heb het weerbericht niet gehoord
ik hehp heht **wayr**bericht neet ghe**hoart**

◀ It's going to rain/hail/snow
We krijgen regen/hagel/sneeuw
we **kraiy**ghen **ray**ghen/**hah**ghel/snayoo

◀ It's going to freeze/thaw
Het gaat vriezen/dooien
heht ghaht **vree**zen/**doa**yen

The sky is clouding over, ...
De lucht betrekt, ...
de lught be**trehkt**, ...

.... it's going to rain/there's going to be a thunderstorm/a gale is blowing up
.... het gaat regenen/onweren/stormen
.... heht ghaht **ray**ghenen/**on**wayren/**stor**men

The wind is rising/falling
De wind steekt op/gaat liggen
de wint staykt op/ghaht **li**ghen

It's hot/chilly/sultry/cold today
Het is vandaag warm/koel/drukkend/koud
heht is van**dahgh** warm/kool/**dru**kent/kout

The sun is coming out again/doesn't shine
De zon schijnt weer/niet
de zon sghaiynt wayr/neet

The sky is clear/clouded
De hemel is onbewolkt/bewolkt
de **hay**mel is **on**bewolkt/be**wolkt**

* Note that on the Continent the Celsius system is being used; the degrees used in weather forecasts are always according to the Celsius and never to the Fahrenheit system.

atmospheric pressure	luchtdruk	**lught**druk
changeable	onbestendig	onbe**stehn**degh
climate	klimaat	klee**maht**
depression	lagedrukgebied	lah-ghe-**druk**-ghebeet
downpour	wolkbreuk	**wolk**brøk
drizzle	motregen	**mot**rayghen
easterly wind	oostenwind	**oas**tenwint
fog	mist	mist
frost	vorst	vorst
glazed frost	ijzel	**aiy**zel
heat	hitte	**hi**te
high pressure zone	hogedrukgebied	hoaghe**druk**ghebeet
ice	ijs	aiys
(black) ice on the road	gladheid	**ghlat**haiyt
lightning	bliksem	**blik**sem
northern wind	noordenwind	**noar**denwint
precipitation	neerslag	**nayr**slagh
sea breeze	zeewind	**zay**wint
shower	regenbui	**ray**ghenbœ
southern wind	zuidenwind	**zœ**denwint
storm alarm	stormwaarschuwing	**storm**wahr-sghew-wing
storm clouds	regenwolken	**ray**ghenwolken
sunny spells	opklaringen	**op**klahringen
thaw	dooi	doay
thunder	donder	**don**der
twilight, dusk, dawn	schemering	**sghay**mering
variable	veranderlijk	ver**an**derlek
variable cloudiness	wisselend bewolkt	**wi**selent be**wolkt**
weather forecast	weersverwachting	**wayrs**verwaghting
western wind	westenwind	**wehs**tenwint
wind	wind	wint

Winter in Nederland

1 Volkssport nummer 1
2 Een bevroren sloot
3 Het aanbinden van schaatsen
4 Warme drankjes te koop
5 Een flinke sneeuwbui
6 Kale bomen
7 Sinterklaas en Zwarte Piet*

Winter in Holland

The Dutch national sport
A frozen ditch
Fastening one's skates
Hot drinks for sale
Heavy snowfall
Bare trees
Saint Nicholas and Black Pete

* Sint Nicolaas or Sinterklaas is the Dutch equivalent of Father Christmas/Santa Claus. On December the 5th, on the eve of his birthday, he hands out presents and candy to the children (in fact everyone is buying one another presents). Black Pete is the helper of this great friend of all children.

ARRIVAL

PASSPORT CONTROL

◄ **May I see your passport/car documents/green card?**
Mag ik uw paspoort/autopapieren/groene kaart zien?
magh ik eww **pas**poort/**out**oa pahpeeren/**ghroo**ne kahrt zeen?

Here you are
Alstublieft
alstew**bleeft**

◄ **Your passport/visa has expired/is not valid**
Uw pas/visum is verlopen/niet geldig
eww pas/**vee**sem is ver**loa**pen/neet **ghehl**degh

◄ **Your passport will soon expire**
Uw paspoort verloopt binnenkort
eww **pas**poart ver**loapt** binnen**kort**

◄ **You need a visa/transit permit**
U heeft een visum/doorreisvisum nodig
ew hayft en **vee**sem/**door**raiysveesem **noa**degh

◄ **How long do you intend to stay in Holland?**
Hoe lang blijft u in Nederland?
hoo lang blaiyft ew in **nay**derlant?

◄ **Are you here for business or pleasure?**
Bent u hier als toerist of voor zaken?
behnt ew heer als too**rist** of voar **zah**ken?

◄ **Are you passing through?**
Bent u op doorreis?
behnt ew op **door**raiys?

How much is a visa?
Wat kost een visum?
wat kost en **vee**sem?

Where can I have passport photos made?
Waar kan ik pasfoto's laten maken?
wahr kan ik **pas**foatoas **lah**ten **mah**ken?

DOUANE	CUSTOMS
PASCONTROLE	IMMIGRATION
E.G.-ONDERDANEN	EC CITIZENS
ANDERE NATIONALITEITEN	OTHER NATIONALITIES
NIETS AAN TE GEVEN	NOTHING TO DECLARE
AANGIFTE	ANYTHING TO DECLARE
HIER WACHTEN A.U.B.	WAIT HERE PLEASE
HIER OPSTELLEN	QUEUE HERE
PERSONENAUTO'S	PASSENGER CARS
VRACHTVERKEER	FREIGHT TRAFFIC

ARRIVAL

◄ **Would you please fill in this form?**
Wilt u dit formulier invullen?
wilt ew dit formew**leer in**vullen?

◄ **Would you please follow me?**
Wilt u even meekomen?
wilt ew **ay**ven **may**koamen?

◄ **We must send you back**
Wij moeten u terugsturen
waiy **moo**ten ew te**rugh**stewren

◄ **Would you please wait here?**
Wilt u hier even wachten?
wilt ew heer **ay**ven **wagh**ten?

◄ **You cannot enter the country**
U mag ons land niet binnen
ew magh ons lant neet **bi**nen

CUSTOMS

◄ **Would you please pull over/dismount?**
Wilt u hier even parkeren/afstappen?
wilt ew heer **ay**ven par**kay**ren/**af**stapen?

◄ **Do you have anything to declare?**
Hebt u iets aan te geven?
hehpt ew eets ahn te **ghay**ven?

◄ **Please open this suitcase**
Wilt u deze koffer openmaken?
wilt ew **day**ze **ko**fer **oa**penmahken?

◄ **You have to pay duty on this**
U moet hiervoor invoerrechten betalen
ew moot heer**voar in**voor-rehghten be**tah**len

Where can I pay?
Waar kan ik betalen?
wahr kan ik be**tah**len?

◄ **Would you please open the boot?**
Wilt u de kofferruimte openmaken?
wilt ew de **ko**fer-rœmte **oa**penmahken?

◄ **Is this your suitcase/rucksack/bag?**
Is deze koffer/rugzak/tas van u?
is **day**ze **ko**fer/**rugh**zak/tas van ew?

◄ **It's not allowed to import/export this**
U mag dit niet invoeren/uitvoeren
ew magh dit neet **in**vooren/**œt**vooren

How much do I owe you?
Hoeveel moet ik betalen?
hoovayl moot ik be**tah**len?

◄ **We'll confiscate this property**
Dit nemen we in beslag
dit **nay**men we in be**slagh**

◄ **Do you have a vaccination certificate for your dog/cat?**
Hebt u een inentingsbewijs voor uw hond/poes?
hehpt ew en **in**ehn-tings-bew**aiys** voar eww hont/poos?

◄ **You may proceed/go through**
U kunt doorrijden/doorlopen
ew kunt **doar**raiyden/**doar**loapen

TRAVELLING AROUND

TRANSPORTATION

Private transportation:

English	Dutch	Pronunciation
(motor) car	auto	**ou**toa
passenger car	personenauto	pehr**soa**nen-outoa
car and trailer	auto met aanhanger	**ou**toa meht **ahn**hanger
car and caravan	auto met caravan	**ou**toa meht 'caravan'
lorry	vrachtauto	**vraght**outoa
heavy lorry	vrachtauto met aanhanger	**vraght**outoa meht **ahn**hanger
articulated lorry	truck met oplegger	'truck' meht **op**lehgher
containerized truck	truck met container	'truck' meht 'container'
van	bestelauto	be**stehl**outoa
minibus	minibus	**mee**neebus
motor cycle	motorfiets	**moa**torfeets
sidecar machine	motor met zijspan n	**moa**tor meht **zaiy**span
motor scooter	scooter	'scooter'
moped	bromfiets	**brom**feets
bicycle	fiets	feets
racing cycle	racefiets	**rays**feets
touring bicycle	toerfiets	**toor**feets
tandem	tandem	'tandem'
lady's bike	damesfiets	**dah**mesfeets
gents' bike	herenfiets	**hay**renfeets
child's bicycle	kinderfiets	**kin**derfeets
mountain bike	ATB (mountain bike)	aa tay bay ('mountain bike')
BMX	BMX (crossfiets)	bay ehm iks (**kros**feets)

Public and group transport:

English	Dutch	Pronunciation
airplane	vliegtuig n	**vleegh**tœg
boat	boot	boat
car ferry	autoveerpont	**ou**toa-vayrpont
pleasure boat (city cruises)	rondvaartboot	**ront**vahrtboat
pleasure steamer	cruiseschip n	**kroos**-sghip
(local) bus	(stads)bus	(**stats**)bus

41

trolley bus	trolleybus	**troll**eebus
(motor) coach	touringcar	**too**ringkar
underground	metro	**may**troa
taxi, cab	taxi	**ta**xee
shared taxi	groepstaxi	**ghroops**taxee
train	trein	traiyn
carriage, coach	koets	koots

CAR RENTAL

(for information on how to rent a bicycle, see the chapter on 'Sports and recreation')

I'd like to hire a car
Ik wil een auto huren
ik wil en **ou**toa **hew**ren

◄ Which brand/type of car do you prefer?
Hebt u een voorkeur voor een bepaald merk/type?
hehpt ew en **voar**kør voar en be**pahlt** mehrk/**tee**pe?

How much is it per day/week?
Wat kost dit per dag/week?
wat kost dit pehr dagh/wayk?

What's included in the price?
Wat is bij de prijs inbegrepen?
wat is baiy de praiys **in**beghraypen?

comprehensive car insurance	all risk-verzekering	'all risk' ver**za**ykering
fuel	brandstof	**brant**stof
full tank	volle tank	**vol**le 'tank'
rate per kilometer	tarief per kilometer	tah**reef** pehr **kee**loamayter

Do I have to pay a deposit?
Moet ik een borgsom betalen?
moot ik en **borgh**som be**tah**len?

◄ May I see your driving license?
Mag ik uw rijbewijs zien?
magh ik eww **raiy**bewaiys zeen?

◄ Here are the keys/your car papers
Hier zijn de sleutels/uw autopapieren
heer zaiyn de **slø**tels/eww **ou**toa-pahpeeren

◄ The car is standing .....
U vindt de auto .....
ew vint de **ou**toa ....

◄ The registration number is ....
Het kenteken is ....
heht **kehn**tayken is ....

Where can I return the car?
Waar kan ik de auto terugbezorgen?
wahr kan ik de **ou**toa te**rugh**-bezorghen?

What time will the office close?
Tot hoe laat is het kantoor open?
tot hoo laht is heht kan**toar oa**pen?

The Dutch road system

The Netherlands is criss-crossed by a dense network of motorways (*autosnelwegen*), indicated by the letter **A + number** (NB: the British equivalent is therefore the M-ways, not the A roads - their Dutch equivalents are designated with an **N** for 'national'). Secondary roads are also generally good; you'll hardly find any dirt roads in the Netherlands. Given the relentlessly flat, water-dominated Dutch countryside, many roads are on or beside dykes and may be risky for towing a caravan in very windy conditions (in fact on the two main ones this will frequently be prohibited). The two most striking features about Belgian motorways is that they often seem to be virtually empty (certainly compared to Holland and Britain) and that they're brilliantly illuminated for long stretches.

British visitors will regard Dutch cyclists as a pampered breed, and will look on in envy at the special cycle paths all over the towns and countryside. Paths signposted *fietspad* (cycle path) **can** but do not **have** to be used by cyclists, and are prohibited for mopeds and other motorbikes. Paths indicated by a circular blue sign **are** compulsory, both for cyclists and moped riders. In the urban centres cyclists have their own lanes, which are often in a different colour to the road. Motorists are supposed to stay off these lanes but in reality there's a lot of cowboy parking. Watch out for the special cyclists' traffic lights (although cyclists, especially in the main cities, frequently ignore red lights of all descriptions). Motorists should know that when it comes to turning right or left, cyclists and motorcyclists going straight on have priority!

Another important point is that when two roads of equal status merge, a car approaching from the right has priority (i.e. as in the French 'priorité à droite' system). Officially, motor vehicles have priority over cyclists in this situation, but in practice the cyclist will tend to sail on regardless (the technique is deliberate refusal to make eye contact!).

ASKING FOR DIRECTIONS

How do I get from here to ....?
Hoe kom ik van hier naar ....?
hoo kom ik van heer nahr ....?

Do I take the motorway/toll road?
Is dat via de snelweg/tolweg?
is dat **vee**yah de **snehl**wehgh/**tol**wegh?

Is there a scenic route?
Is er een mooie route naar toe?
is ehr en **moa**ye **roo**te nahr too?

Is the road flat or hilly?
Is de weg vlak of zijn er hellingen?
is de wehgh vlak of zaiyn ehr **heh**lingen?

Can I drive there with a caravan/trailer?
Kan ik er met een caravan/aanhanger over rijden?
kan ik ehr meht en 'caravan'/**ahn**hanger **oa**ver **raiy**den?

Can you point it out on the map?
Kunt u dit op de kaart aanwijzen?
kunt ew dit op de kahrt **ahn**waiyzen?

Is this the way to ....?
Is dit de weg naar ....?
is dit de wehgh nahr ....?

Is the road in good condition?
Is de weg goed berijdbaar?
is de wehgh ghoot be**raiyt**bahr?

Is there a cycle path?
Is er een fietspad?
is ehr en **feets**pat?

What's the name of this town/area?
Hoe heet deze plaats/streek?
hoo hayt dayze plahts/strayk?

Are there any sights around here?
Is hier in de buurt iets te zien?
is heer in de bewrt eets te zeen?

I'am lost
Ik ben verdwaald
ik behn ver**dwahlt**

◀ From here you must.....
U moet van hier af ....
ew moot van heer af ....

go straight on	rechtdoor	rehghtdoar
turn to the right	rechtsaf	rehghtsaf
turn to the left	linksaf	linksaf
turn around	keren	**kay**ren
drive back	terugrijden	te**rugh**raiyden ....
to the motorway	naar de snelweg	nahr de **snehl**wehgh
to the main road	naar de hoofdweg	nahr de **hoaft**wehgh
and leave the town	de stad uit	de stat œt
and leave the village	het dorp uit	heht dorp œt
through the tunnel	de tunnel door	de **tu**nel doar
and cross the railway	de spoorbaan oversteken	de **spoar**bahn **oa**verstayken
along the river	langs de rivier	langs de ree**veer**
through the woods	door het bos	doar heht bos

44

through the valley	door het dal	doar heht dal
till the crossing	tot de kruising	tot de **krœs**ing
till the fork	tot de splitsing	tot de **splits**ing
till the roundabout	tot de rotonde	tot de roa**ton**de

PARKING, FINES

Where can I park?
Waar kan ik hier parkeren?
wahr kan ik heer par**kay**ren?

Is there a parking lot/(multi-storey) car park?
Waar is een parkeerplaats/parkeergarage?
wahr is en par**kayr**plahts/par**kayr**-ghah-rah-zhe?

Where can I pay?
Waar moet ik betalen?
wahr moot ik be**tah**len?

Is there a ticket machine/parking meter?
Is er een parkeerautomaat/parkeermeter?
is ehr en par**kayr**-outoamaht/par**kayr**mayter?

◀ **You are not allowed to park here**
U mag hier niet parkeren
ew magh heer neet par**kay**ren

◀ **Your parking time has expired**
Uw parkeertijd is verstreken
eww par**kayr**taiyt is ver**stray**ken

◀ **May I see your driving license?**
Mag ik uw rijbewijs zien?
magh ik ew **raiy**bewaiys zeen?

PARKEERVERBOD	NO PARKING
UITRIT	EXIT
NEEM HIER UW PARKEERKAART	TAKE YOUR PARKING CARD
HIER BETALEN	PAY HERE
INWORP	INSERT
... PER UUR	... PER HOUR
WERKDAGEN TOT 18.00 UUR	ON WEEKDAYS UNTIL 6 PM
PARKEERTERREIN VOL	CAR PARK FULL
PARKEERSCHIJF VERPLICHT	PARKING DISC OBLIGATORY
GERESERVEERD VOOR	RESERVED FOR ....
TAXISTANDPLAATS	TAXI RANK

◄ You will be fined for ....
U krijgt een bekeuring wegens ....
ew kraiyght en be**kø**ring **way**ghens ....

unauthorized parking	fout parkeren	fout par**kay**ren
exceeding the parking limit	te lang parkeren	te lang par**kay**ren
speeding	te snel rijden	te snelh **raiy**den
within the built-up area	binnen de bebouwde kom	**bi**nen de be**bou**de kom
dangerous driving	gevaarlijk rijden	ghe**vahr**lek **raiy**den
illegal crossing	verkeerd oversteken	ver**kayrt oa**verstayken
passing through amber	door geel licht rijden	doar ghayl light **raiy**den
jumping the lights	door rood (licht) rijden	doar roat (light) **raiy**den
failing to give right of way	geen voorrang verlenen	ghayn **voa**rang ver**lay**nen
failing to indicate a	geen richting aangeven	ghayn **righ**ting **ahn**ghayven
change of direction		
unauthorized overtaking	verkeerd inhalen	ver**kayrt in**hahlen

◄ You're not allowed to drive here
U mag hier niet rijden
ew mahgh heer neet **raiy**den

◄ The fine is fifty guiders
De boete bedraagt vijftig gulden
de **boo**te be**drah**ght vaiyftegh **ghul**den

◄ You can pay to me
U kunt aan mij betalen
ew kunt ahn maiy be**tah**len

◄ You must come to the office
U moet naar het bureau komen
ew moot nahr heht bew**roa koa**men

◄ I'll only give you a warning this time
Ik geef u alleen een waarschuwing
ik ghayf ew a**layn** en **wahr**sghew-wing

NOTICES AND DIRECTIONS

AFGESLOTEN VOOR	CLOSED TO ....
AFSLAG	EXIT
ALLEEN VOOR	.... ONLY
ALLE RICHTINGEN	ALL DIRECTIONS
BEBOUWDE KOM	BUILT-IN AREA
BROMFIETSERS	MOPED RIDERS
CENTRUM	CENTRE
DOODLOPENDE WEG	DEAD END
DOORGAAND RIJVERKEER	NO THOROUGHFARE
GESTREMD	
EIGEN WEG	PRIVATE ROAD

ER KAN NOG EEN TREIN KOMEN	ANOTHER TRAIN MAY FOLLOW
FIETSERS	CYCLISTS
FIETSERS OVERSTEKEN	CYCLISTS' CROSSING
FIETSPAD	CYCLE TRACK
FILE	TAILBACK
GA TERUG!	GO BACK!
GEEN DOORGAAND VERKEER	NO THROUGH TRAFFIC
GELDT NIET VOOR	NOT APPLYING TO ....
GESLOTEN	CLOSED
GEVAARLIJKE STOFFEN	DANGEROUS SUBSTANCES
HIER OPSTELLEN	LINE UP HERE
HIER OVERSTEKEN	CROSS HERE
LANGZAAM RIJDEN	DRIVE SLOWLY
LET OP	ATTENTION
LICHTEN ONTSTEKEN	SWITCH ON LIGHTS
MAXIMUM SNELHEID	SPEED LIMIT
M.U.V.	WITH THE EXCEPTION OF
NA 100 M	AFTER 100 METERS
NIET PARKEREN	NO PARKING
OMLEIDING	DIVERSION
P + R	PARKING FOR RAIL PASSENGERS
POLITIE	POLICE
SCHOOL	SCHOOL
SMALLE WEG	NARROW ROAD
STOPLICHTEN	TRAFFIC LIGHTS
TEGENLIGGERS	ONCOMING TRAFFIC
.... TOEGESTAAN	.... ALLOWED
TOL	TOLL
TRAM	TRAM, STREETCAR
UIT	EXIT
UITRIT VRIJLATEN	PLEASE KEEP THE EXIT CLEAR
VEERPONT	FERRY
VERBODEN TOEGANG	NO ENTRY
VERBODEN TOEGANG VOOR ONBEVOEGDEN	NO TRESPASSING
VERKEERSDREMPEL	SPEED RAMP
VOETGANGERS	PEDESTRIANS
VOETGANGERS- OVERSTEEKPLAATS	PEDESTRIAN CROSSING
VOLG ROUTE NR. 3	FOLLOW ROUTE NUMBER 3
VOORSORTEREN	GET IN LANE

WEGOMLEGGING	DIVERSION
WERK IN UITVOERING	ROAD WORKS AHEAD
WIELRIJDERS	CYCLISTS
*WOONERF	RESIDENTIAL AREA
ZACHTE BERM	SOFT VERGES

*In a residential area marked as 'woonerf' motorists should drive slowly and give way to cyclists and pedestrians.

HITCHHIKING

Are we allowed to hitchhike here?
Mogen we hier liften?
moaghen we heer **lif**ten?

◀ **Not alongside the motorway/slip road**
Niet langs de snelweg/oprit
neet langs de **snehl**wehgh/**op**rit

Can you take us to ....?
Kunt u ons meenemen naar ....?
kunt ew ons **may**naymen nahr ....?

Shall I pay part of the expenses?
Zal ik een deel van de onkosten vergoeden?
zal ik en dayl van de **on**kosten ver**ghoo**den?

Thanks for the ride
Bedankt voor de lift
be**dankt** voar de lift

PUBLIC TRANSPORT

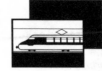

BUS, TRAM, UNDERGROUND

Where is the tube station/central bus terminal?
Waar is het metrostation/centrale busstation?
wahr is heht **meh**troa-stahsyon/sehn**trah**le **bus**-stahsyon?

Where is the nearest bus stop?
Waar stopt hier een bus?
wahr stopt heer en bus?

Is there a bus/tram going to ....?
Gaat er een bus/tram naar ...?
ghaht ehr en bus/'tram' nahr ...?

Which number do I take?
Welk nummer moet ik nemen?
wehlk **nu**mer moot ik **nay**men?

What time does the first/last bus/tram leave?
Hoe laat gaat de eerste/laatste bus/tram?
hoo laat ghaht de **ayr**ste/**laht**ste bus/'tram'?

Do I have to change (busses/trains, etc.)?
Moet ik overstappen?
moot ik **oa**verstapen?

Where can I buy a ticket?
Waar kan ik een kaartje kopen?
wahr kahn ik en **kahr**tye **koa**pen?

◀ From the driver/at the bus station
Bij de chauffeur/op het busstation
baiy de shoa**før**/op heht **bus**-stahsyon

One single to .... please
Een enkele reis naar .... alstublieft
en **ehn**kele raiys nahr .... alstew**bleeft**

DEUR OPENEN	DOOR BUTTON - PUSH TO OPEN
GEEN UITGANG	NO EXIT
HIER GEEN STAANPLAATSEN	DO NOT STAND HERE
KAARTVERKOOP BIJ DE BESTUURDER	TICKETS CAN BE PURCHASED FROM THE DRIVER
NIET SPREKEN MET DE BESTUURDER	DO NOT SPEAK TO THE DRIVER
NOODREM	ALARM, EMERGENCY BRAKE
VERBODEN TE ROKEN	NO SMOKING

The 'strippenkaart'

The Dutch have a unique ticketing system based on the *strippenkaart* ('strip ticket'). This can be used for all buses, trams, the underground and a few overground trains (although usually only on local and short-distance suburban routes).

The ticket is divided into a number of 'strips', each of which represents a public transport zone. (The entire Netherlands is divided into these zones, and theoretically you could travel from one end of the country to the other using strip tickets.)

Calculate how many zones you're travelling through (there'll be a map in the tram or tube, or just ask a helpful local) and stamp the appropriate strip on your ticket. The stamping machines are located in the trams and on the underground and train platforms; in buses, tickets are stamped by the driver. If you're travelling, say, three zones you stamp the fourth strip down on your ticket - you don't need to stamp the three sections above.

The strip ticket can be used by more than one person - for two people travelling across three zones, therefore, you'd need to stamp the fourth and the eighth strips down. Your stamped strip ticket will be valid for at least an hour's travel, longer for multi-zone journeys (the details are on the back of the ticket,

return ticket	retour *n*	re**toor**
day ticket	dagkaart	**dagh**kahrt
children's ticket	kinderkaartje *n*	**kin**derkahrtye
monthly season ticket	maandabonnement	**mahnt**-a-bo-ne-mehnt
to stamp	afstempelen	**af**stehmpelen
stamping machine	stempelautomaat	**stehm**pel-outoamaht

Could you notify me when we arrive at ....?
Wilt u mij waarschuwen als we bij .... zijn?
wilt ew maiy **wahr**sghew-wen als we baiy .... zaiyn?

Can I take the dog with me in the bus?
Mag de hond mee in de bus?
magh de hont may in de bus?

(e.g. 2-4 strips = 1 hour, 5-7 strips = 1.5 hours, etc.).
By the way, this system enables you to interrupt your journey and then continue on the same stamped strip. Make sure your time hasn't run out, though. If it has you'll need to stamp more strips.
You can purchase 3- or 10-strip tickets from bus and tram drivers (some tram lines also have a conductor who sits in the back). However, you're better off buying the considerably cheaper 15- or 45-strip tickets available at post offices, railway stations and some shops (usually tobacconists). Just say: *Een strippenkaart alstublieft*. These outlets also sell half-price tickets for children of up to twelve years old and discount tickets for holders of senior citizens' passes. The public transport operators provide English-language leaflets (available at their information points) explaining how to use the *strippenkaart*.
Finally, it may look temptingly easy to travel without paying - *zwartrijden* ('travelling black'). Don't do it. All of a sudden 3 or 4 *controleurs* (inspectors) can get in and they never accept ANY excuses. The on-the-spot fine is 60 guilders + the price of the ticket you should have bought.

◀ **Your ticket please**
Uw plaatsbewijs alstublieft
eww **plahts**bewaiys alstew**bleeft**

◀ **Your ticket has expired**
Uw plaatsbewijs is verlopen
eww **plahts**bewaiys is ver**loa**pen

◀ **You have to pay a fine**
U moet een boete betalen
ew moot en **boo**te be**tah**len

◀ **Terminus, all change here!**
Eindpunt, uitstappen alstublieft
aiyntpunt, œtstapen alstew**bleeft**

◀ **You cannot sit here, this is the first class**
U mag hier niet zitten, dit is de eerste klas
ew magh heer neet **zi**ten, dit is de **ayr**ste klas

◀ **Your ticket is not valid**
Uw plaatsbewijs is niet geldig
eww **plahts**bewaiys is neet **ghehl**degh

◀ **We stop over for ten minutes**
We houden hier tien minuten pauze
we **hou**den heer teen mee**new**ten **pou**ze

driver	bestuurder	be**stewr**der
number	(lijn)nummer *n*	(**laiyn**)numer
seat	zitplaats	**zit**plahts
standing room	staanplaats	**stahn**plahts
stop	halte	**hal**te
ticket collector	controleur	kontroa**lør**

TRAIN

Where is the station?
Waar is het station?
wahr is heht stah**syon**?

One single to ...., please
Mag ik een enkele reis naar ....?
magh ik en **ehn**kele raiys nahr ....?

Do I have to make a reservation?
Moet ik een plaats reserveren?
moot ik en plahts rayser**vay**ren?

Do I have to transfer?
Moet ik overstappen?
moot ik **oa**verstapen?

Can I take my bicycle with me into the train?
Kan ik mijn fiets in de trein meenemen?
kan ik maiyn feets in de traiyn **may**naymen?

What time does the train to .... leave?
Hoe laat gaat de trein naar ....?
hoo laht ghaht de traiyn nahr ....?

timetable	dienstregeling	**deenst**ray-ghe-ling
arrival	aankomst	**ahn**komst
departure	vertrek *n*	ver**trehk**
weekdays	werkdagen	**wehrk**dahghen
Sundays and bank holidays	zon- en feestdagen	zon en **fayst**dahghen
track	spoor *n*	spoar
platform	perron *n*	peh**ron**
international train	internationale trein	internahshoa**nah**le traiyn
Inter-city train	intercity(trein)	'inter-city'(traiyn)
express train	sneltrein	**snehl**traiyn
local train	stoptrein	**stop**traiyn
through train	doorgaande trein	**doar**ghahnde traiyn
ticket counter	loket *n*	loa**keht**
surcharge	toeslag	**too**slagh
first class	eerste klas	**ayr**ste klas
second class	tweede klas	**tway**de klas
smoking	roken	**roa**ken
non smoking	niet-roken	neet-**roa**ken
reserved	gereserveerd	gherayser**vayrt**
dining compartment	restauratie	rehstoa**raht**see
dining car/diner	restauratiewagon	rehstoa**raht**see-wahghon

52

ACHTER(STE TREINSTEL)	REAR (TRAIN)
ACHTER/VOOR UITSTAPPEN	GET OUT IN THE BACK/FRONT
BAGAGE(RUIMTE)	LUGGAGE (COMPARTMENT)
BAGAGEKLUIZEN	LOCKERS
BINNENLAND	DOMESTIC
BUITENLAND	INTERNATIONAL
DAMES	LADIES
D-TREIN MET TOESLAG	INTER-CITY EXPRESS WITH SURCHARGE
EERSTE KLASSE	FIRST CLASS
FIETSENSTALLING	BICYCLE SHED
GEEN TOEGANG	NO ENTRY
HEREN	GENTS
INGANG	ENTRANCE
INLICHTINGEN	INFORMATION
KAARTVERKOOP	TICKET OFFICE
METRO	UNDERGROUND
MET TOESLAG	WITH A SURCHARGE
NIET INSTAPPEN	DO NOT GET IN
NIET OPENEN VOORDAT DE TREIN STILSTAAT	DO NOT OPEN UNTIL THE TRAIN HAS COME TO A COMPLETE STOP
NIET ROKEN	NO SMOKING
NOODREM	EMERGENCY BRAKE
NOODUITGANG	EMERGENCY EXIT
OPENEN	OPEN
OP VOL BALKON NIET ROKEN	NO SMOKING WHEN PLATFORM IS FULL
OVERSTAPPEN	CHANGE HERE
ROKEN	SMOKING
SLUIT AUTOMATISCH	DOOR CLOSES AUTOMATICALLY
SLUITEN	CLOSE
SPOOR	TRACK (PLATFORM)
STATIONSRESTAURATIE	STATION RESTAURANT
STOPT NIET IN ...	DOES NOT STOP IN ...
STOPT OP VERZOEK	REQUEST STOP
TOILETTEN	TOILETS
UITGANG	EXIT
VOOR(STE TREINSTEL)	FRONT (TRAIN)
WACHTKAMER	WAITING ROOM

sleeping car/sleeper	slaap-/ligrijtuig n	slahp-/lighraiytœg
luggage van	bagagerijtuig n	bah**ghah**zhe-raiytœgh
berth	couchette	koo**sheht**
seat	zitplaats	**zit**plahts
corridor	gangpad n	**ghang**pat
luggage rack	bagagerek n	bah**ghah**zhe-rehk
ticket collector	conducteur	konduk**tør**
engine driver	machinist	mashee**nist**

◄ **The train only stops at/does not stop at ....**
De trein stopt alleen/niet in ....
de traiyn stopt a**layn**/neet in ....

◄ **You're sitting in the wrong seat**
U zit op de verkeerde plaats
ew zit op de ver**kayr**de plahts

◄ **Your ticket isn't valid**
Uw kaartje is niet geldig
eww **kahr**tye is neet **ghehl**degh

◄ **You're in the wrong train**
U zit in de verkeerde trein
ew zit in de ver**kayr**de traiyn

◄ **You're in the first-class section**
U zit in de eerste klasse
ew zit in de **ayr**ste **kla**se

◄ **The train has a 30 minutes delay**
De trein heeft 30 minuten vertraging
de traiyn hayft **dehr**tegh mee**new**ten ver**trah**ghing

BOAT SERVICE

I'd like to have a ticket to ....
Ik wil een kaartje naar ....
ik wil en **kahr**tye nahr ....

I'd like to reserve a reclining seat/cabin
Ik wil een slaapstoel/hut reserveren
ik wil en **slahp**stool/hut rayser**vay**ren

HIER OPSTELLEN	QUEUE HERE
MOTOR AFZETTEN	SWITCH OFF YOUR MOTOR
REDDINGSVESTEN	LIFE JACKETS
REDDINGSBOTEN	LIFEBOATS
ALLEEN PASSAGIERS	PASSENGERS ONLY
BENEDENDEK	LOWER DECK
TUSSENDEK	BETWEEN DECK
BOVENDEK	UPPER DECK
GEEN TOEGANG	NO ENTRY
NAAR HET AUTODEK	TO THE CAR DECK

on the outside	aan de buitenzijde	ahn de **bœ**tenzaiyde
on the inside	aan de binnenzijde	ahn de **bi**nenzaiyde
with a shower	met douche	meht doosh
for three people	voor 3 personen	voar dree pehr**soa**nen

Can I take my bike aboard?
Kan de fiets mee op de boot?
kan de feets may op de boat?

When will the next boat sail?
Wanneer vaart de eerstvolgende boot af?
wahnayr vahrt de **ayrst**volghende boat af?

How much for a car and two passengers?
Wat kost het vervoer van een auto met 2 inzittenden?
wat kost heht ver**voor** van en **ou**toa meht tway in**zi**tenden?

How long does the passage take?
Hoe lang duurt de overtocht?
hoo lang dewrt de **oa**vertoght?

◀ **Follow the crew's instructions**
U moet de aanwijzingen van de bemanning volgen
ew moot de **ahn**waiyzingen van de be**ma**ning **vol**ghen

CAB

Could you call a cab for me?
Kunt u voor mij een taxi bellen/roepen?
kunt ew voar maiy en **ta**xee **beh**len/**roo**pen?

Is there a taxi rank around?
Waar is hier een taxistandplaats?
wahr is heer en **ta**xee-stantplahts?

To the .... please
Naar de/het .... alstublieft
nahr de/heht .... alstew**bleeft**

airport	vliegveld n	**vleegh**vehlt
railway station	(trein)station n	(**traiyn**)stahsyon
centre	centrum n	**sehn**trum
'Phoenix' Hotel	Hotel n 'Phoenix'	hoa**tehl fø**niks
museum	museum n	mew**say**-yum
hospital	ziekenhuis n	**zee**kenhœs

Could you bring me to this address?
Wilt u mij naar dit adres brengen?
wilt ew maiy nahr dit ah**drehs brehng**en?

How much for the ride?
Wat gaat de rit kosten?
wat ghaht de rit **kos**ten?

55

Could you help me with my luggage?
Kunt u mij helpen met de bagage?
kunt ew maiy **hehl**pen meht de bah**ghah**zhe?

Could you stop here?
Wilt u hier stoppen?
wilt ew heer **sto**pen?

◀ **The meter is out of order**
De meter is defect
de **may**ter is de**fehkt**

Keep the change
Laat maar zitten
laht mahr **zi**ten

I'm not very mobile
Ik ben wat slecht ter been
ik behn wat slehght tehr bayn

How much do I owe you?
Hoeveel ben ik u schuldig?
hoovayl behn ik ew **sghul**degh?

◀ **I don't have any change**
Ik heb geen wisselgeld
ik hehp ghayn **wi**sel-ghehlt

Can I have a receipt?
Mag ik een kwitantie?
magh ik en kwee**tan**see?

TANKING, ACCIDENTS

AT THE PETROL STATION

Fill her up/Five litres* please
Voltanken/Vijf liter alstublieft
voltehnken/vaiyf **lee**ter alstew**bleeft**

Would you please check the ....?
Wilt u de/het .... even nakijken?
wilt ew de/heht .... **ay**ven **nah**kaiyken?

brake fluid	remvloeistof	**rehm**vlooystof
front lights	verlichting vóór	ver**ligh**ting voar
oil level	oliepeil *n*	**oa**leepaiyl
rear lights	verlichting achter	ver**ligh**ting **agh**ter
tyre pressure	bandenspanning	**ban**denspaning
water level	waterpeil *n*	**wah**terpaiyl

Do you have a road map?
Heeft u een wegenkaart?
hayft ew en **way**ghenkahrt?

Are there any toilets here?
Is hier een toilet aanwezig?
is heer en twah**leht** ahn**way**zegh?

NORMAAL	NORMAL (oct. 90)
SUPER	SUPER (oct. 94)
LOODVRIJ	UNLEADED PETROL
DIESEL	DIESEL
LPG	LPG
MENGSMERING	PETROIL/TWO-STROKE MIXTURE
LUCHT	AIR
WATER	WATER
ZELFBEDIENING	SELF-SERVICE
AUTOWASSEN/WASTUNNEL	CAR WASH

* the common fluid measure (5 litres = 1.1 gallon)

Breakdowns and accidents - assistance

In the Netherlands there's a single number **(06-11)** for all three emergency services: *politie* (police), *ambulance* (ambulance) and *brandweer* (fire). There is no charge for these emergency calls.

In Belgium you phone **101** for police assistance and **100** for the fire and ambulance services. Probably from 1994 onwards the general number for emergency services in all EC countries will be **112**.

Along the Dutch motorways you can use the yellow, emergency telephones (*praatpalen* - literally 'talking posts') that are distributed at regular intervals. These phones are provided by the *ANWB*, the Dutch AA. All you do is press the button and explain the problem to the telephonist. If you've broken down you'll be assisted by the organization's *Wegenwacht* service (road assistance). Away from the motorways you can summon assistance by ringing **06-0888** (calls free of charge).
In Belgium the equivalent body is the *Touring Wegenhulp* (its French name is *Touring Secours*), part of the *Touring Club van België/de Belgique (TCB)*. There is also the *Pechdienst* (breakdown service) provided by the *Vlaamse Automobilistenbond (VAB)*, which only operates in Flanders. Only the *TCB* can be contacted using the emergency telephones along the motorways.

Could you please ....?		
Kunt u ....?		
kunt ew ....?		
fill this petrol can	deze jerrycan vullen	**day**ze 'jerry can' **vu**len
repair this tyre	deze band reparen	**day**ze bant raypah**ray**ren
change this tyre	deze band verwisselen	**day**ze bant ver**wi**selen
pump/inflate the tyres	de banden oppompen	de **ban**den **op**-pompen
clean the windows	de ruiten schoonmaken	de **rœ**ten **sghoan**mahken
clean the windscreen	de voorruit schoonmaken	de **voar**œt **sghoan**mahken
give me a receipt	een kwitantie geven	en kwee**tan**see **ghay**ven
wash the car	de auto wassen	de **ou**toa **wa**sen

charge the battery	de accu vullen	de **a**kew **vu**len
change the oil	de olie verversen	de **oa**lee ver**vehr**sen
change the sparking plugs	de bougies verwisselen	de boo**zhees** ver**wi**selen
call a breakdown van/truck	een takelwagen bellen	en **tah**kelwahghen **beh**len

REPAIRS

Where is the nearest garage/bicycle repair shop?
Waar is een garage/fietsenmaker?
wahr is en ghah**rah**zhe/**feet**senmahker?

I have trouble with the ....
Ik heb een defect aan de/het ....
ik hehp en de**fehkt** ahn de/heht ....

I am losing oil/petrol
Ik verlies olie/benzine
ik ver**lees oa**lee/behn**zee**ne

I have a flat front/rear tyre
Ik heb een lekke voorband/achterband
ik hehp en **leh**ke **voar**bant/**ahgh**terbant

I hear a strange noise
Ik hoor een vreemd geluid
ik hoar en vraymt ghe**lœt**

The car won't start
De wagen wil niet starten
de **wah**gen wil neet **star**ten

The engine is overheated
De motor raakt oververhit
de **moa**tor rahkt oaverver**hit**

The battery is flat
De accu is leeg
de **a**kew is laygh

Could you repair/change the ....?
Kunt u de/het .... repareren/verwisselen?
kunt ew de/heht .... raypah**ray**ren/ver**wi**selen

Do you have the parts in stock?
Hebt u de onderdelen in voorraad?
hehpt ew de **on**derdaylen in **voa**raht?

I can have the parts sent in from Britain/America
Ik kan onderdelen uit Engeland/Amerika laten overkomen
ik kan **on**derdaylen œt **ehng**elant/ah**may**reekaa **lah**ten oa**ver**koamen

When will the car/motorcycle/bicycle be ready?
Wanneer is de auto/motor/fiets weer klaar?
wanayr is de **ou**toa/**moa**tor/feets wayr klahr?

Till what time can I pick it up?
Tot hoe laat kan ik hem afhalen?
tot hoo laht kan ik hehm **af**hahlen?

Do you have any idea how much it will be?
Heeft u een idee hoeveel het gaat kosten?
hayft ew en ee**day** hoovayl heht ghaht **kos**ten?

I have come to pick up my car/motorcycle/bicycle
Ik kom mijn auto/motor/fiets afhalen
ik kom maiyn **ou**toa/**moa**tor/feets **af**hahlen

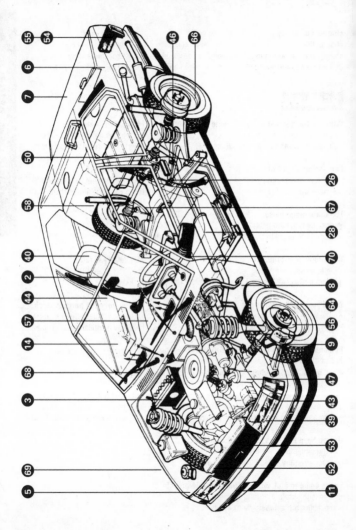

55
54
6
7
50
58
40
2
44
57
14
68
3
69
5
46
66
26
67
28
70
8
64
56
9
47
43
39
53
52
11

60

Have you found the defect?
Heeft u het mankement kunnen vinden?
hayft ew heht **man**kemehnt **ku**nen **vin**den?

Can I pay with a traveller's letter of credit?
Kan ik betalen met de reis- en kredietbrief?
kan ik be**tah**len meht de raiys- ehn kre**deet**breef?

CAR PARTS

(the parts indicated by * are not shown in the illustration)

1	accelerator pedal	gaspedaal n	**ghas**pedahl
2	backrest	rugleuning	**rugh**løning
3	battery	accu	a**kew**
*4	bearing	lager	**lah**gher
5	bonnet	motorkap	**moa**torkap
6	boot	kofferruimte	**ko**fer-rœmte
7	boot lid	kofferdeksel n	**ko**ferdehksel
8	brake, brake pedal	rem, rempedaal n	**rehm**, **rehm**pedahl
9	brake disc	remschijf	**rehm**sghaiyf
10	brake light, stoplight	remlicht n	**rehm**light
11	bumper	bumper	'**bum**per'
	front bumper	voorbumper	**voar**bumper
	rear bumper	achterbumper	**agh**ter-bumper
*12	camshaft	nokkenas	**no**ken-as
13	carburettor	carburateur	karbew**rah**tor
14	car door	portier n	por**teer**
*15	chassis	chassis n	sha**see**
16	clutch pedal	koppelingpedaal n	**ko**pelingpedahl
*17	coachwork	carrosserie	ka-ro-se-**ree**
*18	connecting rod	drijfstang	**draiyf**stang
19	cooling water pipe	koelwaterleiding	**kool**wahterlaiyding
*20	crankshaft	krukas	**kruk**as
*21	cylinder crankcase	cilinderblok n	see**lin**derblok
*22	cylinder head	cilinderkop	see**lin**derkop
23	dashboard	dashboard n	'**dashboard**'
*24	defroster vent	voorruitverwarming	**voa**-rœt-ver-war-ming
*25	dipped beam	dimlicht n	**dim**light
26	door handle	deurkruk	**dør**kruk
27	engine mounting	motorophanging	**moa**tor-ophanging
28	exhaust	uitlaat	**œt**laht
*29	exhaust valve	uitlaatklep	**œt**lahtklehp
30	fan	ventilator	vehntee**lah**tor
31	fan belt	ventilatorriem	vehntee**lah**tor-reem
*32	fan clutch for viscous drive	ventilatorkoppeling	vehntee**lah**tor-kopeling

61

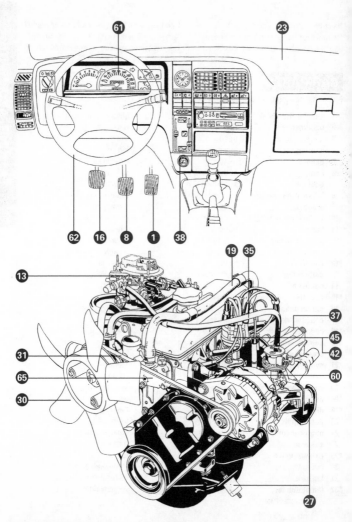

*33	filter	filter *n*	**fil**ter
*34	flywheel	vliegwiel *n*	**vleegh**wheel
35	fuel supply line	brandstofleiding	**brant**stof-laiyding
*36	(multi-speed) gearbox	versnellingsbak	ver**sneh**lings-bak
37	gearing	transmissie	trans**mi**see
38	gear (lever)	versnelling(shandle)	ver**sneh**ling(s-'handle')
39	headlight	koplamp	**kop**lamp
40	headrest	hoofdsteun	**hoaft**støn
*41	horn	claxon	**klak**son
42	ignition distributor	stroomverdeler	**stroam**verdayler
43	indicator light	richtingaanwijzer	**righ**ting-ahnwaiyzer
44	inside rear-view mirror	achteruitkijkspiegel	aghter**œt**kaiyk-speeghel
45	ignition	ontsteking	ont**stay**king
46	lock	slot *n*	slot
47	oil filter	oliefilter	**oa**leefilter
*48	oil pipe	olieleiding	**oa**leelaiyding
*49	oil pump	oliepomp	**oa**leepomp
50	petrol tank	benzinetank	behn**zee**ne-'tank'
*51	piston	zuiger	**zœ**gher
52	radiator	radiator	rah-dee**yah**tor
53	radiator grill	radiatorgrill	rah-dee**yah**tor-ghril
54	reflector	reflector	re**flehk**tor
55	reversing light	achteruitrijlicht *n*	aghter-**œt**-raiy-light
56	rim	velg	vehlgh
57	seat	zitting	**zi**ting
	front seats	voorzitting	**voar**ziting
	rear seats	achterzitting	**agh**ter-ziting
58	shock absorber	schokdemper	**sghok**dehmper
*59	spare wheel	reservewiel *n*	re**sehr**ve-weel
60	sparking plug	bougie	boo**zhee**
61	speedometer	snelheidsmeter	**snehl**haiyts-mayter
62	steering wheel	stuurwiel *n*	**stewr**weel
*63	suspension	vering	**vay**ring
64	tyre	band	bant
65	water pump	waterpomp	**wah**terpomp
66	wheel	wiel *n*	weel
	front wheel	voorwiel *n*	**voar**weel
	rear wheel	achterwiel *n*	**agh**ter-weel
67	window	ruit	rœt
	windscreen	voorruit	**voar**rœt
	side window	zijruit	**zaiy**rœt
	rear window	achterruit	**agh**te-rœt
68	windscreen wiper	ruitewisser.	**rœ**tewisser

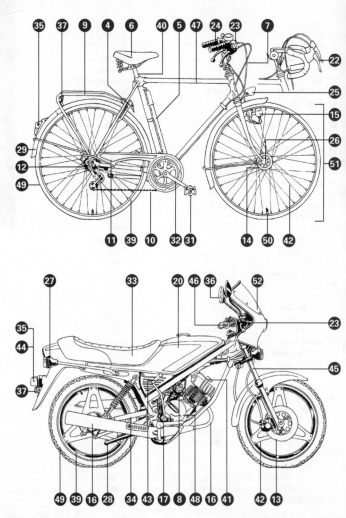

| 69 | wing | spatbord n | **spat**bort |
| 70 | wing mirror | buitenspiegel | **bœ**ten-speeghel |

MOTORCYCLE/BICYCLE PARTS

(the parts indicated by * are not shown in the illustration)

1	axle	as	as
*2	back-pedal brake	terugtraprem	te**rugh**trap-rehm
*3	ball race	kogellager	**koa**ghel-lahgher
4	bicycle lock	fietsslot n	**feets**-slot
5	bicycle pump	fietspomp	**feets**pomp
6	bicycle saddle	zadel n	**zah**del
7	cable	kabel	**kah**bel
	brake cable	remkabel	**rehm**kahbel
	gear cable	versnellingskabel	ver**sneh**lings-kahbel
	throttle cable	gaskabel	**ghas**kahbel
8	carburettor	carburator	karbew**rah**tor
9	(luggage) carrier	bagagedrager	bah**ghah**zhe-drahgher
10	chain	ketting	**keh**ting
11	chain guard	kettingkast	**keh**tingkast
12	chain wheel	kettingwiel n	**keh**tingweel
13	disc brake	schijfrem	**sghaiy**frehm
14	drum brake	trommelrem	**tro**mel-rehm
15	dynamo	dynamo	dee**naa**moa
16	exhaust	uitlaat	**œt**laht
17	footrest	voetsteun	**voot**støn
*18	four-stroke engine	viertaktmotor	**veer**taktmoator
*19	wing/butterfly nut	vleugelmoer	**vlø**ghelmoor
20	fuel tank	brandstoftank	**brant**stof-'tank'
*21	gear-change, gear shift	versnelling	ver**sneh**ling
22	hand brake	knijprem	**knaiy**prehm
23	handlebars	stuur n	stewr
24	handles	handvatten	**hant**vatten
25	headlamp	koplamp	**kop**lamp
26	hub	naaf	nahf
27	indicator (light)	richtingaanwijzer	**righ**ting-ahnwaiyzer
28	kick stand	standaard	**stan**dahrt
29	mudguard	spatbord n	**spat**bort
*30	oil tank	olietank	**oa**lee-'tank'
31	pedal	pedaal n	pe**dahl**
32	pedal crank	crank	'crank'

33	racing-style twin seat	buddyseat	'buddy seat'
34	rear fork	achtervork	**agh**tervork
35	rear light	achterlicht *n*	**agh**terlight
36	rear-view mirror	achteruitkijkspiegel	agh-ter-**œt**-kaiyk-speeghei
37	reflector	reflector	re**flehk**tor
*38	rev counter	toerenteller	**too**rentehler
39	rim	velg	vehlgh
40	seat pillar	zadelpen	**zah**delpehn
41	spark plug	bougie	boo**zhee**
42	spoke	spaak	spahk
43	starter	starter	**star**ter
44	tail light	remlicht *n*	**rehm**light
45	telescopic shock absorber	telescoopvork	tayles**koap**vork
46	throttle twist grip	gashandel	**ghas**-'handle'
47	tubular frame	buisframe *n*	**bœs**fraym
48	two-stroke engine	tweetaktmotor	**tway**taktmoator
49	tyre	band	bant
	front tyre	voorband	**voar**bant
	rear tyre	achterband	**agh**terbant
	(inner) tube	binnenband	**bi**nenbant
	tyre	buitenband	**bœ**tenbant
50	valve, valve tube	ventiel *n*, ventielslang	vehn**teel**, vehn**teel**slang
51	wheel	wiel *n*	weel
	front wheel	voorwiel *n*	**voar**weel
	rear wheel	achterwiel *n*	**agh**terweel
52	windscreen	windscherm *n*	**wint**sghehrm

NATURE OF THE DAMAGE

blocked, clogged	verstopt	ver**stopt**
broken	gebroken	ghe**broa**ken
burnt-out	doorgebrand	**doar**ghebrant
burst	gebarsten	ghe**bars**ten
dirty	vuil	vœl
frozen	bevroren	be**vroa**ren
jammed	geblokkeerd	gheblo**kayrt**
makes a noise	maakt lawaai	mahkt lah**wahy**
not properly set/aligned	verkeerd afgesteld	ver**kayrt** af**gh**estehlt
overheated	oververhit	oaver**verhit**
punctured	lek	lehk
rusty	verroest	ve**roost**

66

short-circuits	maakt kortsluiting	mahkt **kort**slœting
stuck	klemt	klehmt
vibrates	trilt	trilt
worn out	versleten	ver**slay**ten

ROAD ACCIDENTS

(see also 'Problems encountered in town' and 'Medical assistance')

There has been an accident!
Er is een ongeluk gebeurd!
ehr is en **on**gheluk ghe**børt**!

There are (no) casualties
Er zijn (geen) gewonden
ehr zaiyn (ghayn) ghe**won**den

There is only material damage
Er is alleen materiële schade
ehr is a**layn** mah-tay-ree-**yay**-le **sghah**de

Call the police/an ambulance
Waarschuw de politie/een ambulance
wahrsghew de poa**lee**tsee/en ambew**lan**se

May I please call the police?
Kan ik hier de politie bellen?
kan ik heer de poa**lee**tsee **beh**len?

Don't touch him/her
Raak hem/haar niet aan
rahk hehm/hahr neet ahn

Wait for the doctor/ambulance
Wacht op een dokter/ambulance
waght op en **dok**ter/ambew**lan**se

◄ **Who is the driver?**
Wie is de bestuurder?
wee is de be**stewr**der?

◄ **May I see your driving license/insurance papers?**
Mag ik uw rijbewijs/verzekeringspapieren zien?
magh ik ew **raiy**bewaiys/ver**zay**kerings-pahpeeren zeen?

Emergency numbers

	Netherlands	Belgium
Police	06-11	101
Ambulance	06-11	100
Fire	06-11	100

From 1994 onwards all emergency services in EC countries will be available by dialling **112**.

67

◀ **I'll have to book you**
Ik moet een proces-verbaal opmaken
ik moot en proa**sehs**-ver**bahl** op**mah**ken

◀ **Are there any witnesses?**
Zijn er getuigen?
zaiyn ehr ghe**tœ**ghen?

The other party made a mistake
De ander heeft een fout gemaakt
de **an**der hayft en fout ghe**mahkt**

◀ **You are (not) to blame for this accident**
U hebt (geen) schuld aan dit ongeval
ew hehpt (ghayn) sghult ahn dit **on**gheval

◀ **You have ....**
U hebt/bent ....
ew hehpt/behnt ....

been speeding	te snel gereden	te snehl ghe**ray**den
cut in	verkeerd ingevoegd	ver**kayrt in**ghevoogt
failed to give way	geen voorrang verleend	ghayn **voo**rang ver**laynt**
incorrectly overtaken	onjuist ingehaald	on**yœst in**ghe-hahlt
jumped the lights	door rood (licht) gereden	doar roat (light) ghe**ray**den

◀ **You will be fined for this**
U krijgt hiervoor een bekeuring
ew kraiyght heer**voar** en be**kø**ring

◀ **You'll have to come to the office**
U moet even mee naar het bureau
ew moot **ay**ven may nahr heht bew**roa**

◀ **You'll have to take a Breathalyzer test/blood test**
U moet een blaastest doen/bloedproef afleggen
ew moot en **blahs**tehst doon/**bloot**proof **af**lehghen

◀ **You may/are not allowed to drive on**
U mag (niet) verder rijden
ew mahgh (neet) **vehr**der **raiy**den

◀ **You can settle the matter amicably**
U kunt de zaak onderling schikken
ew kunt de zahk **on**derling **sghi**ken

◀ **Your car will be confiscated for inspection**
Uw auto wordt voor controle in beslag genomen
eww **ou**toa wort voar kon**tro**le in be**slagh** ghe**noa**men

I would like to have your details for insurance purposes
Ik wil graag uw gegevens voor de verzekering
ik wil ghrahgh eww ghe**ghay**vens voar de ver**zay**kering

◀ **Would you sign here?**
Wilt u dit tekenen?
wilt ew dit **tay**kenen?

I can't read this
Ik kan dit niet lezen
ik kan dit neet **lay**zen

ACCOMMODATION

Where is the 'Phoenix' Hotel?
Waar is hotel 'Phoenix'?
wahr is hoa**tehl** f**ø**niks?

Is there a hotel/guesthouse around?
Is hier in de buurt een hotel/pension?
is heer in de bewrt en hoa**tehl**/pehn**syon**?

CHECKING IN

I have a room reservation
Ik heb een kamer gereserveerd
ik hehp en **kah**mer gerayser**vayrt**

My name is ....
Mijn naam is ....
maiyn nahm is ....

◀ **Do you have a voucher/confirmation?**
Hebt u een voucher/reserveringsbevestiging?
hehpt ew en en 'voucher'/rayser**vay**rings-be-veh-ste-ghing?

Are there any vacancies?
Heeft u nog kamers vrij?
hayft ew nogh **kah**mers vraiy?

◀ **No, the hotel is fully booked**
Nee, het hotel is vol(geboekt)
nay, heht hoa**tehl** is **vol**(ghebookt)

I'd like to have a ....
Ik wil graag een ....
ik wil ghrahgh en ....

single room	eenpersoonskamer	**ayn**-per-soans-kah-mer
double room	tweepersoonskamer	**tway**-per-soans-kah-mer
apartment	appartement *n*	a**par**temehnt
with a bath	met bad *n*	meht bat
with a shower	met douche	meht doosh
with a toilet	met toilet *n*	meht twah**leht**
with running water	met stromend water *n*	meht **stroa**ment **wah**ter
with a kitchenette	met kitchenette	meht 'kitchenette'
with a double bed	met tweepersoonsbed	meht **tway**-per-soans-beht
with twin beds	met lits-jumeaux	meht lee-zhew**moa**
with an extra bed	met een extra bed	meht en **ehx**trah beht
with a cot	met een kinderbedje *n*	meht en **kin**derbehtye
with air conditioning	met airconditioning	meht 'air conditioning'

69

with a telephone	met telefoon	meht tayle**foan**
with a radio	met radio	meht **rah**deeyoa
with a television	met televisie	meht tayle**vee**see
with a balcony	met balkon *n*	meht bal**kon**
with a terrace	met terras *n*	meht teh**ras**
overlooking/with a view of the sea	met zeezicht *n*	meht **zay**zight
facing the street	aan de straatzijde	ahn de **straht**zaiyde
at the back	aan de achterzijde	ahn de **agh**terzaiyde
on the ground floor	op de begane grond	op de be**ghah**ne ghront
on a low floor	op een lage verdieping	op en **lah**ghe ver**dee**ping
on a high floor	op een hoge verdieping	op en **hoa**ghe ver**dee**ping

I'd like to have ....
Ik wil graag ....
ik wil ghrahgh ....

accommodation only	alleen logies	a**layn** loa**zhees**
bed and breakfast	logies en ontbijt	loa**zhees** ehn ont**baiyt**
half board	half pension	half pehn**syon**
full board	volledig pension	vo**lay**degh pehn**syon**

How much is the room ....?
Hoeveel kost de kamer ....?
hoovayl kost de **kah**mer ....?

a night	per nacht	pehr naght
a week	per week	pehr wayk
a fortnight	per 2 weken	pehr tway **way**ken

I/We will be staying for only one night/... nights
Ik blijf/we blijven alleen deze nacht/... nachten
ik blaiyf/we **blaiy**ven a**layn day**ze naght/... **nagh**ten

I don't know yet how long we will be staying
Ik weet nog niet hoe lang we zullen blijven
ik wayt nogh neet hoo lang we **zu**len **blaiy**ven

Can I pay with a Eurocheque/credit card?
Kan ik betalen met een Eurocheque/credit card?
kan ik be**tah**len meht en ø-roa-shehk/"credit card"?

Do I have to pay some nights in advance?
Moet ik een aantal nachten vooruit betalen?
moot ik en **ahn**tal **nagh**ten voar**œt** be**tah**len?

70

RECEPTIE	RECEPTION
SLEUTELBORD	KEY RACK
KASSIER	CASHIER
ONTBIJTZAAL	BREAKFAST ROOM
RESTAURANT	RESTAURANT
ADMINISTRATIE	ADMINISTRATION
DAMES	LADIES
HEREN	GENTS
KAPPER	HAIRDRESSER
REISBUREAU	TRAVEL AGENCY
LIFT	LIFT

◀ **Would you please fill in this form?**
Wilt u dit formulier invullen?
wilt ew dit formew**leer in**vulen?

◀ **Your room number is ....**
Uw kamernummer is ....
eww **kah**mernumer is ....

◀ **Your room will be ready at .. o'clock**
U kunt vanaf .. uur op uw kamer terecht
ew kunt van**af** .. ewr op eww **kah**mer te**rehght**

◀ **It's on the .... floor**
Het is op de .... verdieping
heht is op de ... ver**dee**ping

Can anybody help me with my luggage?
Kan iemand mij met mijn bagage helpen?
kan **ee**mant maiy meht maiyn bah**ghah**zhe **hehl**pen?

◀ **Your luggage will be brought to your room**
Uw bagage wordt gebracht
eww bah**ghah**zhe wort ghe**braght**

At what time is breakfast being served?
Om hoe laat kan ik ontbijten?
om hoo laht kan ik ont**baiy**ten?

◀ **May I have your passport?**
Mag ik uw paspoort (hebben)?
magh ik eww **pas**poart (**heh**ben)?

◀ **Unfortunately, your room is not ready yet**
De kamer is helaas nog niet vrij
de **kah**mer is hay**lahs** nogh neet vraiy

◀ **Here is your key**
Hier is uw sleutel
heer is eww **slø**tel

◀ **The lift is over there**
Daar vindt u de lift
dahr vint ew de lift

Where will breakfast be served?
Waar wordt het ontbijt geserveerd?
wahr wort heht ont**baiyt** gesehr**vayrt**?

71

Could I have my key? Number ....
Mag ik mijn sleutel hebben? Nummer ....
magh ik maiyn **slø**tel **heh**ben? **Nu**mer ....

I would like to check out
Ik wil uitchecken
ik wil **œt**shehken

Could I have the bill, please?
Wilt u de rekening voor mij opmaken, alstublieft?
wilt ew de **ray**kening voar maiy **op**mahken, alstew**bleeft**?

Could you send the bill to this address?
Wilt u de rekening sturen naar dit adres?
wilt ew de **ray**kening **stew**ren nahr dit ah**drehs**?

INFORMATION, SERVICE, COMPLAINTS

Where can I park my car?
Waar kan ik de auto parkeren?
wahr kan ik de **ou**toa par**kay**ren?

◀ **We have our own car park** (indoors/outdoors)
We hebben een eigen parkeerterrein/parkeergarage
we **heh**ben en **aiy**ghen par**kayr**tehraiyn/par**kayr**-ghah-rah-zhe

◀ **That will cost an extra ... guilders a day**
Dat kost u ... gulden extra per dag
dat kost ew ... **ghul**den **ehx**trah pehr dagh

Does the hotel have its own restaurant?
Heeft het hotel een eigen restaurant?
hayft heht hoa**tehl** en **aiy**ghen rehstoa**rant**?

Can you recommend a good/cheap restaurant?
Kunt u een goed/goedkoop restaurant aanbevelen?
kunt ew en ghoot/ghoot**koap** rehstoa**rant** **ahn**bevaylen?

Can you book a table for us?
Kunt u voor ons een tafel reserveren?
kunt ew voar ons en **tah**fel rayser**vay**ren?

Can I use room service?
Kan ik gebruik maken van de room service?
kan ik ghe**brœk mah**ken van de "room service"?

Do you have a map of the town?
Heeft u een plattegrond van de stad?
hayft ew en platte**ghront** van de stat?

Do you have a list of events?
Heeft u een evenementenlijst?
hayft ew en ayvene**mehn**tenlaiyst?

Can you reserve tickets for us?
Kunt u plaatskaarten reserveren?
kunt ew **plahts**kahrten rayser**vay**ren?

Can I book an excursion?
Kan ik boeken voor een excursie?
kan ik **boo**ken voar en ehx**kur**see?

72

Could you order a taxi for me?
Kunt u voor mij een taxi bestellen?
kunt ew voar maiy en **ta**xee be**steh**len?

I would like an outside line
Ik wil graag een buitenlijn
ik wil ghrahgh en **bœ**tenlaiyn

Can I have breakfast/lunch/dinner in my room?
Kan ik op de kamer ontbijten/lunchen/dineren?
kahn ik op de **kah**mer ont**baiy**ten/**lun**shen/dee**nay**ren?

Has anyone left a message for me?
Is er een boodschap voor mij achtergelaten?
is ehr en **boat**sghap voar maiy **agh**ter-ghelahten?

I would like to make a phone call to ....
Ik wil graag een telefoongesprek met ....
ik wil ghrahgh en taylefoanghesprehk meht ....

Could you wake me tomorrow at ....?
Wilt u mij morgen wekken om ....?
wilt ew maiy **mor**ghen **weh**ken om ....?

I am expecting a visitor
Ik verwacht een bezoeker
ik ver**waght** en be**zoo**ker

I'll wait ....
Ik wacht ....
ik waght ....

here	hier	heer
in the bar	in de bar	in de bar
in the lounge	in de lounge	in de 'lounge'
in the restaurant	in het restaurant	in heht rehstoa**rant**
in my room	op mijn kamer	op maiyn **kah**mer

I have an appointment with ....; is he/she in his/her room?
Ik heb een afspraak met ....; is hij/zij op zijn/haar kamer?
ik hehp en **af**sprahk meht ....; is haiy/zaiy op zaiyn/hahr **kah**mer?

Could you put this in the safe?
Kunt u dit in de safe bewaren?
kunt ew dit in de 'safe' be**wah**ren?

Can I change money/cash cheques here?
Kan ik hier geld wisselen/cheques verzilveren?
kan ik heer ghehlt **wis**selen/shehks ver**zil**veren?

The room has not been cleaned
De kamer is niet schoongemaakt
de **kah**mer is neet **sghoan**ghemahkt

Can I leave my luggage here?
Kan ik deze bagage hier laten staan?
kan ik **day**ze bah**ghah**zhe heer **lah**ten stahn?

The bed linen has not been changed
Het beddegoed is niet verschoond
heht **beh**deghoot is neet ver**sghoant**

73

I have no ....
Ik heb geen ....
ik hehp ghayn ....

towel	handdoek	**han**dook
bath towel	badhanddoek	**bat**handook
soap	zeep	zayp
plug	afvoerstop	**af**voorstop
toilet paper	toiletpapier *n*	twah**leht**pahpeer
wastepaper basket	prullenbak	**prul**-en-bak
pillow case	kussensloop *n*	**kus**-en-sloap
coat hangers	klerenhangers	**klay**ren-hangers

The .... doesn't/don't work
Er is een defect aan de/het ....
ehr is en de**fehkt** ahn de/heht ....

air conditioning	airconditioning	'air conditioning'
heating	verwarming	ver**warm**ing
lights	verlichting	ver**lich**ting
television set	televisietoestel *n*, t.v.	tayle**vee**see-toostehl, tay-vay
shower	douche	doosh
drainage	afvoer	**af**voor

The window cannot be opened/closed
Het raam kan niet open/dicht
heht rahm kan neet **oa**pen/dight

Could you send up a chambermaid/repairman?
Kunt u een kamermeisje/reparateur sturen?
kunt ew en **kah**mermaiysye/raypahrah**tør** stew**ren**?

I would like to have an extra blanket/pillow
Ik wil graag een extra deken/kussen
ik wil ghrahgh en **eh**xtrah **day**ken/**kus**en

My room has been broken into/Something has been stolen
Er is bij mij ingebroken/Er is iets gestolen
ehr is baiy maiy **in**ghebroaken/ehr is eets ghe**stoa**len

I would like to have another room	**I am moving into another hotel**
Ik wil graag een andere kamer	Ik neem een ander hotel
ik wil ghrahgh en **an**dere **kah**mer	ik naym en **an**der hoa**tehl**

ON THE CAMP SITE/IN THE YOUTH HOSTEL

Is camping allowed here?
Mag men hier vrij kamperen?
magh mehn heer vraiy kam**pay**ren?

May I camp on your land?
Mag ik op uw grond kamperen?
magh ik op ew ghront kam**pay**ren?

Is it allowed to spend the night in the car/caravan?
Mag men hier in de auto/caravan overnachten?
magh mehn heer in de **ou**toa/'caravan' oaver**nagh**ten?

How do I get to the camp site/youth hostel?
Hoe kom ik op de camping/bij de jeugdherberg?
hoo kom ik op de **kehm**ping/baiy de **jøght**-hehr-behrgh?

◄ **Check in here please**
Hier melden a.u.b.
heer **mehl**den alstew**bleeft**

I am looking for a spot to put a ...
Ik zoek een plaats voor een ...
ik zook en plahts voar en ...

small tent	kleine tent	**klaiy**ne tehnt
large tent	grote tent	**ghroa**te tent
car with a caravan	auto met caravan	**ou**toa meht 'caravan'

Do you have room for .. people?
Heeft u plaats voor .. personen?
hayft ew plahts voar .. pehr**soa**nen?

◄ **This is a private camp site**
Dit is een besloten camping
dit is en be**sloa**ten **kehm**ping

◄ **I am afraid the camp site/youth hostel is full**
De camping/jeugdherberg is helaas vol
de **kehm**ping/**jøght**-hehr-behrgh is hay**lahs** vol

How much is it per/for each ....?
Wat kost het per ....?
wat kost heht pehr ....?

night	nacht	naght
week	week	wayk
person	persoon	pehr**soan**
adult	volwassene	vol**was**ene
child	kind *n*	kint
tent	tent	tehnt
caravan	caravan	'caravan'
car	auto	**ou**toa
motorcycle	motor	**moa**tor
bicycle	fiets	feets

Are there any dogs allowed on the camp site?
Mag de hond op de camping komen?
magh de hont op de **kehm**ping **koa**men?

◀ **May I see your camping carnet/membership card?**
Mag ik uw kampeercarnet/lidmaatschapskaart zien?
magh ik eww kam**payr**karneht/**lit**-maht-sghaps-kahrt zeen?

◀ **You can become a temporary member**
U kunt een tijdelijk lidmaatschap aangaan
ew kunt en **taiy**delek **lit**-maht-sghap **ahn**ghahn

Is the camp site guarded?
Is de camping bewaakt?
is de **kehm**ping be**wahkt**?

Is there a/Are there any .... on the camp site?
Is er op de camping een ....?
is ehr op de **kehm**ping en ....?

camp site shop	kampwinkel	**kamp**winkel
children's playground	kinderspeelplaats	**kin**der-spaylplahts
cooking facilities	kookgelegenheid *sg.*	**koak**-ghe-lay-ghen-haiyt
washrooms	wasgelegenheid *sg.*	**was**-ghe-lay-ghen-haiyt
showers	douchegelegenheid *sg*	**doosh**-ghe-lay-ghen-haiyt
toilet	toilet *n*	twah**leht**
bicycle shed	fietsenstalling	**feet**sen-stal-ing
postbox	brievenbus	**bree**venbus

Can I rent a tent/bungolow/caravan/linen here?
Kan ik hier een tent/bungalow/caravan/linnegoed huren?
kan ik heer en tehnt/'bungalow'/'caravan'/**lin**neghoot **hew**ren?

Is there any electricity here?
Is er een aansluiting voor elektriciteit?
is ehr en **ahn**slœting voar ay-lehk-tree-see-**taiyt**?

Can I have my gas cylinders filled/replaced here?
Kan ik hier gasflessen laten vullen/omwisselen?
kan ik heer **ghas**flehsen **lah**ten **vul**en/**om**wisselen?

EATING OUT

Eating habits

A Dutch breakfast (*ontbijt*) usually consists of sandwiches
(*boterhammen*) - white or brown bread (*wit of bruin brood*) with
butter (*boter*), *margarine* or *halvarine* (low-fat margarine) and
something savoury like cheese (*kaas*), *ham* and sausage (*worst*)
or sweet such as *jam* or honey (*honing*). You can even sprinkle
hagelslag - chocolate 'hailstorm' - on your bread! More
familiarly, you can order an egg (*ei*) - hard-boiled (*hardgekookt*),
soft-boiled (*zachtgekookt*) or fried (*gebakken*, also known as
spiegelei). In many hotels you will be served an English or
American breakfast with toast, bacon, etc. on request. Besides
cornflakes you'll also see many other types of cereal, muesli and
crispbreads (often UK imports). Coffee (*koffie*) or tea (*thee*) and
fruit juice (*vruchtesap*) will also be served.

Lunch (*middageten*) is between 12.30 and 1.30 p.m. Most
working people generally take sandwiches (although many large
firms have their own canteens). The evening meal (*avondeten*) is
on the early side - usually between 6 and 7 p.m. It generally
consists of two or three hot courses.

PLACES TO EAT AND DRINK

automatiek (automat)	self-service snack machines (taking guilders and 25-cent coins) in and outside snackbars; the Dutch refer to this as *eten uit de muur* ('eating out of the wall'). See the list of snacks below;
bistro	small restaurants with a French atmosphere and a limited but reasonably priced choice;
broodjeszaak	snack bars specialising in rolls and sandwiches. See snacks below;
bruin café ('brown café')	these resemble British pubs; you find them in the big cities and they are highly popular with the locals. They are called 'brown' after the colour of the wooden wall covering; while sipping your (alcoholic) drink you can play billiards, darts or cards; small snacks are also available;

café	a cross between a simple bar (serving alcohol, mainly beer) and a coffee shop;
cafetaria	a snack bar or small restaurant, usually self-service and relatively cheap; hot meals available;
Chinees-Indisch restaurant	a legacy of Holland's colonial past when it controlled the former Dutch East Indies (Nederlands Indië or just Indië, now Indonesia and not to be confused with India). These relatively cheap restaurants are frequently run by (Hong Kong) Chinese and serve both Chinese and Indonesian food (see list below); they often have a take away service (afhaalloket), and like the British, the Dutch talk about 'going for a Chinese' (Wij gaan vanavond chinezen);
croissanterie	French-inspired café-type establishments specialising in croissants and French bread, coffee and tea;
eethuis (eating house/eatery)	usually relatively inexpensive and simple restaurants;
haringkraam (herring stall)	fish stall in the street; you can eat your purchase on the spot (hold the fish by the tail and swallow it) or take it away. A speciality in late spring is fresh, young herring (Hollandse nieuwe or nieuwe haring) - relatively expensive, especially in the first few days after the catch, but delicious. The herring are eaten raw, usually with chopped onions (uitjes);
koffieshop (coffee shop)	usually in shopping centres or department stores serving coffee, tea, soft drinks, cakes and pastries; in several big cities - notably Amsterdam - many coffee shops (most using the English term) sell soft drugs. Strictly speaking the trade is illegal but tolerated by the authorities in the interests of separating the markets for soft and hard drugs;
pannekoekenhuisje (pancake house)	these restaurants might be small but the pancakes are enormous (served with savoury or sweet toppings); popular with children;
patatkraam (chip/fries stall)	besides chips (cut in the French way) also serving other snacks (to eat on the spot or take away); the Flemish often use the term frituur;
poffertjeskraam (pancake stall)	'poffertjes' are small pancakes fried in butter and sprinkled with icing sugar; again, very popular with children;
restaurant	restaurants in Holland are high quality and generally cheaper than in the UK, and some also offer an inexpensive Tourist Menu There are also lots of very good foreign restaurants: Chinees-Indisch (see above), Surinaams (from Surinam, the former Dutch Guiana), Grieks (Greek), Turks (Turkish), Italiaans (Italian), Spaans (Spanish), etc.;
snackbar	wide selection of fast food to take away or consume on the premises. Many of these snackbars have fruit machines;

wegrestaurant   sometimes self-service; cannot be described as cheap.
(wayside restaurant)

Do you have a table for us?
Heeft u een tafel vrij?
hayft ew en **tah**fel voar ons vraiy?

A table for two please
Een tafel voor 2 personen alstublieft
en **tah**fel voar tway pehr**soa**nen alstew**bleeft**

◄ **Do you have a reservation?**
Heeft u gereserveerd?
hayft ew gerayser**vayrt**?

I made a reservation for a table for two
Ik heb een tafel voor 2 personen gereserveerd
ik hehp en **tah**fel voar tway pehr**soa**nen gerayser**vayrt**

◄ **Unfortunately all tables are occupied**
We hebben helaas geen tafel meer vrij
we **heh**ben hay**lahs** ghayn **tah**fel mayr vraiy

◄ **You can come back in half an hour**
U kunt over een half uur terugkomen
ew kunt **oa**ver en half ewr te**rugh**koamen

◄ **The restaurant does not open until seven**
Het restaurant gaat pas om zeven uur open
heht rehstoa**rant** ghaht pas om **zay**ven ewr **oa**pen

◄ **The kitchen is already closed**
De keuken is al gesloten
de **køk**en is al ghe**sloa**ten

The menu/wine list please
De menukaart/wijnkaart alstublieft
de me**new**kahrt/**waiyn**kahrt alstew**bleeft**

I only eat vegetarian dishes
Ik eet alleen vegetarische maaltijden
ik ayt a**layn** vayghe**tah**reese **mahl**taiyden

Can you recommend anything?
Kunt u iets aanbevelen?
kunt ew eets **ahn**bevaylen?

We'd like small portions for our children
Voor onze kinderen graag een kinderportie
voar **on**ze **kin**deren ghrahgh en **kin**derporsee

I would like to try a regional dish
Ik wil graag een streekgerecht proeven
ik wil ghrahgh en **strayk**gherehght **proo**ven

We don't have any cutlery/plates
We hebben geen bestek/borden
we **heh**ben ghayn be**stehk**/**bor**den

(also see 'Some useful expressions')

Could you open this bottle for me?
Wilt u deze fles voor mij openen?
wilt ew **day**ze flehs voar maiy **oa**penen?

◄ **Enjoy your meal!**
Eet smakelijk!
ayt **smah**kelek!

◄ **Did you enjoy your meal?**
Heeft het gesmaakt?
hayft heht ghe**smahkt**?

◄ **Can I clear the table?**
Kan ik afruimen?
kan ik **af**rœmen?

79

Waiter!	**The bill please**	**I would like to pay**
Ober!	De rekening alstublieft	Ik wil graag betalen
oaber!	de **ray**kening alstew**bleeft**	ik wil ghraagh be**tah**len

We'd like to have separate bills	**Where's the toilet/cloakroom?**
We willen graag apart betalen	Waar is het toilet/de garderobe?
we **wi**len ghraagh a**part** be**tah**len	wahr is heht twah**leht**/de gharde**ro**be?

SOME USEFUL EXPRESSIONS

ashtray	asbak	**as**bak
bottle	fles	flehs
cutlery	bestek *n*	be**stehk**
fork	vork	vork
glass	glas *n*	ghlas
knife	mes *n*	mehs
napkin	servet *n*	sehr**veht**
salt and pepper	peper- en zoutstel *n*	**pay**per- ehn **zout**stehl
spoon	lepel	**lay**pel

Enjoy your meal!	Eet smakelijk!	ayt **smah**kelek!
Cheers, here's to your health!	Proost! Op uw gezondheid!	proast! op eww ghe**zont**hayt!
And here's to you!	Op de uwe!	op de **ew**we!
I hope you have enjoyed your meal!	Moge het u wel bekomen!	**moa**ghe heht ew wehl be**koa**men!

A DUTCH MENU

VOORGERECHTEN	STARTERS
ansjovis	anchovy
ganzeleverpastei	pâté de foie gras
garnalencocktail	prawn cocktail
gevulde eieren	stuffed eggs
(Ardenner) ham	(Ardennes) ham, a very tasty kind of ham
haring	herring, a Dutch delicacy, usually eaten salted, sometimes pickled
huzarensalade	a salad consisting of meat (usually ham), vegetables, potatoes and mayonnaise
mosselen	mussels, usually eaten boiled or fried
oesters	oysters

80

omelet	omelette
pasteitje	a pastry shell stuffed with hot ragout
paté	pâté
Russisch ei	egg mayonnaise

SOEPEN — SOUPS

aspergesoep	asparagus soup
(bruine) bonensoep	(trad.; winter) a rich soup made of red kidney beans, vegetables and meat
bouillon	broth
consommé	consommé, clear soup
erwtensoep	(trad.; winter) a typical Dutch delicacy: a thick soup made of green peas, leek, celeriac, pork and smoked sausage
groentesoep	vegetable soup
kerriesoep	curry soup
kervelsoep	chervil soup
kippesoep	chicken soup
koninginnesoep	cream of chicken soup
ossestaartsoep	oxtail soup
soep van de dag	soup of the day
tomatensoep	tomato soup
uiensoep	onion soup
vermicellisoep	clear noodle soup
vissoep	fish soup

VIS EN SCHAALDIEREN — FISH AND SEAFOOD

baars	perch
bokking	smoked herring, comparable to kippers
forel	trout
garnalen	shrimps, prawns
haring	(trad.) herring, a typical Dutch delicacy, for example maatjesharing (young herring, Hollandse nieuwe (new herring), rolmops (pickled herring), panharing (fried herring)
heilbot	halibut
inktvis	squid, octopus
kabeljauw	cod
karper	carp
kreeft	lobster
makreel	mackerel, usually eaten smoked
mosselen	mussels, usually eaten boiled or fried
paling	(trad.) eels, a real specialty, for example gerookte paling (smoked eels), paling in het groen (a typical Belgian dish, consisting of stewed eels served in chervil sauce)

rivierkreeft	crayfish
schelvis	haddock
schol	plaice
snoek	pike
snoekbaars	pikeperch
stokvis	stockfish, cured cod or haddock
tarbot	turbot
tong	sole
tonijn	tuna
wijting	whiting
zalm	salmon
zeekreeft	lobster
zeetong	sole

WILD EN GEVOGELTE	GAME AND FOWL
duif	pigeon
eend	duck
fazant	pheasant
fricassee	fricassee
gans	goose
haantje	chicken
haas	hare
hazepeper	jugged hare, hare stew
houtsnip	woodcock
kalkoen	turkey
kip	chicken, for example gebraden kip (fried chicken), kippeborst (chicken breast), kipfilet (fillet of chicken), kippelevertjes (chicken liver)
konijn	rabbit
patrijs	partridge
reerug	venison
waterzooi	(Belg.) chicken casserole

VLEESGERECHTEN	MEAT
biefstuk	steak: biefstuk van de haas (fillet steak), biefstuk tartaar (steak tartare)
blinde vink	(trad.) slice of veal rolled up and stuffed with minced meat
entrecote	entrecôte, rib steak
filet	fillet, tenderloin
gehaktbal	meat ball, a very common dish, usually not served in restaurants but only eaten at home
hachee	hash, a meat stew with lots of onions
hersenen	brains

82

hete bliksem	(trad.) literally 'hot lightning', a dish consisting of stewed potatoes, apples and meat
hutspot met klapstuk	(trad.; winter) mashed potatoes, carrots and onions, served with boiled beef
jachtschotel	meat casserole with mashed potatoes and apples
kalfsvlees	veal, for example kalfsborst (breast of veal), kalfsbout (leg of veal), kalfsoester (veal escalope), kalfsschenkel (knuckle of veal)
karbonade	pork chop
kotelet	cutlet
lamsvlees	lamb
lendestuk	sirloin
lever	liver
nieren	kidneys
ossehaas	tenderloin
pastei	pie
pens	tripe
ragout	ragout
rollade	rolled meat
rolpens	spiced minced meat in tripe
rookworst	(trad.) smoked sausage, eaten with almost all typical Dutch winter dishes
rosbief	roast beef
rundvlees	beef, for example: runderlapje (braised slice of beef), runderrollade (rolled beef, a popular dish at Christmas)
schapevlees	mutton
spek	bacon
tong	tongue, for example ossetong (ox tongue), rundertong (beef tongue)
tournedos	fillet steak
varkensvlees	pork, for example varkenshaas (pork tenderloin), varkenskarbonade (pork chop), varkenspoot (pettitoes)

CHINEES-INDONESISCHE GERECHTEN — CHINESE AND INDONESIAN DISHES

A small selection (the spelling may vary):

atjar tjampoer	a side dish: a sweet-and-sour vegetable mixture
babi pangang	grilled pork in a sweet-and-sour sauce
bami goreng	fried noodles and vegetables, pork and omelette, sometimes served with 'saté'
haaievinnesoep	literally translated: 'shark-fin soup', a jelly-like soup, usually not made of shark fins but of chicken
foe jong hai	omelette with vegetables, sometimes also with meat

83

gado gado	a variety of vegetables covered with a peanut sauce
kroepoek	a side dish: prawn crackers
mie goreng	fried noodles
miesoep	noodle soup
nasi goreng	fried rice with meat, onions, chicken, prawns and a fried egg on top
nasi rames	a mini 'rijsttafel' (see 'rijsttafel')
oedang	prawns
Pekingeend	Peking duck, a Chinese delicacy
pisang goreng	fried bananas
rijsttafel	(min. 2 pers.) a sumptuous meal, a remnant of Dutch colonial times in Indonesia, consisting of white rice served with numerous small meat and vegetable dishes
roedjak manis	cucumber and/or apple in soy sauce
sambal	(sometimes extremely) hot pepper paste
sajoer kerrie	soup-like curry dish, eaten with white rice
sajoer lodeh	soup-like vegetable dish with meat or shrimps
saté (sateh) babi/ajam	grilled cubes of pork or chicken on skewers, served with a peanut sauce
seroendeng	side dish consisting of ground peanuts and coconut
teloer reboes	egg dish
tjap tjoy	chop suey, vegetables served in a special sauce

WIJZE VAN BEREIDEN	METHODS OF PREPARATION
aan het spit	roasted on the spit, barbecued
gaar	done
gebakken	fried: goed doorbakken (well-done), half doorbakken (medium), in de oven gebakken (baked)
gebraden	roasted
gegarneerd met ...	garnished with ...
gegrild	grilled
gehakt	chopped
gekookt	boiled
gekruid	spicy
gelardeerd met ...	larded with ...
gemarineerd	marinated
gepaneerd	breaded
gerookt	smoked
geroosterd	broiled
gesmoord	braised
gestoofd	stewed
gestoomd	steamed
gevuld met ...	stuffed with ...

84

gezouten	salted
koud	cold
mager	lean
rauw	raw
scherp	spicy, hot
vers	fresh

GROENTEN — VEGETABLES

andijvie	endive
artisjokken	artichoke
(rode) bietjes	beetroot
bloemkool	cauliflower
boerenkool met worst	(trad.; winter) dish of kale and potatoes, served with smoked sausage
(witte/bruine) bonen	(haricot/kidney) beans
Brussels lof	chicory
champignons	mushrooms
(dop)erwten	(green) peas
hutspot met klapstuk	(trad.; winter) boiled potatoes, carrots and onions mixed together, served with boiled beef
kapucijners	marrow peas
komkommer	cucumber
peulen	sugar peas, mangetout
postelein	purslane
prei	leek
radijs	radishes
rode kool	red cabbage
selderij	celery
sla	lettuce
snijbonen	sliced green beans
sperciebonen/ prinsessebonen	French beans
spinazie	spinach
spruitjes	Brussels sprouts
tomaten	tomatoes
uien	onions
zuurkool met spek	(trad.; winter) sauerkraut and potatoes mixed together, served with bacon

SAUSEN, KRUIDEN E.D. — SAUCES, HERBS, ETC.

azijn	vinegar
bieslook	chives
citroen	lemon

85

dille	dill
gelei	jelly, aspic
kaassaus	cheese sauce
kaneel	cinnamon
ketchup	(tomato) ketchup
knoflook	garlic
komijn	cummin
kruiden	herbs
kruidnagel	cloves
laurierbladeren	bay leaves
mayonaise	mayonnaise
mierikswortel	horseradish
mosterd(saus)	mustard (sauce)
nootmuskaat	nutmeg
olie	oil
olijven	olives
paprika(poeder)	paprika
peterselie	parsley
peper	pepper
room	cream
rozemarijn	rosemary
rozijnen	raisins
slagroom	whipped cream
witte wijnsaus	sauce made of white wine, flour and cream
zout	salt

TAFELGEREI	**CUTLERY**
asbakje *n*	ashtray
bestek *n*	cutlery
bierglas *n*	beer glass
bord *n*	plate
borrelglaasje *n*	spirit glass
gebakvorkje *n*	cake fork
glas *n*	glass
karaf	decanter
kop en schotel	cup and saucer
lepel	spoon
melkkannetje *n*	cream jug
mes *n*	knife
peper- en zoutstel *n*	salt and pepper pots
servetjes	napkins
suikerpot	suger bowl
tafellaken *n*	tablecloth

86

theelepeltje n	tea spoon
vork	fork
wijnglas n	wine glass
zoutvaatje n	saltcellar

NAGERECHTEN/DESSERTS DESSERTS

fruit	fruit, for example appels (apples), peren (pears), bananen (bananas), perziken (peaches), pruimen (prunes), mandarijnen (tangerines), sinaasappels (oranges), grapefruits (grapefruits), ananas (pineapple), aardbeien (strawberries), meloen (melon), bosbessen (blueberries), bramen (blackberries), druiven (grapes), dadels (dates) etc.
gebak, koekjes	pastry, cookies, usually served with coffee or tea at the end of a meal; a few Dutch specialities are: amandelgebak, appelgebak/appelpunt met slagroom, tompoes, moorkop, bitterkoekjes, kokosmakronen, Arnhemse meisjes, bokkepootjes
ijs	various kinds of icecream; for children you could order the kinderijsje, a small portion of ice cream, usually accompanied by a small gift or surprise
kaas	cheese; in restaurants at the end of a meal one usually serves French and Swiss geitekaas or schapekaas; Dutch cheese is labelled either jonge kaas, belegen kaas or oude kaas according to its age; most kinds of cheese are named after the town in which they used to be traded in the old days: Goudse kaas, Edammer kaas, Leidse kaas (the latter contains komijn) or the region where they are made Texelaar, Maaslander, Friese nagelkaas
pannekoeken	pancakes, if so desired served with stroop (syrop), gember (ginger) or some other ingredient; small, thin pancakes are called flensjes; tiny, thick ones are called poffertjes and are served with butter and icing sugar
pudding	milk pudding
vlaai	a speciality from the southern province of Limburg: a large flat pie filled with fruit (cherries, strawberries, prunes, apricots, etc.)
vruchtencompote	stewed fruit
yoghurt	yoghurt

DRANKEN	DRINKS
Alcoholische dranken	Alcoholic drinks
advocaat	a typical ladies' drink: egg liqueur served with whipped cream, which can't be drunk but is eaten with a small spoon
Berenburg	a strong herbal gin from the northern province of Friesland
bier	beer, the most popular kind being lager, called Pilsener bier in Dutch or pils in short; other kinds of beer are bokbier (a seasonal beer), moutbier (malt beer) and oud bruin (a dark, sweet stout); Dutch beer brands (Amstel, Heineken, Grolsch, Bavaria) are renowned, but many connoisseurs prefer beer from the southern provinces of Holland and especially from Belgium (this beer can be bought in many Dutch cafés nowadays), for example geuzenlambiek, kriekenlambiek (cherry-flavoured beer) and trappist (a malt beer brewed in Trappist monasteries)
borrel(tje)	almost synonymous with 'jenever', but also the term used to indicate alcoholic drinks in general or even a small five o'clock party during which alcoholic drinks are served
brandewijn (met suiker)	brandy (served with sugar)
jenever	a juniper-flacoured spirit, comparable to gin; there are several kinds, like oude jenever or jonge jenever, popularly referred to as oude/jonge klare; there are also flavoured kinds like bessenjenever (blackcurrant gin, especially popular with women) and citroenjenever (lemon gin, popularly also called: citroentje met suiker)
likeur	liqueur; the Curaçao (orange-flavoured liqueur) is renowned
wijn	wine; you can buy almost all kinds of wine in Holland: Frans (French), Italiaans (Italian), Duits (German), Spaans; (Spanish); you have a choice of rode wijn (red wine), witte wijn (white wine), rosé (rosé), droge wijn (dry wine), zoete wijn (sweet wine), mousserende wijn (sparkling wine), port(wijn) (port), sherry (sherry), etc.

cognac, rum and *whisky* have no Dutch names

Niet-alcoholische dranken	Non-alcoholic drinks
alcoholvrij bier	low alcohol beer (brand names: Buckler, Stender, Bavaria Malt etc.)

88

chocolademelk	chocolate-flavoured milk; warme chocolademelk (hot chocolate) can be served if one so wishes with slagroom (whipped cream); koude chocolademelk (cold chocolate-flavoured milk) is usually referred to as Chocomel (a brand name)
frisdranken	soft drinks; numerous kinds of soft drinks and all well-known international brands are available
koffie	coffee; you can choose from bonenkoffie, filterkoffie or oploskoffie (instant coffee); if you don't want any cream in your coffee you must order zwarte koffie (black coffee), although nowadays the cream is usually served separately; koffie verkeerd is coffee with a lot of hot milk, koffie met slagroom is coffee with whipped cream; espresso, cappuccino, Wiener melange and other foreign specialities are available in most restaurants and coffee bars nowadays; Dutch people like to have some kind of pastry with their coffee (see desserts), whereas Belgium is renowned for its bonbons/pralines, chocolates of an exceptionally high quality
melk	milk; milk is subdivided according to fat content in volle melk, halfvolle melk or magere melk; other dairy products are karnemelk, kwark, (Duitse) hüttenkäse and umer, which are more often eaten or drunk at breakfast than as a dessert
mineraalwater	mineral water, almost always carbonated; the most popular brand is 'Spa', named after the Belgian town of that name and all waiters will know exactly what you mean if you order een spaatje; (Spa rood is carbonated, Spa blauw is not, Spa groen is lemon-flavoured; the colour refers to the colour of the label and not to the colour of the water, which is clear, although coloured Spa with blueberry, orange or apple flavour is becoming popular)
thee	tea, can be sterk (strong) or slap (weak), just like coffee, and is being served without milk, unless you explicitly ask for thee met melk; tea with lemon is called thee met citroen in the major cities you will find theehuizen which serve numerous kinds of tea
tomatensap	tomato juice
vruchtesap	fruit juice; the most popular being jus d'orange (orange juice), but you can also buy appelsap (apple juice), citroensap (lemon juice), grapefruitsap or druivesap (grape juice), or a combination of various kinds of juice

SNACKS	SNACKS
patat (patates frites)	chips, served with mayonaise or pindasaus (peanut sauce). You could also try patat speciaal (chips covered with tomato ketchup, mayonnaise and onions)
croquet/kroket	meat croquettes
frikadel	sausage made of minced meat and, if so desired, served with mayonnaise, tomato ketchup and onions
bal gehakt	meatball
bamischijf	(Indon.) kind of square, flat croquette made of chow mein
milkshake	milkshake
nasibal	(Indon.) kind of square, flat croquette made of fried rice with meat, spices and vegetables
hamburger	hamburger
loempia	(Indon./Chin.) spring roll
saté	(Indon.) meat on a skewer, served with a peanut sauce

Most snack bars and cafeterias also serve a wide variety of belegde broodjes (rolls stuffed with various fillings): you can choose from broodje ham (roll stuffed with ham), kaas (cheese), ei (egg), gezond (a health-food roll stuffed with ham, cheese, lettuce, tomato, cucumber), lever (liver), tartaar (minced steak) or halfom (a popular combination of liver and salted meat).

GOING OUT

Do you have a list of events/theatre performances?
Heeft u een lijst met evenementen/theatervoorstellingen?
hayft ew en laiyst meht ayvene**mehn**ten/tay-**ah**-ter-voar-steh-ling-en?

Is there anything special going on in town today/tonight?
Is er vandaag/vanavond iets bijzonders te zien in de stad?
is ehr van**dahgh**/van**ah**vont eets bee**zon**ders te zeen in de stat?

ballet	ballet n	bal**eht**
ballroom, dance hall	danszaal	**dans**zahl
cinema	bioscoop	bee-yos**koap**
circus performance	circusvoorsteling	**sir**kus-voarstehling
concert hall	concertzaal	kon**sehrt**zahl
dance	dansavond	**dans**ahvont
discotheque	discotheek	diskoa**tayk**
film	film	film
folkloristic performance	folkloristische voorstelling	folkloa**aris**teese **voar**stehling
musical	musical	'musical'
open-air cinema	openluchtbioscoop	oapen**lught**-beeyoskoap
open-air concert	openluchtconcert	oapen**lught**konsehrt
open-air theatre	openluchttheater	oapen**lught**-tay-ah-ter
opera	opera	**oa**pe-rah
operetta, light opera	operette	oape**reht**e
parade, pageant	optocht	**op**toght
performance of	optreden van	**op**trayden van ....
play	toneelstuk n	toa**nayl**stuk
rock concert, gig	popconcert n	**pop**konsehrt
sound-and-light show	klank- en lichtspel n	klank-ehn-**light**spehl
theatre	schouwburg, theater n	**sghou**burgh, tay-**ah**ter
variety show	variété n	vah-ree-yay-**tay**

CINEMA AND THEATRE

Is there a cinema nearby?
Is hier in de buurt een bioscoop?
is heer in de bewrt en beeyos**koap**?

Are foreign films being dubbed?
Worden buitenlandse films nagesynchroniseerd?
worden **boe**tenlantse films **nahg**he-sin-ghroa-nee-sayrt?

◀ **No, they come with Dutch subtitles***
Nee, ze hebben Nederlandse ondertitels
nay, ze **heh**ben **nay**derlantse **on**derteetels

* In Belgium films often get both Dutch and French subtitles; in the French speaking
regions many foreign films are being imported from France, where they have been dubbed.

What's on tonight?
Wat draait er vanavond?
wat drayt ehr van**ah**vont?

What kind of film is it?
Wat is het voor een soort film?
wat is heht voar en soart film?

American	Amerikaans	ahmayree**kahns**
adventure film	avonturenfilm	ahvon**tew**renfilm
cartoon	tekenfilm	**tay**kenfilm
children's film	kinderfilm	**kin**derfilm
comedy	komedie	koa**may**dee
crime/action film	misdaadfilm	**mis**dahtfilm
Dutch	Nederlands	**nay**derlants
English	Engels	**ehng**els
French	Frans	frans
Italian	Italiaans	ee-tah-lee-**ahns**
musical	musical	'musical'
science fiction	science fiction	'science fiction'
thriller	thriller	'thriller'
tragedy	drama	**drah**mah
western	western	'western'

What time does the performance start?
Hoe laat begint de voorstelling?
hoo laht be**ghint** de **voar**stehling?

Is the film suitable for children?
Is de film geschikt voor kinderen?
is de film ghe**sghikt** voar **kin**deren?

Is there a play in any other language than Dutch?
Is er een toneelstuk in een andere taal dan Nederlands?
is ehr en toa**nayl**stuk in en **an**dere tahl dan **nay**derlants?

Who are performing?
Wie treedt er op?
wee trayt ehr op?

Where can I buy tickets?
Waar kan ik kaarten krijgen?
wahr kan ik **kahr**ten **kraiy**ghen?

◀ **At the box office/booking office**
Aan de kassa/bij het bespreekbureau
ahn de **ka**sah/baiy heht be**sprayk**bewroa

Two tickets for tonight's show, please
Twee kaartjes alstublieft voor de voorstelling van vanavond
tway **kahr**tyes alstew**bleeft** voar de **voar**stehling van van**ah**vont

in the back	achteraan	agh-ter-ahn
in the front	vooraan	voar**ahn**
in the middle	in het midden	in heht **mid**den
box, loge	loge	**loa**zhe
gallery	balkon	bal**kon**
stalls	zaal	zahl

◀ **The show is sold out**
De voorstelling is uitverkocht
de **voar**stehling is **œt**verkoght

DANCING AND DISCOTHEQUE

Is there a nice discotheque around?
Is hier een leuke dancing/disco(theek)?
is heer en **lœ**ke 'dancing'/diskoa(**tayk**)?

◀ **This is a private club**
Dit is een besloten club
dit is en be**sloa**ten klup

Do they charge an admission fee?
Moet er entree betaald worden?
moot ehr ehn**tray** be**tahlt wor**den?

What kind of music do they usually play?
Wat voor muziek wordt er meestal gespeeld?
wat voar mew**zeek** wort ehr **mays**tal ghe**spaylt**?

Is there live music or do they play records?
Is het live muziek of van platen?
is heht 'live' mew**zeek** of van **plah**ten?

Is there a good d.j.?
Is er een goede d.j.?
is ehr en **ghoo**de 'd.j.'?

Can we go ballroom-dancing here as well?
Kunnen we hier ook stijldansen?
kunen we heer oak **staiyl**dansen?

Would you like to go to the disco?
Ga je mee naar de disco?
ghah ye may nahr de **dis**koa?

May I have this dance, please?
Mag ik deze dans van u?
magh ik **day**ze dans van ew?

This music is far out!
Wat een onwijs gave muziek!
wat en on**waiys ghah**ve mew**zeek**!

Let's step out
Laten we naar buiten gaan
lahten we nahr **bœ**ten ghahn

Let's go somewhere/someplace else
Laten we ergens anders heen gaan
lahten we **ehr**ghens **an**ders hayn ghahn

May I take you to your seat?
Mag ik u naar uw plaats brengen?
magh ik ew nahr eww plahts **brehng**en?

Shall I take you home/to the hotel?
Zal ik je naar huis/het hotel brengen?
zal ik ye nahr hœs/heht hoa**tehl brehng**en?

93

Thank you for a lovely evening
Bedankt voor de leuke avond
be**dankt** voar de l**ø**ke **ah**vont

OUTINGS WITH THE CHILDREN

Is there a nice place for children to go to?
Is er iets leuks voor de kinderen?
is ehr eets løks voar de **kin**deren?

amusement park	pretpark *n*	**preht**park
aquarium	aquarium *n*	ah-**kwah**-ree-yum
children's museum	museum *n* voor kinderen	mew**say**-um voar **kin**deren
circus	circus *n*	**sir**kus
miniature town	miniatuurstad	meeneeyah**tewr**stat
mini zoo	kinderboerderij	**kin**derboorderaiy
play area	speelweide	**spayl**waiyde
playground	speeltuin	**spayl**tœn
round trip by plane	rondvlucht	**ront**vlught
sightseeing cruise	rondvaart	**ront**vahrt
steam train	stoomspoorlijn	**stoam**spoarlaiyn
swimming pool	zwembad *n*	**zwehm**bat
swimming pool and leisure centre	waterpretpark *n*	**wah**terprehtpark
terrarium	terrarium *n*	teh**rah**reeyum
Wild West village	wild west-dorp *n*	wilt wehst dorp
zoo	dierentuin	**dee**rentœn

PROBLEMS IN TOWN

ASKING FOR DIRECTIONS

Could you show me the way to the/a ... ?
Kunt u mij de weg wijzen naar de/het/een ... ?
kunt ew maiy de wehgh **waiy**zen nahr de/heht/en ...?

amusement park	pretpark n	**preht**park
bank	bank	bank
bus terminal	busstation n	**bus**-stahsyon
cathedral	kathedraal, dom	ka-te-**drahl**, dom
centre	centrum n	**sehn**trum
doctor	dokter	**dok**ter
exit	uitgang	**œt**ghang
hospital	ziekenhuis n	**zee**kenhœs
market	markt	markt
museum	museum n	mew**say**-um
open-air museum	openluchtmuseum n	oa-pen-**lught**-mew-say-um
police station	politiebureau n	poa**lee**tsee-bewroa
post office	postkantoor n	**post**kantoar
this address	dit adres	dit ah**drehs**
station	station n	stah**syon**
tourist information	VVV-kantoor n	vay-vay-vay-kan**toar**

◀ **No, I'm afraid I'm a stranger here**
Nee, ik ben hier helaas niet bekend
nay, ik behn heer hay**lahs** neet be**kehnt**

◀ **From here you go ....**
U gaat hier....
ew ghaht heer ...

straight on	rechtuit	**rehght**œt
to the right	rechtsaf	**rehghts**af
to the left	linksaf	**links**af
round the corner	de hoek om	de hook om

95

◀ **as far as/up to ....**
.... en dan tot aan ....
.... ehn dan tot ahn ....

the crossing	de kruising	de **krœ**sing
the large square	het grote plein	heht **ghroa**te plaiyn
the roundabout	de rotonde	de roa**ton**de
the bridge	de brug	de brugh
the church	de kerk	de kehrk
the first turning on the right	de eerste zijstraat rechts	de **ayr**ste **zaiy**straht rehghts
the third turning on the left	de derde zijstraat links	de **dehr**de **zaiy**straht links
on your left	aan uw linkerhand	ahn eww **lin**kerhant
on your right	aan uw rechterhand	ahn eww **rehght**erhant
right in front of you	recht vóór u	rehght voar ew
across the road and a little to the left/right	schuin (links/rechts) aan de overzijde	sghœn (links/rehghts) ahn de **oa**verzaiyde
behind/beyond that	daarachter	dah**ragh**ter
next to that	daarnaast	dahr**nahst**
200 meters* from here/there	na 200 meter	nah **tway**hondert **may**ter
half an hour on foot	een half uur lopen	en half ewr **loa**pen
around the corner	om de hoek	om de hook

◀ **You'd better ask again from there**
Vraag het dan nog maar een keer
vrahgh heht dan nogh mahr en kayr

How far is it on foot?
Hoe ver is het lopen?
hoo vehr is heht **loa**pen?

Is it far from here?
Is het ver van hier?
is heht vehr van heer?

◀ **You had better take bus number 4****
U kunt beter met bus nummer 4 gaan
ew kunt **bay**ter meht bus **nu**mer veer ghahn

◀ **You had better take a taxi/cab**
U kunt beter een taxi nemen
ew kunt **bay**ter en **ta**xi **nay**men

I am lost
Ik ben de weg kwijt
ik behn de wehgh kwaiyt

◀ **You have taken the wrong way**
U bent verkeerd gelopen
ew behnt ver**kayrt** ghe**loa**pen

◀ **They've sent you in the wrong direction**
Men heeft u de verkeerde weg gewezen
mehn haiyft ew de ver**kayr**de wehgh ghe**way**zen

---

* On the continent **meters** and **kilometers** are used instead of feet, yards and miles
(1 kilometre = 0.62 miles).
**All bus and tram services are indicated by numbers; the underground is named after its
destination (for example 'Gaasperplas').

Can you show me on the map where I am now?
Kunt u op de plattegrond aanwijzen waar ik nu ben?
kunt ew op de pla-te-**ghront ahn**waiyzen wahr ik new behn?

◄ You are now here
U staat nu hier
ew staht new heer

Could you walk part of the way with me?
Kunt u een eindje met mij meelopen?
kunt ew en **aiyn**tye meht maiy **may**loapen?

ACCIDENTS/POLICE

A fire has broken out/There has been an accident
Er is brand uitgebroken/Er is een ongeluk gebeurd
ehr is brant **œt**ghebroaken/ehr is en **on**gheluk ghe**børt**

Would you please call the police/an ambulance/the fire brigade?
Wilt u de politie/ambulance/brandweer bellen?
wilt ew de poa**lee**tsee/ambew**lan**se/**brant**wayr **bel**en?

I urgently need help
Ik heb snel hulp nodig
ik hehp snehl hulp **noa**degh

Help! Stop thief!
Help! Houd de dief!
hehlp! hout de deef!

Emergency telephone numbers

	Netherlands	Belgium
Police	06-11	101
Ambulance	06-11	100
Fire	06-11	100

From 1994 onwards all emergency services in EC countries will be available by dialling **112**.

By the way, bicycle theft is the most frequently occurring type of crime in the big cities. **Always** lock your bike **and** attach it to something (fence, lamp post) as well. Use a *fietsenstalling* (cycle shed) or *fietsenrek* (cycle stand/rack) wherever possible. You see them everywhere. There are also supervised sheds (for which a charge is made). Always report theft to the police, even though it is unlikely that anything can be done to get your bicycle back.

Where is the police station?
Waar is het politiebureau?
wahr is heht poa**lee**tseebewroa?

I'd like to report (a/an) ....
Ik wil aangifte doen van ....
ik wil **ahn**ghifte doon van ....

arson	brandstichting	**brant**stighting
assault	aanranding	**ahn**randing
battery	mishandeling	mis**han**deling
breaking and entering	inbraak	**in**brahk
damage	schade	**sghah**de
extortion	afpersing	**af**pehrsing
fraud	oplichting	**op**lighting
loss	verlies *n*	ver**lees**
pickpocketing	zakkenrollerij	**zak**-en-rol-e-raiy
rape	verkrachting	ver**kragh**ting
robbery/theft	beroving/diefstal	ber**oa**ving/**deef**stal
shoplifting	winkeldiefstal	**win**keldeefstal
that my car has been broken into	openbreken van de auto	**oa**penbrayken van de **ou**toa
vandalism	vernieling	ver**nee**ling

My .... has been stolen/I lost my ....
Ik ben beroofd van mijn ..../Ik ben mijn .... verloren
ik behn be**roaft** van maiyn ..../ik behn maiyn .... ver**loa**ren

banker's card	betaalpas	be**tahl**pas
camera	fototoestel *n*	**foa**toa-toostehl
car radio	autoradio	**ou**toa-rahdeeyoa
cheques	cheques	shehks
credit card	credit card	'credit card'
hand bag	handtasje *n*	**hant**-ta-sye
luggage	bagage	bah**ghah**zhe
passport	paspoort *n*	**pas**poart
purse	portemonnee	portemo**nay**
suitcase	koffer	**kof**fer
travel documents	reisdocumenten	**raiys**doa-kew-mehn-ten
wallet	portefeuille	porte**fœ**ye

My car/bicycle/caravan/trailer has been stolen
Mijn auto/fiets/caravan/aanhanger is gestolen
maiyn **ou**toa/feets/'caravan'/**ahn**hanger is ghe**stoa**len

I have been harassed
Ik ben lastig gevallen
ik behn **las**tegh ghe**val**en

98

◄ I am being followed
Ik word achtervolgd
ik wort ahgter**volgt**

◄ Do you want to report a crime/make a statement?
Wilt u aangifte doen/een verklaring afleggen?
wilt ew **ahn**ghifte doon/en ver**klah**ring **af**lehghen?

◄ We will make a report
Wij zullen proces-verbaal opmaken
waiy **zul**en proa**sehs**-vehrbahl **op**mahken

◄ Are there any witnesses?
Hebt u getuigen?
hehpt ew ghe**toe**ghen?

◄ We can't do anything just yet
Wij kunnen er voorlopig niets aan doen
waiy **kun**en ehr voar**loa**pegh neets ahn doon

◄ We will take the matter into investigation
Wij zullen de zaak onderzoeken
waiy **zul**en de zahk onder**zoo**ken

◄ You can inquire at the lost and found office
U kunt navraag doen bij het bureau voor gevonden voorwerpen
ew kunt **nah**vrahgh doon baiy heht bew**roa** voar ghe**von**den **voar**wehrpen

◄ Would you fill in/sign this form?
Wilt u dit formulier invullen/ondertekenen?
wilt ew dit formew**leer in**vulen/onder**tay**kenen?

I can't read it
Ik kan het niet lezen
ik kan heht neet **lay**zen

I'd like to have an interpreter/see a police woman
Kan er een tolk/vrouwelijke agent bijkomen?
kan ehr en tolk/vrou-we-le-ke ah**ghehnt baiy**koamen?

I can't sign this
Ik kan dit niet ondertekenen
ik kan dit neet onder**tay**kenen

I retract my report/statement
Ik trek de aangifte/verklaring in
ik trehk de **ahn**ghifte/ver**klah**ring in

◄ Your car has been towed away
Uw auto is weggesleept
eww **ou**toa is **wehgh**-gheslaypt

◄ You can collect it there
U kunt hem daar afhalen
ew kunt hehm dahr **af**hahlen

◄ May I see your passport/driving license/ID?
Mag ik uw paspoort/rijbewijs/een legitimatie zien?
magh ik eww **pas**poart/**raiy**bewaiys/en lay-ghee-tee**mah**tsee zeen?

◄ You must come along to the police station
U moet mee naar het bureau
ew moot may nahr heht bew**roa**

◄ You are trespassing
U bevindt zich op verboden terrein
ew be**vint** zigh op ver**boa**den teh**raiyn**

◄ You're not allowed to take pictures here
U mag hier niet fotograferen
ew magh heer neet foa-toa-ghrah**fay**ren

99

◄ You are suspected of ..../arrested for ....
U wordt verdacht van ..../gearresteerd wegens ....
ew wort ver**daght** van ..../ghe-arehs**tayrt** wayghens ....

an act of violence	geweldpleging	ghe**wehlt**playghing
being guilty of causing an accident	schuld aan een ongeval	sghult ahn en **on**gheval
having illegally entered the country	illegale grensoverschrijding	**ee**lay-ghah-le **ghrehns**oaver-sghraiyding
possesion of drugs	bezit van verdovende middelen	be**zit** van ver**doa**vende **mid**-e-len
public drunkenness	openbare dronkenschap	**oa**penbahre **dron**kensghap
smuggling	smokkel	**smok**el
theft	diefstal	**deef**stal
vandalism	vernieling	ver**nee**ling
violation of the public order	verstoring van de openbare orde	ver**stoa**ring van de **oa**penbahre **or**de

I'd like to see a lawyer/someone from the embassey
Ik wil een advocaat/iemand van de ambassade spreken
ik wil en atvoa**kaht**/**ee**mant van de am-ba-**sah**-de **spray**ken

◄ We're placing you under arrest
Wij nemen u in voorlopige hechtenis
waiy **nay**men ew in voor**loa**peghe **hehgh**tenis

◄ We're taking you into custody
Wij nemen u in hechtenis
waiy **nay**men ew in **hehgh**tenis

◄ You will have to go to court
U wordt voorgeleid
ew wort **voar**ghelaiyt

I'm innocent/have nothing to do with this
Ik ben onschuldig/heb hier niets mee te maken
ik behn on**sghul**degh/hehp heer neets may te **mah**ken

accused, defendant	beklaagde	be**klahgh**de
criminal investigation department	recherche	re**syehr**sye
judge	rechter	**rehgh**ter
magistrate in a juvenile court	kinderrechter	**kin**der-rehghter
public prosecutor	officier van justitie	of-ee-**seer** van jus**teet**see
suspect	verdachte	ver**daghte**
traffic police	verkeerspolitie	ver**kayrs**poaleetsee
vice squad	zedenpolitie	**zay**denpoaleetsee

MEDICAL CARE

ASKING FOR HELP

I (urgently) need a doctor/dentist
Ik heb (dringend) een dokter/tandarts nodig
ik hehp (**dring**ent) en **dok**ter/**tant**arts **noa**degh

Could you call a doctor/ambulance for me?
Kunt u voor mij een dokter/ambulance bellen?
kunt ew voar maiy en **dok**ter/ambew**lan**se **be**len?

Where can I find a first-aid post/outpatients' clinic?
Waar is een eerste hulp-post/de polikliniek?
wahr is en **ayr**ste hulp-post/de **poa**lee-kleeneek?

Is there a night/weekend service?
Is er nachtdienst/weekenddienst?
is ehr **naght**deenst/'weekend'-deenst?

I have to get to a hospital quickly
Ik moet snel naar een ziekenhuis
ik moot snehl nahr en **zee**kenhœs

Where does the doctor live?
Waar woont de dokter?
wahr woant de **dok**ter?

I'd like to make an appointment with the/a ....
Ik wil een afspraak maken met de/een ....
ik wil en **af**sprahk **mah**ken meht de/en ....

dentist	tandarts	**tant**arts
dermatologist	huidarts	**hœt**arts
doctor	arts	arts
ear, nose and throat specialist	keel-, neus- en oorarts	kayl-, nøs- ehn **oar**arts
general practitioner, GP	huisarts	**hœs**arts
gynaecologist	vrouwenarts, gynaecoloog	**vrou**-wenarts, ghee-nah-koa**loagh**
internist	internist	inter**nist**
neurologist	zenuwarts	**zay**neww-arts
ophthalmologist	oogarts	**oagh**arts
paediatrician	kinderarts	**kin**der-arts
urologist	uroloog	ewroa**loagh**

When is the surgery open?
Hoe laat heeft de dokter spreekuur?
hoo laht hayft de **dok**ter **sprayk**ewr?

Is the doctor in?
Is de dokter aanwezig?
is de **dok**ter ahn**way**zegh?

101

Does the doctor speak English?
Spreekt de dokter Engels?
spraykt de **dok**ter **eng**els?

◀ **Would you please take a seat in the waiting room?**
Wilt u in de wachtkamer plaats nemen?
wilt ew in de **wagh**tkahmer plahts **nay**men?

◀ **Do you have insurance?**
Bent u verzekerd?
behnt ew ver**zay**kert?

◀ **Next please!**
Volgende patiënt!
volghende pah**syehnt**!

IN THE DOCTOR'S/DENTIST'S OFFICE

I suffer from ....
Ik heb last van ....
ik hehp last van ....

My .... is hurting
Ik voel pijn in mijn ....
ik vool paiyn in maiyn ...

I can't move my ....
Ik kan mijn .... niet bewegen
ik kan maiyn .... neet be**way**ghen

I have been bitten by a dog/an insect
Ik ben gebeten door een hond/insect
ik behn ghe**bay**ten doar en hont/in**sehkt**

Could you examine me?
Kunt u mij onderzoeken?
kunt ew maiy onder**zoo**ken?

I'm .. months pregnant
Ik ben .. maanden zwanger
ik behn .. **mahn**den **zwang**er

I am a diabetic/have a heart condition/am allergic to ....
Ik ben diabeticus/hartpatiënt/allergisch voor ....
ik behn dee-yah-**bay**-tee-kus/**hart**pah-syehnt/a**lehr**ghees voar ....

I have been treated/operated for this before
Ik ben al eerder behandeld/geopereerd hiervoor/hieraan
ik behn al **ayr**der be**han**delt/ghe-oa-pe-**rayrt** heer**voar**/heer**ahn**

◀ **Sit/Lie down here**
Gaat u hier zitten/liggen
ghaht ew heer **zi**ten/**li**ghen

◀ **You can undress yourself overthere**
U kunt zich daar uitkleden
ew kunt zigh dahr **œt**klayden

◀ **How long have you been suffering from this?**
Hoe lang hebt u hier al last van?
hoo lang hehpt ew heer al last van?

◀ **Do you use any medication?**
Gebruikt u medicijnen?
ghe**brœkt** ew maydee**saiy**nen?

◀ **Where does it hurt?**
Waar doet het pijn?
wahr doot heht paiyn?

◀ **Does this hurt?**
Doet dit pijn?
doot dit paiyn?

102

◀ **Take a deep breath**
Zucht eens diep
zught ayns deep

◀ **Breathe in, than slowly breathe out**
Inademen en langzaam uitademen
inah-de-men ehn **lang**zahm œt̶ah-de-men

◀ **You should have an X-ray**
U moet een röntgenfoto laten maken
ew moot en 'röntgen'-foatoa **lah**ten **mah**ken

◀ **I have to refer you to a specialist**
Ik moet u naar een specialist verwijzen
ik moot ew nahr en **spay**syah-list ver**waiy**zen

◀ **You need to go to a hospital ....**
U moet hiermee naar een ziekenhuis .....
ew moot heer**may** nahr en **zee**kenhœs ....

for a blood test	voor een bloedproef	voar en **bloot**proof
for a urinalysis	voor een urinetest	voar en ew**ree**netest
for further examinations	voor nader onderzoek	voar **nah**der **on**derzook

◀ **You must rest for a few days**
U moet een paar dagen rust houden
ew moot en pahr **dah**ghen rust **hou**den

◀ **You must stay in bed for a few days**
U moet een paar dagen in bed blijven
ew moot en pahr **dah**ghen in beht **blaiy**ven

◀ **You may not use/move this for a few days**
U mag dit een paar dagen niet gebruiken/bewegen
ew magh dit en pahr **dah**ghen neet ghe**brœ**ken/be**way**ghen

◀ **It's nothing serious**
Het is niets ernstigs
heht is neets **ehrn**steghs

◀ **You are suffering from ....**
U lijdt aan ....
ew laiyt ahn ....

◀ **I shall write out a prescription**
Ik zal u een recept geven
ik zal ew en re**sehpt ghay**ven

◀ **I'll give you a painkiller/a sedative/sleeping pills**
Ik geef u een pijnstiller/een kalmerend middel/een slaapmiddel
ik ghayf ew en **paiyn**sti-ler/en kal**may**rent **mi**del/en **slahp**mi-del

◀ **You must take a tablet .....**
U moet een tablet nemen .....
ew moot en tah**bleht nay**men ....

on an empty stomach	op de nuchtere maag	op de **nugh**tere mahgh
three times a day	driemaal daags	**dree**mahl dahghs
before each meal	vóór elke maaltijd	voar **ehl**ke **mahl**taiyt
after each meal	na elke maaltijd	nah **ehl**ke **mahl**taiyt
before you go to bed	vóór het slapengaan	voar heht **slah**penghahn
with some water	met wat water	meht wat **wah**ter

MEDICAL CARE

◄ See me again in 3 days
Komt u over 3 dagen nog eens terug
komt ew **oa**ver dree **dah**ghen nogh ayns te**rugh**

I have ..../You have ....
Ik heb .... /U hebt ....
ik hehp ..../ew hehpt ....

a toothache	kiespijn/tandpijn	**kees**paiyn/**tant**paiyn
bleeding gums	bloedend tandvlees *sg.*	**bloo**dent **tant**vlaiys
an inflammation of the	ontstoken tandvlees *sg.*	ont**stoa**ken **tant**vlays
gums		
caries	een gaatje/.. gaatjes	en **ghah**tye/.. **ghah**tyes
neuritis	een zenuwontsteking	en **zay**new-ontstayking
a broken tooth	een afgebroken tand	en **af**ghebroaken tant

I lost a filling/I broke my dentures
Ik heb een vulling verloren/Ik heb mijn kunstgebit gebroken
ik hehp en **vul**ing ver**loa**ren/ik hehp maiyn **kunst**ghebit ghe**broa**ken

◄ I'll have to pull/fill/drill this tooth
Ik moet deze kies trekken/vullen/boren
ik moot **day**ze kees **treh**ken/**vul**en/**boa**ren

◄ I'll give you a(n) ....
Ik geef u een ....
ik **ghayf** ew en ....

anaesthetic	verdoving	ver**doa**ving
crown	kroon	kroan
fluoride rinse	fluorspoeling	**flew**or-spooling
injection	injectie	in**jehk**see
temporary filling	noodvulling	**noat**vul-ing
root canal treatment	wortelkanaalbehandeling	**wor**tel-kahnahl-be**han**deling
root canal work	zenuwbehandeling	**zay**new-behandeling

◄ Rinse your mouth with this
U moet hiermee de mond spoelen
ew moot **heer**may de mont **spoo**len

◄ Consult your GP/dentist/specialist on returning home
U moet na thuiskomst uw huisarts/tandarts/specialist raadplegen ·
ew moot nah **tœs**komst eww **hœs**arts/**tant**arts/**spay**shah-list **raht**playghen

◀ **You must pay cash**
U moet contant betalen
ew moot kon**tant** be**tah**len

Could I have a receipt for the insurance company?
Kan ik een bewijsje krijgen voor de verzekering?
kan ik en be**waiys**ye **kraiy**ghen voar de ver**zay**kering?

SYMPTOMS

abscess	abces *n*	ap**sehs**
appendicitis	blindedarmontsteking	blinde**darm**ontstayking
asthma	astma	**as**mah
backache	rugpijn	**rugh**paiyn
bellyache	buikpijn	**bœk**paiyn
bleeding, haemorrhage	bloeding	**bloo**ding
bruise	bloeduitstorting	**bloot**œtstorting
burns	brandwond	**brant**wont
cold	verkoudheid	ver**kout**haiyt
concussion	hersenschudding	**hehr**sen-sghu-ding
constipation	verstopping	ver**sto**ping
cramp, spasm	kramp	kramp
depression	neerslachtigheid	nayr-**slagh**-tegh-haiyt
diarrhoea	diarree	dee-ya-**ray**
earache	oorpijn	**oar**paiyn
fever	koorts	koarts
flu	griep	ghreep
food poisoning	voedselvergiftiging	**voot**sel-vergifteghing
gastroenteritis	buikgriep	**bœk**ghreep
graze	schaafwond	**sghahf**wont
haemorrhoids	aambeien	**ahm**baiy-en
headache	hoofdpijn	**hoaft**paiyn
infection	infectie	in**fehk**see
inflammation of the jaw	kaakontsteking	**kahk**ont-stay-king
insect bite	insektenbeet	in**sehk**ten-bayt
insomnia	slapeloosheid	slahpe**loas**haiyt
itch	jeuk	yøk
laryngitis	keelontsteking	**kayl**ont-stay-king
lumbago	spit	spit
nausea	misselijkheid	**mi**-se-lek-haiyt
pneumonia	longontsteking	**long**ont-stay-king
qualms	braakneigingen	**brahk**naiy-ghing-en
(the) shivers	rillerigheid *sg.*	**ri**-le-regh-haiyt
sinusitis	voorhoofdsholteontsteking	**voar**hoafts-holte-ont**stay**king
sore muscles	spierpijn *sg.*	**speer**paiyn
stomachache	maagpijn	**mahgh**paiyn

105

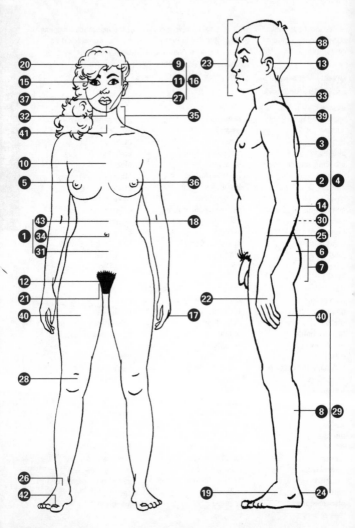

106

sunburn	zonnebrand	**zo**-ne-brant
sunstroke	zonnesteek	**zo**-ne-stayk
toothache	kiespijn	**kees**paiyn
ulcer	maagzweer	**mahgh**zwayr
wound	wond	wont

◄ **This bone has been fractured/cracked/injured**
Dit bot is gebroken/gescheurd/gekneusd
dit bot is ghe**broa**ken/ghe**sghørt**/ghe**knøst**

◄ **You've torn/pulled a muscle**
De spier is gescheurd/verrekt
de speer is ghe**sghørt**/veh**rehkt**

◄ **This must be ....**
Dit moet worden ....
dit moot **wor**den ....

bandaged	verbonden	ver**bon**den
operated on	geopereerd	ghe-oa-pe-**rayrt**
removed	verwijderd	ver**waiy**dert
rubbed	ingesmeerd	**in**ghe-smayrt
splint	gespalkt	ghe**spalkt**
stitched	gehecht	ghe**hehght**

PARTS OF THE BODY

1	abdomen	buik	bœk
2	arm	arm	arm
3	armpit	oksel	**ok**sel
4	back	rug	rugh
5	breast	borst	borst
6	buttock	bil	bil
7	buttocks, backside	zitvlak *n*	**zit**vlak
8	calf	kuit	kœt
9	cheek	wang	wang
10	chest	borstkas	**borst**kas
11	chin	kin	kin
12	crotch	kruis *n*	krœs
13	ear	oor *n*	oar
14	elbow	elleboog	**eh**-le-boagh
15	eye	oog *n*	oagh
16	face	gezicht *n*	ghe**zight**
17	finger	vinger	**ving**er
18	flank	zij	zaiy
19	foot	voet	voot
20	forehead	voorhoofd *n*	**voar**hoaft

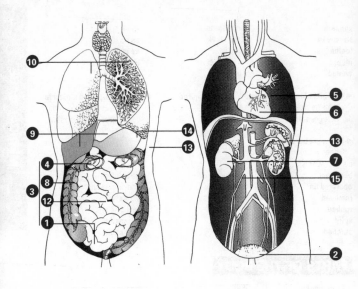

21	groin	lies	lees
22	hand	hand	hand
23	head	hoofd _n_	hoaft
24	heel	hiel	heel
25	hip	heup	høp
26	instep	wreef	wrayf
27	jaw	kaak	kahk
28	knee	knie	knee
29	leg	been _n_	bayn
30	loin	lende	**lehn**de
31	lower abdomen	onderbuik	**on**derbœk
32	mouth	mond	mont
33	nape	nek	nehk

34	navel	navel	**nah**vel
35	neck	hals	hals
36	nipple	tepel	**tay**pel
37	nose	neus	nøs
38	occiput	achterhoofd *n*	**agh**terhoaft
39	shoulder	schouder	**sghou**der
40	thigh	dij	daiy
41	throat	keel	kayl
42	toe	teen	tayn
43	upper abdomen, epigastrium	bovenbuik	**boa**venbœk

INTERNAL ORGANS

1	appendix	blinde darm	**blin**de darm
2	bladder	blaas	blahs
3	bowel, intestine	darm	darm
4	gall bladder	galblaas	**ghal**blahs
5	heart	hart *n*	hart
6	heart valve	hartklep	**hart**klehp
7	kidney	nier	neer
8	large intestine	dikke darm	**di**ke darm
9	liver	lever	**lay**ver
10	lung	long	long
11	pancreas	alvleesklier	**al**vlayskleer
12	small intestine	dunne darm	**du**ne darm
13	spleen	milt	milt
14	stomach	maag	mahgh
15	ureter	urineleider	ew-**ree**-ne-laiy-der

BONES, JOINTS, MUSCLES

abdominal muscle	buikspier	**bœk**speer
Achilles tendon	achillespees	a-**ghi**-les-pays
cervical vertebra	halswervel	**hals**wehrvel
cheekbone	jukbeen *n*	**juk**bayn
chest, thorax	borstkas	**borst**kas
collar bone	sleutelbeen *n*	**slø**telbayn
dorsal muscle	rugspier	**rugh**speer
fibula	kuitbeen *n*	**kœt**bayn
gluteus maximus	bilspier	**bil**speer

gullet	slokdarm	**slok**darm
metacarpal bone	middenhandsbeentje n	**mi**-den-hants-bayn-tye
metatarsus	middenvoetsbeentje n	**mi**-den-voots-bayn-tye
muscle, muscular system	spier, spierstelsel n	speer, **speer**stehlsel
nasal bone	neusbeen n	**nøs**bayn
nasal cavity	neusholte	**nøs**holte
patella	knieschijf	**knee**sghaiyf
pelvis	bekken n	**beh**ken
phalanx (finger)	vingerkootje n	**ving**er-koatye
phalanx (toe)	teenkootje n	**tayn**-koatye
rib	rib	rip
scapula, shoulder blade	schouderblad n	**sghou**derblat
skull	schedel	**sghay**del
spine	wervelkolom	**weh**rvelkolom
sural muscle	kuitspier	**kœt**speer
thighbone, femur	dijbeen n	**daiy**-bayn
tibia, shinbone	scheenbeen n	**sghayn**-bayn
tongue	tong	tong
tympanic membrane	trommelvlies n	**tro**melvlees
upper arm	bovenarm	boavenarm

AT THE CHEMIST'S

(for items which can be bought without prescription, see 'Toiletries and medicines' in the chapter on 'Shopping')

Is there a dispensing chemist's with a night/weekend service?
Is er een apotheek met nachtdienst/weekeinddienst?
is ehr en ahpoa**tayk** meht **naght**deenst/'weekend'-deenst?

Could you prepare this prescription for me?
Kunt u dit recept voor mij klaarmaken?
kunt ew dit re**sehpt** voor maiy **klahr**mahken?

What time can I pick it up?
Wanneer kan ik het afhalen?
wanayr kan ik heht **af**halen?

DIT MIDDEL BEÏNVLOEDT DE RIJVAARDIGHEID	THIS MEDICINE AFFECTS YOUR ABILITY TO DRIVE
BUITEN BEREIK VAN KINDEREN HOUDEN	KEEP OUT OF REACH OF CHILDREN
NIET OM IN TE NEMEN	DO NOT INGEST/SWALLOW

◀ **It can be prepared while you're waiting**
U kunt erop wachten
ew kunt ehr**op wagh**ten

Can you make out a receipt?
Wilt u een kwitantie uitschrijven?
wilt ew en kwee**tan**see **œt**sghraiven?

HOSPITAL

◀ **You will be hospitalized in the .... ward**
U wordt hier opgenomen op de afdeling ....
ew wort heer **op**ghenoamen op de **af**dayling ....

◀ **You will be treated in the outpatients' department**
U wordt poliklinisch behandeld
ew wort poalee-**klee**-nees be**han**delt

◀ **You will probably have to stay for .. days**
U moet waarschijnlijk .. dagen blijven
ew moot wahr-**sghaiyn**lek .. **dah**ghen **blaiy**ven

◀ **You will be operated on ....**
U wordt .... geopereerd
ew wort .... ghe-oape**rayrt**

◀ **We will only run some tests on you**
U blijft alleen voor onderzoek
ew blaiyft a**layn** voar **on**derzook

◀ **You may leave the hospital on ....**
U mag .... het ziekenhuis weer verlaten
ew magh .... heht **zee**kenhœs wayr ver**lah**ten

◀ **You can be transported to England/America**
U mag naar Engeland/Amerika worden vervoerd
ew magh nahr **eng**elant/ah**may**reekah **wor**den ver**voort**

What time are visiting hours?
Wanneer is het bezoekuur?
wanayr is heht be**zook**ewr?

Can the children come along?
Mogen kinderen meekomen?
moaghen **kin**deren **may**koamen?

◀ **The patient is not allowed to receive any visitors**
De patiënt mag geen bezoek ontvangen
de pah**syehnt** magh ghayn be**zook** ont**vang**en

Prinsjesdag*	'Princes' Day'
1 De Ridderzaal in Den Haag	The Knights' Hall in The Hague
2 Een enthousiaste menigte	An enthusiastic crowd
3 Rechtstreeks op de t.v.	Broadcast live on TV
4 De gouden koets	The Queen's golden coach
5 De koetsier	The coachman
6 De palfrenier	The groom
7 Het Binnenhof	The Inner Court (houses of parliament)

* Every third Tuesday in September is 'Prinsjesdag', the official opening of the Dutch parliamentary year by the Queen. She and her family make a short tour of The Hague in her golden coach, eventually arriving at the Inner Court, where she delivers the opening speech in the Knights' Hall.

BANKS, POST OFFICES

AT THE BANK

Dutch banks are usually open from 9 a.m. to 5 p.m. Small branches sometimes close earlier. Some banks in shopping centres in the cities stay open longer for *koopavond* (see 'Shopping'). There are also private bureaux de change in heavily touristed areas. Check to see if a commission is charged because this may make a considerable difference (your best bet is the *Grenswisselkantoren* at major stations, airports, border crossing points, etc). You can cash Eurocheques and traveller's cheques at virtually all banks. Giro cheques and money orders must be presented at the *Postbank* (no offices of their own, but all post offices serve as Postbank branches).

The large banks and the *Postbank* have their own cash dispensers, some of which also accept the leading international credit cards (Eurocard, Visa).

Where can I find a bank?
Waar kan ik een bank vinden?
wahr kan ik en bank **vin**den?

Could you change these pounds/dollars for me?
Wilt u deze ponden/dollars voor mij wisselen?
wilt ew dayze **pon**den/'dollars' voar maiy **wis**-e-len?

What's the exchange rate?
Wat is de wisselkoers?
wat is de **wis**-el-koors?

How many guilders/franks do I get for twenty pounds?
Hoeveel gulden/franken krijg ik voor twintig pond?
hoovayl **ghul**den/**frahn**ken kraiygh ik voar **twin**tegh pond?

Do you also take coins?
Neemt u ook munten aan?
naymt ew oak **mun**ten ahn?

Could you cash this Eurocheque/traveller's cheque?
Kunt u deze Eurocheque/reischeque verzilveren?
kunt ew **day**ze ø-roa-shehk/**raiys**-shehk ver**zil**veren?

I'd like to have three 100 guilder notes, five 50 guilder notes ....
Graag 3 biljetten van 100 gulden, 5 van 50 ....
ghrahgh dree bil**yeh**ten van **hon**dert **ghul**den, vaiyf van **vaiyf**tegh ....

.... and the balance in small change
.... en de rest in kleingeld
.... ehn de rehst in **klaiyn**ghelt

I prefer money of small denominations
Het liefst in kleine coupures
heht leefst in **klaiy**ne koo**pew**res

Dutch money

The national unit of currency is the *gulden* (guilder, florin), which is divided into 100 *centen* (cents). The currency is frequently symbolized by *f* or Fl.; in international banking, NLG is used.

The Dutch coins are for 5, 10 and 25 cent and 1, 2.50 and 5 gulden. The banknotes are in denominations of 10, 25, 50, 100, 250 and 1000 guilders. Most shops don't accept the 1000-guilder notes for security reasons.

Some of the coins have names: *stuiver* (5 ct), *dubbeltje* (10 ct), *kwartje* (25 ct) and *rijksdaalder* (*f* 2.50). It's as well to recognise these terms since they crop up all the time in shops.

The use of credit cards is growing but still limited mainly to hotels, restaurants and department stores. Most banks and the Postbank issue their customers with a *betaalpas* (cheque guarantee card - literally 'pay pass'). Some stores have facilities for you to enter your PIN code; elsewhere you need an accompanying, signed cheque. Whatever the arrangement though, these betaalpassen are universally accepted.

Belgian money

The national unit of currency is the *(Belgische) frank* (Belgian franc), divided into 100 *centimes*. The usual abbreviations are BFr., F. and Fr.; banks use BEF. The coins in circulation are for 50 centimes and for 1, 5, 10 and 20 frank. The banknotes are in denominations of 100, 500, 1000 and 5000 frank.

◀ **May I see your passport/banker's card?**
Mag ik uw paspoort/betaalpas zien?
magh ik eww **pas**poart/be**tahl**pas zeen?

◀ **Would you sign here, please?**
Wilt u hier tekenen?
wilt ew heer **tay**kenen?

Where do I sign?
Waar moet ik tekenen?
wahr moot ik **tay**kenen?

◀ **You can collect the money from the cashier**
U kunt het geld krijgen bij de kas
ew kunt heht ghehlt **kraiy**ghen baiy de kas

GELD WISSELEN	CHANGE
(HOOFD)KAS	(HEAD)CASHIER'S DESK
INLICHTINGEN	INFORMATION
KREDIETEN	LOANS
SPAARBANK	SAVINGS BANK
UITBETALINGEN	PAY-COUNTER

I'd like to transfer this amount of money (by wire/telephone) to ....
Ik wil dit bedrag (telegrafisch/telefonisch) overmaken naar .....
ik wil dit be**dragh** (tayle**ghrah**fees/tayle**foa**nees) **oa**vermahken nahr ....

Has there any money been transferred to me?
Is er geld voor mij overgemaakt?
is ehr ghelt voar maiy **oa**verghemahkt?

American dollars	Amerikaanse dollars	ahmayree**kahn**se 'dollars'
amount, sum	bedrag n	be**dragh**
banker's commission	bankprovisie	**bank**proaveesee
bank notes	bankbiljetten	**bank**-bil-yeh-ten
bank order	bankopdracht	**bank**-op-draght
bill of exchange	wisselbriefje n	**wis**-el-breef-ye
British/Irish pounds*	Britse/Ierse ponden	**brit**se/**eer**se **pon**den
cash	contant geld n	kon**tant** ghelt
cash dispenser	geldautomaat	**ghelt**-ou-toa-maht
coins	munten	**mun**ten
counter	loket n	loa**keht**
credit card	credit card	'credit card'
current account	rekening-courant	**ray**kening-koo**rant**
current rate, today's rate	dagkoers	**dagh**koors
(of exchange)		
to deposit	storten	**stor**ten
exchange rate	wisselkoers	**wis**-el-koors
foreign currency	deviezen	de**vee**zen
form	formulier n	formew**leer**
identity papers	legitimatie(bewijs)	lay-gheetee-**mah**see(be-waiys)
opening hours	openingstijden	**oa**pe-nings-taiy-den
receipt	kasbewijs n, kwitantie	**kas**bewaiys, kwee**tan**see
savings account	spaarrekening	**spahr**-ray-ke-ning
savings account record	spaarbankboekje n	**spahr**-bank-book-ye
small change	kleingeld n	**klaiyn**ghelt

* Most people are not familiar with Scottish pounds; please offer only British bank notes.

stock	effecten	eh**fehk**ten
to transfer	overmaken	**oa**vermahken
transfer form	overschrijvingsformulier n	**oa**-ver-sghraiy-vings-for-mew-leer
traveller's cheques	reischeques	**raiys**-shehks
to withdraw	opnemen	**op**naymen

AT THE POST OFFICE

The privatised Dutch postal service, *PTT Post*, has a dense network of branches. As you would expect, it handles not only postal business but also offers a variety of other services, such as issuing fishing licences and selling lottery tickets. Often, you can also order foreign exchange and sometimes there'll even be a travel agent's corner. The post offices also handle deposits and payouts for *Postbank*, which is engaged largely in money transfers. Opening hours depend on the size of the branch, but most are open from 8.30 a.m. to 5 p.m. Only the main post offices are open on Saturday mornings. Letter boxes are red and emptied three times a day. There are always two slots, one for local mail and the other for all other destinations, including those abroad (*overige bestemmingen*).

Where is the nearest post office?
Waar is het dichtstbijzijnde postkantoor?
wahr is heht **dightst**-baiy-zaiyn-de **post**kantoar?

Where can I find a letter box?
Waar is een brievenbus?
wahr is en **bree**venbus?

Can I cash travelers' cheques here?
Kan ik hier reischeques verzilveren?
kan ik heer **raiys**-shehks ver**zil**veren?

◄ No, you have to go to a bank
Nee, daarvoor moet u bij een bank zijn
nay, **dahr**voar moot ew baiy en bank zaiyn

How much am I allowed to draw?
Hoeveel kan ik opnemen?
hoovayl kan ik **op**naymen?

Can I also fill in a lower amount?
Kan ik ook een lager bedrag invullen?
kan ik oak en **lah**gher be**dragh** in-vu-len?

◄ May I see you banker's card and your passport?
Mag ik uw betaalpas en uw paspoort zien?
magh ik ew be**tahl**pas ehn eww **pas**poart zeen?

116

Addressing letters

In the Netherlands you frequently use the recipient's initials rather than writing out the first names in full. The name is preceded by **Dhr.** (de Heer = Mr) or **Mevr.** (Mevrouw = Mrs, Ms). Usage is rather more flexible in Belgium, where people also often write their surname first. Postcodes consist of four digits (two for the place, two for the postal district), in Holland followed by two letters (denoting the part of the street).

Dhr. J.H. van Vliet
Wezelrade 102
1054 SH AMSTERDAM
Nederland

Mevr. Verbiest Jeanne
Oude Steenweg 42
2000 ANTWERPEN
België

Some house numbers also have an additional **II** (or **"**), meaning 'second floor', or **hs (huis** - 'house', meaning ground floor and originally used to indicate flats in the same building as a shop).

How much is a stamp for a letter/postcard to England/America?
Hoeveel moet er op een brief/ansichtkaart naar Engeland/Amerika?
hoovayl moot ehr op en breef/**an**sightkahrt nahr **eng**elant/ah**may**reekah?

Do you have any special stamps?
Heeft u ook bijzondere postzegels?
hayft ew oak bee**zon**dere **post**-zay-ghels?

I'd like to have this series
Ik wil graag deze serie
ik wil ghrahgh **day**ze **say**ree

Three 60/80 cent stamps, please
Drie zegels van zestig/tachtig cent alstublieft
dree **zay**ghels van **zehs**tegh/**tagh**tegh sehnt alstew**bleeft**

Is there any poste restante for me?
Is er poste restante voor mij aangekomen?
is ehr post reh**stant** voar maiy **ahn**ghekoamen?

I'd like to send a cable
Ik wil graag een telegram verzenden
ik wil ghrahgh en tayle**gram** ver**zehn**den

What's the rate per word?
Wat is het tarief per woord?
wat is heht tah**reef** pehr woart?

◄ Would you fill in/complete this form?
Wilt u dit formulier invullen?
wilt ew dit formew**leer in**-vu-len?

117

addressee	geadresseerde	ghe-ah-dreh-**sayr**-de
air mail	luchtpost	**lught**post
cable, telegram	telegram n	tayle**ghram**
collection	lichting	**ligh**ting
congratulatory telegram	gelukstelegram n	ghe**luks**tayleghram
express post	exprespost	'express'-post
letter	brief	breef
letter box, postbox	brievenbus	**bree**venbus
money order	postwissel	**post**-wi-sel
opening hours	openingstijden	**oa**-pe-nings-taiy-den
parcel	pakket n	pa**keht**
parcel post	pakketpost	pa**keht**post
PO box	postbus	**post**bus
postage paid by addressee	kosten ontvanger	**kos**ten ont**vang**er
postal code	postcode	**post**koade
postcard	briefkaart	**breef**kahrt
(picture) postcard	ansichtkaart	**an**sightkahrt
printed matter	drukwerk n	**druk**wehrk
recorded mail	post met ontvangstbevestiging	post meht ont-**vangst**-be-vehs-te-ghing
registered	aangetekend	**ahn**-ghe-tay-kent
sample	monster n zonder waarde	**mon**ster **zon**der **wahr**de
sender	afzender	**af**zehnder
stamp	postzegel	**post**zayghel
stamp(-vending) machine	postzegelautomaat	**post**zayghel-outoamaht

TELEPHONING

Dutch public phone boxes (*telefooncellen*) are painted green. You can make international calls from these phones. Most are still coin-operated but the number of card-only phones is growing rapidly. You can buy a phone card (*telefoonkaart*) at some shops as well as the post offices, the latter also having public telephones. In central Amsterdam there's a 'telephone shop' where you phone first and pay later. Reverse-charge calls and similar services are available.

Where can I find a telephone booth?
Waar is een telefooncel?
wahr is en tayle**foan**sehl?

Where can I make a phone call?
Waar kan ik telefoneren?
wahr kan ik taylefoa**nay**ren?

I'd like to make a phone call to Britain/America
Ik wil graag een gesprek met Engeland/Amerika voeren
ik wil ghrahgh en ghe**sprehk** meht **ehng**elant/ah**may**reeka **voo**ren

Do you know the international access code/international dialing code/dialing code?
Weet u het internationaal toegangsnummer/landnummer/kengetal?
wayt ew heht **in**ter-na-syoa-nahl **too**ghangs-nu-mer/**lant**nu-mer/**kehn**ghetal?

◄ **Booth number 5 is vacant**
Cel 5 is vrij
sehl **nu**mer vaiyf is vraiy

◄ **It will take 30 minutes**
Dat duurt nog 30 minuten
dat dewrt nogh **dehr**tegh mee**new**ten

◄ **You can dial the number yourself**
U kunt zelf het nummer draaien
ew kunt zehlf heht **nu**mer **drah**yen

How much is the call per minute?
Hoeveel kost het gesprek per minuut?
hoovayl kost heht ghe**sprehk** pehr mee**newt**?

How much do I owe you?
Hoeveel ben ik u schuldig?
hoovayl behn ik ew **sghul**degh?

I can't get through
Ik krijg geen verbinding
ik kraiygh ghayn ver**bin**ding

The line is engaged
De lijn is bezet
de laiyn is be**zeht**

There's no reply
Ik krijg geen gehoor
ik kraiygh ghayn ghe**hoar**

◄ **Hold on please**
Blijft u aan de lijn
blaiyft ew ahn de laiyn

The line is bad/has been disconnected
De verbinding is slecht/verbroken
de ver**bin**ding is slehght/ver**broa**ken

◄ **One moment please**
Een moment alstublieft
en moa**meht** alstew**bleeft**

Could I speak to Mr/Mrs Jansma?
Kan ik met de heer/mevrouw Jansma spreken?
kan ik meht de hayr/me**vrou jan**smah **spray**ken?

◄ **I'll put you through**
Ik verbind u door
ik ver**bint** ew doar

◄ **He/She is not in**
Hij/Zij is niet aanwezig
haiy/zaiy is neet ahn**way**zegh

Can he/she call me back?
Kan hij/zij mij terugbellen?
kahn haiy/zaiy maiy te**rugh**behlen?

busy, engaged	bezet	be**zeht**
call	gesprek n	ghe**sprehk**
to call	opbellen	**op**behlen
coins	munten	**mun**ten
dialling code	kengetal n	**kehn**ghetal
direct	automatisch	outoa**mah**tees
insert	inwerpen	**in**wehrpen

How to use the phones

The Dutch and Belgian telephone systems are fully automated. You'll find instructions in English in every phone box. If you're in Holland and you want to ring, say, Central London, first dial **09** and wait for the dialling tone (it takes about a second). Then dial **44** for Britain, **71** for Central London (you don't need to dial the zero from abroad) and then the person's number. If you're phoning from Belgium, you start by dialing **00** (which the Dutch are also likely to start using in 1994 instead of 09). The number for phoning to the Netherlands is **31**, Belgium **32**.

You can make reverse-charge calls from both Belgium and Holland (the term *collect call* is used in Dutch). This is usually done via the Dutch or Belgian operator, but direct contact with the operator abroad is sometimes also possible.

The Dutch and Dutch-speaking Belgians usually answer the phone by saying *met* ('with') + their name or simply their name. They don't just say 'hello' or reel off their phone number. There is no official Dutch telephone alphabet.

When looking up numbers in the telephone book (*telefoonboek*), it's important to bear in mind that the alphabetic arrangement takes no account of the words *de*, *van*, *van de(r)*, etc, which occur in many Dutch names. For **Van der Bildt**, therefore, you would look under B and not V. (In Belgium, however, the words are often written together, e.g., Vandenberg, which would be listed under V). The Dutch equivalent of Britain's 'Yellow Pages' is the *Gouden Gids* (literally 'golden guide'), a separate directory.

international	internationaal	inter-nah-syoa-nahl
local	lokaal	loa**kahl**
out of order	defect	de**fehkt**
refund	teruggave	te**rugh**-ghahve
subscriber's number	abonneenummer *n*	a-bo-**nay**-nu-mer
telephone booth	telefooncel	tayle**foan**sehl
telephone directory	telefoonboek *n*	tayle**foan**book
telephone exchange	centrale	sehn**trah**le
trunk, long-distance	interlokaal	interloa**kahl**

SPORTS AND RECREATION

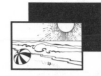

ON THE BEACH/IN THE SWIMMING POOL

The Dutch and Belgian coasts are extremely prone to erosion. The centuries-old struggle the Dutch have had to wage against the sea is of course as celebrated as their windmills and tulips. Only along some parts of the coast are there naturally occurring dunes (*duinen*), and these have been planted with resilient grass types. It's strictly forbidden (*VERBODEN TOEGANG*) to leave the official paths in the dune areas. Elsewhere, the authorities have constructed breakwaters (*golfbrekers, strekdammen*). These structures, consisting of basalt blocks, project into the sea and diminish the power of the waves. Since the breakwaters give rise to strong currents, swimming in their vicinity is extremely hazardous! Altogether, be careful about where you swim along the North Sea coast. Always choose a beach with a coastguard (*strandwacht*) rather than a quiet stretch of water.

How far is it to the beach/swimming pool?
Hoe ver is het naar het strand/zwembad?
hoo vehr is heht nahr heht strant/**zwehm**bat?

◀ You're not allowed to swim here
U mag hier niet zwemmen
ew magh heer neet **zweh**men

Is the beach steep here?
Loopt het strand steil af?
loapt heht strant staiyl af?

What's the temperature of the water?
Hoe warm is het water?
hoo warm is heht **wah**ter?

Is swimming allowed here?
Mag hier worden gezwommen?
magh heer **wor**den ghe**zwo**men?

Is there a dangerous current?
Is er een gevaarlijke stroming?
is ehr en ghe**vahr**leke **stroa**ming?

How deep is the water here?
Hoe diep is het hier?
hoo deep is heht heer?

Is it dangerous here for children?
Is het hier gevaarlijk voor kinderen?
is heht heer ghe**vahr**lek voar **kin**deren?

121

Is there any supervision?
Is er toezicht?
is ehr **too**zight?

The sea is calm/turbulent
De zee is kalm/woelig
de zay is kalm/**woo**legh

The waves are high
Er zijn hoge golven
ehr zaiyn **hoa**ghe **ghol**ven

There is a storm coming up
Er komt storm
ehr komt storm

Are dogs allowed here?
Mogen hier honden komen?
moaghen heer **hon**den **koa**men?

I find the water too cold
Het water is mij te koud
heht **wah**ter is maiy te kout

I can't swim
Ik kan niet zwemmen
ik kahn neet **zweh**men

How much is the entrance fee for two adults and one child?
Hoeveel is de entree voor twee volwassenen en een kind?
hoovayl is de ehn**tray** voar tway vol**wa**senen ehn en kint?

Two tickets please
Twee kaartjes alstublieft
tway **kahr**tyes alstew**bleeft**

One child's ticket please
Een kinderkaartje alstublieft
en **kin**derkahrtye alstew**bleeft**

Is there a children's pool here?
Is hier een kinderbadje?
is heer en **kin**derbatye?

Is it an indoor/open-air/heated pool?
Is het zwembad overdekt/onoverdekt/verwarmd?
is heht **zwehm**bat oaver**dehkt**/**on**oaverdehkt/ver**warmt**?

I'd like to rent ....
Ik wil graag .... huren
ik wil ghrahgh .... **hew**ren

an air mattress	een luchtbed	en **lught**bet
a deck chair	een ligstoel	en **ligh**stool
a pedal boat	een waterfiets	en **wah**terfeets
a sunshade	een parasol	en pahrah**sol**
swimwear	badkleding	**bat**klayding

How much is it per hour?
Wat kost dat per uur?
wat kost dat pehr ewr?

Could you keep an eye on my things?
Kunt u even op mijn spullen letten?
kunt ew **ay**ven op maiyn **spu**len **leh**ten?

bather	badgast	**bat**ghast
bathing cap	badmuts	**bat**muts
bathing towel	badhanddoek	**bat**handook
bathing/swimming trunks	zwembroek	**zwehm**brook
bikini	bikini	bee**kee**nee
changing cubicles	omkleedcabines	**om**klayt-kah-bee-nes

BADSTRAND	BATHING BEACH	
VRIJ TOEGANKELIJK	OPEN TO THE PUBLIC	
ZWEMMEN VERBODEN	NO SWIMMING	
GEVAARLIJKE STROMING	DANGEROUS CURRENT	
(OPENLUCHT)ZWEMBAD	(OPEN-AIR) SWIMMING POOL	
BADMEESTER	SWIMMING POOL ATTENDANT	
OMKLEEDCABINES	CHANGING CUBICLES	
TOILETTEN	TOILETS	
DOUCHES	SHOWERS	
DAMES	LADIES	
HEREN	GENTS	
HONDEN NIET TOEGELATEN	NO DOGS ALLOWED	
KINDERBAD	CHILDREN'S POOL	
NATURISTENSTRAND	NUDIST BEACH	

chute	waterglijbaan	**wah**ter-glaiy-bahn
fine sand	fijn zand n	faiyn zant
lifeguards	reddingsbrigade	**reh**dings-bree-ghah-de
open-air swimming pool	openluchtbad n	oapen**lught**bat
pebbly beach	kiezelstrand n	**kee**zelstrant
sandy beach	zandstrand n	**zant**strant
shells	schelpen	**sghehl**pen
showers	douches	**doo**syes
surf	branding	**bran**ding
swimming pool attendant	badmeester	**bat**mayster
swimming pool with artificial waves	golfslagbad n	**gholf**slagh-bat
swimsuit	(eendelig) badpak n	(**ayn**daylegh) **bat**pak
walk along the beach	strandwandeling	**strant**wan-de-ling
water temperature	watertemperatuur	**wah**ter-tehm-pay-rah-tewr

WATER SPORTS

boardsailing, windsurfing	plankzeilen, windsurfen	**plank**zaiylen, **wint**surfen
canoeing	kanovaren	**kah**noavahren
diving	duiken	**dœ**ken
motor boat sailing	motorbootvaren	**moa**tor-boat-vah-ren
rowing	roeien	**roo**yen
sailing	zeilen	**zaiy**len
surfriding	brandingsurfen	**bran**ding-surfen
waterskiing	waterskiën	**wah**ter-skee-yen

123

Is there a marina nearby?
Is hier een jachthaven in de buurt?
is heer en **yacht**hahven in de bewrt?

Where is the harbour master's office?
Waar is het havenkantoor?
wahr is heht **hah**venkantoar?

How much for a berth?
Wat kost hier een ligplaats?
wat kost heer en **ligh**plahts?

Can I rent ....?
Kan ik .... huren?
kan ik .... **hew**ren?

diving gear	duikspullen	**dœk**spu-len
a motor boat	een motorboot	en **moa**torboat
a rowing boat	een roeiboot	en **rooy**boat
a sailing boat, yacht	een zeilboot	en **zaiyl**boat
a surfboard	een zeilplank, surfplank	en **zaiyl**plank, **surf**plank
water skis	waterski's	**wah**terskees

Is diving allowed here?
Mag hier gedoken worden?
magh heer ghe**doa**ken **wor**den?

Is a permit required?
Is daar een vergunning voor nodig?
is dahr en ver-**ghu**-ning voar **noa**degh?

Is there a surfing/waterskiing school?
Is hier een surfschool/waterskischool?
is heer en **surf**sghoal/**wah**ter-skee-sghoal?

How much for a lesson?
Wat kost een les?
wat kost en lehs?

berth	ligplaats	**ligh**plahts
buoy	boei	booy
decompression chamber	decompressiekamer	daykom**preh**seekahmer
diving mask	duikbril	**dœk**bril
jetty, mole	havenhoofd, steiger	**hah**venhoaft, **staiy**gher
harbour master	havenmeester	**hah**venmayster
lifebuoy	reddingsboei	**reh**dingsbooy
life jacket	zwemvest *n*	**zwehm**vehst
oars	roeiriemen	**rooy**reemen
outboard motor	buitenboordmotor	bœten**boart**moator
paddles	peddels	**peh**dels
rowing boat	roeiboot	**rooy**boat
sailing boat, yacht	zeilboot, jacht *n*	**zaiyl**boat, yaght
snorkel	snorkel	**snor**kel
speedboat	speedboat	'speedboat'
oxygen cylinder	zuurstoffles	**zewr**stof-flehs

124

HORSE RIDING

Is there a riding school around?
Is hier een manege/rijschool?
is heer en mah**nay**zhe/**raiy**sghoal?

Can I rent a horse/pony?
Kan ik een paard/pony huren?
kan ik en pahrt/**pon**nee **hew**ren?

Are there lessons for children?
Kunnen kinderen hier les krijgen?
ku-nen **kin**deren heer lehs **kraiy**ghen?

How much is the rent/a lesson per hour?
Wat kost de huur/een les per uur?
wat kost de hewr/en lehs pehr ewr?

I can't ride yet
Ik kan nog niet paardrijden
ik kan nogh neet **pahrt**raiyden

This horse is too wild for me
Het paard is mij te wild
heht pahrt is maiy te wilt

RENTING A BICYCLE

Where can I rent a bike?
Waar kan ik een fiets huren?
wahr kan ik en feets **hew**ren?

How much is it a day/an hour?
Wat kost dit per dag/uur?
wat kost dit pehr dagh/ewr?

◀ **You must pay a deposit**
U moet een borgsom betalen
ew moot en **borgh**som be**tah**len

◀ **Do you have any identification?**
Kunt u zich legitimeren?
kunt ew zigh lay-ghee-tee-**may**-ren?

I would like a bike ....
Ik wil een fiets ....
ik wil en feets ....

with back-pedal brakes	met terugtrapremmen	meht te**rugh**trap-rehmen
with drum brakes	met trommelremmen	meht **tro**melrehmen
with (three-speed) gear-change	met (3) versnellingen	meht (dree) ver**sneh**lingen
with hand brakes	met knijpremmen	meht **knaiyp**rehmen

Could you adjust the saddle for me?
Wilt u het zadel voor mij afstellen?
wilt ew heht **zah**del voar maiy **af**stehlen?

It's too high/too low
Het staat te hoog/te laag
heht staht te hoagh/te lahgh

Do you have a cyclists' map?
Heeft u een fietskaart?
hayft ew en **feets**kahrt?

Do you have any information on cycle routes?
Heeft u informatie over fietsroutes?
hayft ew infor**mah**tsee **oa**ver **feets**rootes?

125

bicycle lock	fietsslot n	**feets**-slot
children's bicycle	kinderfiets	**kin**derfeets
child's seat	kinderzitje n	**kin**derzitye
combination lock	ringslot n	**ring**slot
gent's bike/bicycle	herenfiets	**hay**renfeets
lady's bike	damesfiets	**dah**mesfeets
mountain bike	mountain bike	'mountain bike'
rent-a-bike	fietsverhuur	**feets**verhewr
tandem	tandem	'tandem'

(see also 'Bicycle parts')

OTHER SPORTS

Where is the ....?
Waar is de/het ....?
wahr is de/heht ....?

circuit	circuit	sir**quee**
golf course/links	golfbaan	**gholf**bahn
race track	draf- en renbaan	draf- ehn **rehn**bahn
soccer stadium	voetbalstadion n	**voot**bal-stah-dee-yon
sports hall/centre	sporthal	**sport**hal
sports park	sportpark n	**sport**park
tennis court	tennisbaan	'tennis'-bahn

Is there an interesting match today?
Is er vandaag een leuke wedstrijd?
is ehr van**dahgh** en **lø**ke **weht**straiyt?

What time does it start?
Hoe laat begint het?
hoo laht be**ghint** heht?

One seat/terrace please
Een zitplaats/staanplaats alstublieft
en **zit**plahts/**stahn**plahts alstew**bleeft**

The English/Scottish team plays better/worse
Engeland/Schotland speelt beter/slechter
ehngelant/**sghot**lant spaylt **bay**ter/**slehgh**ter

The referee is just awful!
Wat een slechte scheidsrechter!
wat en **slehgh**te **sghaiyts**rehghter!

athletics	atletiek	atle**teek**
badminton	badminton	'badminton'
baseball	honkbal	**honk**bal
basketball	basketbal	**bas**ketbal
bicycle racing	wielrennen	**weel**rehnen
billiards	biljarten	bil**yar**ten

126

(tenpin) bowling	bowling	'bowling'
boxing	boksen	**box**en
chess	schaken	**sghah**ken
cricket	cricket	'cricket'
fencing	schermen	**sghehr**men
football	voetbal	**voot**bal
golf	golf	gholf
handball	handbal	**hant**bal
hockey	hockey	'hockey'
(ice) hockey	(ijs)hockey	**(ice)**-'hockey'
horse racing	draf- en rensport	draf- ehn **rehn**sport
jogging	joggen	'jog'-en
judo	judo	**yew**doa
karate	karate	kah**rah**te
motor sports	autosport, motorsport	**ou**toasport, **moa**torsport
mountaineering	bergklimmen	**bergh**-kli-men
riding	paardrijden	**pahrt**raiyden
rowing	roeien	**roo**-yen
rugby league	rugby (13-tallen)	**rugh**bee (**dehr**teen-ta-len)
rugby union	rugby (15-tallen)	**rugh**bee (**vaiyf**teen-ta-len)
soccer	voetbal	**voot**bal
swimming	zwemmen	**zweh**men
table tennis	tafeltennis	**tah**fel-'tennis'
tennis	tennis	'tennis'
volleyball	volleybal	'volley'-bal
break	pauze, rust	**pou**ze, rust
corner	hoekschop, corner	**hook**sghop, 'corner'
defeat	nederlaag, verlies n	**nay**derlahgh, ver**lees**
defence	verdediging, achterhoede	ver-**day**-de-ghing, **agh**ter-hoo-de
draw, tie	gelijkspel n	ghe-laiyk-**spehl**
extra time	verlenging	ver**lehng**ing
forward line	voorhoede, aanval	**voar**hoode, **ahn**-val
free kick	vrije schop	**vraiy**-e sghop
game, match	wedstrijd	**wet**straiyt
goal (area)	doel	dool
goal (point scored)	doelpunt, goal	**dool**punt, 'goal'
goal keeper	doelman, keeper	**dool**man, 'keeper'
half	(speel)helft	**(spayl)**-hehlft
half-time	rust	rust
jury	jury	**zhew**ree
linesman	grensrechter	**ghrehns**rehghter
midfield player	middenveldspeler	**mi**-den-vehlt-spay-ler

127

Sport in the Netherlands

Holland is of course a major football (soccer) and skating power. Cycling, too, is highly popular. This applies not only to the major competitions (only a few of which are held in the Netherlands) but also the *kermiskoers*. These are local events consisting of many runs through a village to coincide with, say, a fair. World famous cyclists are often attracted. Belgium has even more competitions like these. One or other of the two countries is also world *korfbal* (korfball) champion. This is hardly surprising given that it's really only here that the sport is played on any scale. A team consists of twelve players (six women, six men). The game resembles basketball (and the basket is a real wooden one, hanging on a pole), although one team will rarely score more than fifteen points.

Kortebaanschaatsen (sprint skating) is very popular in winter, especially in the Dutch province of Friesland. Two skaters race each other over 100 metres and the winner goes through to the following round. The biggest event in the Dutch skating calendar is the *Elfstedentocht*, a 200-kilometre marathon along canals and across lakes that takes in eleven towns in Friesland. This exhausting event, in which thousands of skaters participate, can be held only in severe winters.

The Friesians have other sports peculiar to themselves, such as *kaatsen* (related to squash and fives) and *fierljeppen*. Here, the athlete jumps over a ditch or canal using a pole - you stand the pole in the water, jump, wriggle to the top of the pole and then let yourself fall down on the other side of the water. Get it wrong and you land in the water, but a good jump can carry you 17-18 metres.

offside	buitenspel	bœten**spehl**
penalty (kick)	strafschop, penalty	straf**s**ghop, 'penalty'
red card	rode kaart	**roa**de kahrt
referee, umpire	scheidsrechter	s**ghaiyts**-rehghter
victory	overwinning, winst	oaver**wi**ning, winst
yellow card	gele kaart	**ghay**le kahrt

Opening hours

Most Dutch and Belgian shops open at 8.30 or 9 a.m. and close at 6 p.m. (butchers usually earlier, tobaconnists later). In the Netherlands, shops have to display their opening hours on a yellow card on the door or window. On Saturdays, most Dutch shops close at 5.30 or 6 p.m.; most shops remained closed until 11 a.m. or 1 p.m. on Mondays. In the evenings only specially licenced shops are open. In the big cities (at least in the centres) there's a *koopavond* (late-night shopping) once a week, with the shops staying open till 9 p.m. Only in the smaller towns and villages do shops close for lunch, and that includes supermarkets. As you would expect, there are supermarkets everywhere. Belgian supermarkets are frequently located on greenfield sites outside the urban centres. Both Holland and Belgium have lots of small, immigrant-run shops where you can find all sorts of ingredients, foods and other items that 'mainstream' shops don't stock.

Where do I find a shopping street/supermarket/shopping centre?
Waar vind ik hier een winkelstraat/supermarkt/winkelcentrum?
wahr vint ik heer en **win**kelstraht/**su**permarkt/**win**kelsehntrum?

What time do the shops open/close?
Hoe laat gaan de winkels hier open/dicht?
hoo laht ghahn de **win**kels heer **oa**pen/dight?

Where do I find a market/flee market?
Waar vind ik een markt/vlooienmarkt?
wahr vint ik en markt/**vloa**yenmarkt?

Do they close for lunch/are they open at night?
Is er een middagpauze/koopavond?
is ehr en **mi**daghpouze/**koap**ahvont?

Is there a shop which is open on sundays/at night?
Is er een winkel die op zondag/'s avonds open is?
is ehr en **win**kel dee op **zon**dagh/**sah**vonts **oa**pen is?

Dutch-English

AANBIEDING	SPECIAL OFFER
ANTIEK	ANTIQUES
APOTHEEK	DISPENSING CHEMIST'S
BAKKERIJ	BAKERY
BANKET	CONFECTIONARY
BIJOUX	JEWELS
BLOEMEN	FLOWERS
BOEKEN	BOOKS
BOEKHANDEL	BOOKSHOP
BROOD	BREAD
CADEAUARTIKELEN	GIFTS
CHEMISCH REINIGEN	DRY-CLEANER
CURIOSA	BRIC-A-BRAC
DAMESKAPPER	LADIES' HAIRDRESSER
DAMESKLEDING	LADIES' WEAR
DAMESKLEERMAKER	DRESSMAKER
DEKENS	BLANKETS
DELICATESSENHANDEL	DELICATESSEN
FRUIT	FRUIT
GEOPEND	OPEN
GESLOTEN	CLOSED
GLAS	GLASSWARE
GOUD(SMID)	GOLD(SMITH)
GROENTEHANDEL	GREENGROCER'S
HANDWERK	HANDICRAFT
HERENKAPPER	BARBER
HERENKLEDING	MEN'S WEAR
HORLOGER	WATCHMAKER
INGANG	ENTRANCE
JUWELEN	JEWELRY
KANTOORBOEKHANDEL	STATIONER
KAPPER	HAIRDRESSER
KINDERKLEDING	CHILDREN'S WEAR
KLEERMAKER	TAILOR
KUNSTNIJVERHEID	ARTS AND CRAFTS
LEDERWAREN	LEATHER GOODS

MELKHANDEL	DAIRY
MEUBELS	FURNITURE
MUNTEN	COINS
OPTICIEN	OPTICIAN
OVERHEMDEN	(MEN'S) SHIRTS
PAPIERWAREN	STATIONERY
PORSELEIN	CHINA
POSTZEGELS	STAMPS
REISARTIKELEN	TRAVEL SUPPLIES
REISBUREAU	TRAVEL AGENCY
ROOKWAREN	TOBACCO
SCHOENEN	SHOES
SCHOENMAKER	COBBLER
SCHOONHEIDSSALON	BEAUTY PARLOUR
SLAGER	BUTCHER
SLIJTERIJ	OFF-LICENCE
SPEELGOED	TOYS
STOMERIJ	DRY-CLEANER'S
TWEEDEHANDS ARTIKELEN	SECOND HAND GOODS
TIJDSCHRIFTEN	MAGAZINES
UITGANG	EXIT
UITVERKOCHT	SOLD OUT
UITVERKOOP	SALE
VISHANDEL	FISHMONGER'S
VLEESWAREN	COLD MEATS
WARENHUIS	DEPARMENT STORE
WASSERETTE	LAUNDERETTE
WERKDAGEN	WEEKDAYS
WONINGINRICHTING	HOME FURNISHINGS
WIJNHANDEL	WINE SHOP
IJZERWAREN	HARDWARE
ZON- EN FEESTDAGEN	SUNDAYS AND PUBLIC HOLIDAYS

English-Dutch

ANTIQUES	ANTIEK
ARTS AND CRAFTS	KUNSTNIJVERHEID
BAKERY	BAKKERIJ
BARBER	HERENKAPPER
BEAUTY PARLOUR	SCHOONHEIDSSALON
BLANKETS	DEKENS
BOOKS	BOEKEN
BOOKSHOP	BOEKHANDEL
BREAD	BROOD
BRIC-A-BRAC	CURIOSA
CHILDREN'S WEAR	KINDERKLEDING
CHINA	PORSELEIN
CLOSED	GESLOTEN
COBBLER	SCHOENMAKER
COINS	MUNTEN
COLD MEATS	VLEESWAREN
CONFECTIONARY	BANKET
DAIRY	MELKHANDEL
DELICATESSEN	DELICATESSENHANDEL
DEPARTMENT STORE	WARENHUIS
DISPENSING CHEMIST'S	APOTHEEK
DRESSMAKER	DAMESKLEERMAKER
DRY-CLEANER'S	STOMERIJ
DRY-CLEANING	CHEMISCH REINIGEN
ENTRANCE	INGANG
EXIT	UITGANG
FISHMONGER'S	VISHANDEL
FLOWERS	BLOEMEN
FRUIT	FRUIT
FURNITURE	MEUBELS
GIFTS	CADEAUARTIKELEN
GLASSWARE	GLAS
GOLD(SMITH)	GOUD(SMID)
GREENGROCER'S	GROENTEHANDEL
HAIRDRESSER	KAPPER
HANDICRAFT	HANDWERK
HARDWARE	IJZERWAREN
HOME FURNISHINGS	WONINGINRICHTING
JEWELRY	JUWELEN
JEWELS	BIJOUX

LADIES' HAIRDRESSER	DAMESKAPPER
LADIES' WEAR	DAMESKLEDING
LAUNDERETTE	WASSERETTE
LEATHER GOODS	LEDERWAREN
MAGAZINES	TIJDSCHRIFTEN
MEN'S SHIRTS	OVERHEMDEN
MEN'S WEAR	HERENKLEDING
OFF-LICENCE	SLIJTERIJ
OPEN	OPEN
OPTICIAN	OPTICIEN
SALE	UITVERKOOP
SECOND HAND GOODS	TWEEDEHANDS ARTIKELEN
SHIRTS	OVERHEMDEN
SHOES	SCHOENEN
SOLD OUT	UITVERKOCHT
SPECIAL OFFER	AANBIEDING
STAMPS	POSTZEGELS
STATIONER	KANTOORBOEKHANDEL
STATIONERY	PAPIERWAREN
SUNDAYS AND PUBLIC HOLIDAYS	ZON- EN FEESTDAGEN
TAILOR	KLEERMAKER
TOBACCO	ROOKWAREN
TOYS	SPEELGOED
TRAVEL AGENCY	REISBUREAU
TRAVEL SUPPLIES	REISARTIKELEN
WATCHMAKER	HORLOGER
WEEKDAYS	WERKDAGEN
WINE SHOP	WIJNHANDEL

CONVERSATIONS WITH SHOP ASSISTANTS

◄ **Can I help you?**
Kan ik u ergens mee helpen?
kan ik ew **ehr**ghens may **hehl**pen?

Do you have a .... for me?
Heeft u voor mij een ....?
hayft ew voar maiy en ....?

I am only browsing
Ik kijk zo maar wat rond
ik kaiyk zoa mahr wat ront

Do you also sell ....?
Heeft u ook ....?
hayft ew oak ....?

133

◄ **No, we don't sell that/I'm afraid it's sold out**
Nee, dat hebben we niet/dat is helaas uitverkocht
nay, dat **heh**ben we neet/dat is hay**lahs** œtverkoght

Do you have another ....?
Heeft u een andere ....?
hayft ew en **an**dere ....?

How much is this one?
Wat kost dit/deze?
wat kost dit/**day**ze?

That's too expensive for me
Dat is mij te duur
dat is maiy te dewr

Do you have anything cheaper?
Heeft u iets goedkopers?
hayft ew eets ghoot**koa**pers?

I'll take this one
Dit/deze neem ik
dit/**day**ze naym ik

This one doesn't fit
Dit/deze past mij niet
dit/**day**ze past maiy neet

It's too ....
Hij/Het is te ....
haiy/heht is te ....

long	lang	lang
loose	wijd	waiyt
narrow	smal	smal
short	kort	kort
small	klein	klaiyn
tight	nauw	nou
wide	breed	brayt

Could this be sent directly to Britain/America?
Kan dit rechtstreeks naar Engeland/Amerika worden gestuurd?
kan dit **rehght**strayks nahr **en**gelant/ah**may**reekah **wor**den ghe**stewrt**?

This is the address
Dit is het adres
dit is heht ah**drehs**

Could you wrap it for me?
Wilt u het voor me inpakken?
wilt ew heht voar me **in**pak-en?

◄ **Do you want anything else?**
Nog iets van uw dienst?
nogh eets van eww deenst?

No thank you, that will be all
Nee dank u, dat was het
nay dank ew, dat was heht

◄ **You can pay at the cash register**
U kunt betalen aan de kassa
ew kunt be**tah**len ahn de **kas**ah

◄ **You can change it within 8 days**
U kunt het binnen 8 dagen ruilen
ew kunt heht **bin**en aght **dah**ghen **rœ**len

Can I pay with a Eurocheque/credit card?
Kan ik betalen met een Eurocheque/credit card?
kan ik be**tah**len meht en **ø**roa-shehk/'credit card'?

◄ **Do you have an account here?**
Hebt u hier een rekening (lopen)?
hehpt ew heer en **ray**kening (**loa**pen)?

134

I'd like to exchange this
Ik wil dit graag ruilen
ik wil dit ghrahgh **rœ**len

Here is the receipt
Hier is de kassabon
heer is de **kas**ahbon

◄ **You can exchange this at the exchange counter/customer service**
U kunt dit ruilen bij de ruilbalie/klantenservice
ew kunt dit **rœ**len baiy de **rœl**bahlee/**klan**ten"service"

Could I have a refund?
Kan ik het geld terugkrijgen?
kan ik heht ghehlt te**rugh**kraiyghen?

◄ **No, you will receive a credit note**
Nee, u krijgt een tegoedbon
nay, ew kraiyght en te**ghoot**bon

COLORS, PATTERNS, FABRICS

See the list under 'Clothes and shoes'.

WEIGHTS, MEASURES, QUANTITIES

a box	een doos	en doas
a tin, can	een blik *n*	en blik
a packet	een pak *n*	en pak
one piece	één stuk *n*	ayn stuk
a pair	een paar *n*	en pahr
a set	een set	en seht
a bottle	een fles	en flehs
a roll	een rol	en rol
a tube	een tube	en **tew**be
a bag	een zak	en zak

FOODSTUFFS, VEGETABLES, FRUIT, ETC.

(see also the chapter on 'Food and drink' and 'Travel and camping equipment')

apples	appels	**a**pels
apricots	abrikozen	ahbree**koa**zen
bananas	bananen	bah**nah**nen
beer	bier *n*	beer
biscuits	koekjes	**kook**yes
bread	brood *n*	broat
butter	boter	**boa**ter

cake	koek	kook
candy	snoep *n*	snoop
cash register	kassa	**kas**ah
cheese	kaas	kahs
cherries	kersen	**keh**rsen
chicken	kip *f*, haantje *n*	kip, **hahn**tye
chocolate	chocolade	shoakoa**lah**de
coffee	koffie	**kof**ee
instant coffee	oploskoffie	**op**loskofee
filter coffee	filterkoffie	**fil**terkofee
cold meats	vleeswaren	**vlays**wahren
cottage cheese	kwark	kwark
cream	room	roam
sour cream	zure room	**zew**re roam
whipped cream	slagroom	**slagh**roam
dairy products	zuivelprodukten	**zœ**velproadukten
eggs	eieren	**aiy**-ye-ren
flower	meel *n*	mayl
fruit juice	vruchtesap *n*	**vrugh**te-sap
grapes	druiven	**drœ**ven
ham	ham	ham
hamburger	hamburger	**ham**burgher
ice cream	ijs *n*	aiys
lettuce	sla	slah
matches	lucifers	**lew**seefehrs
mayonnaise	mayonaise	mah-yoa-**nay**-se
melon	meloen	me**loon**
honeydew melon	suikermeloen	**sœ**kermeloon
water melon	watermeloen	**wah**termeloon
(whole) milk	(volle) melk	(**vol**-e) mehlk
buttermilk	karnemelk	**kar**ne-mehlk
low-fat milk	halfvolle melk	**half**vol-e mehlk
mineral water	mineraalwater *n*	meene**rahl**wahter
mustard	mosterd	**mos**tert
spicy/mild	scherp/mild	sghehrp/milt
napkins	servetten	sehr**veh**ten
oranges	sinaasappels	**see**nahs-ap-els
pastry	gebak *n*	ghe**bak**
peach	perzik	**pehr**zik
pears	peren	**pay**ren
pickles	augurken	ou**ghur**ken
plastic bag	plastic zak	'plastic' zak
potatoes	aardappelen	**ahr**tap-e-len

136

raspberries	frambozen	fram**boa**zen
rolls	broodjes	**broat**yes
salad	salade	sah**lah**de
soft drinks	frisdranken	**fris**dranken
tinned food	conserven	kon**sehr**ven
salt	zout *n*	zout
soup	soep	soop
sugar	suiker	**sœ**ker
tea	thee	tay
tea bags	theezakjes	**tay**zakyes
tomatoes	tomaten	toa**mah**ten
trolley	winkelwagentje *n*	**win**kel-wah-ghen-tye
wine	wijn	waiyn
yoghurt	yoghurt	**yo**ghurt

TOILETRIES/MEDICINES

(see also 'At the hairdresser', 'In the beauty parlour' and 'At the dispensing chemist's')

Do you have a remedy against ....?
Heeft u een middel tegen .... ?
hayft ew en **mid**el **tay**ghen ....?

burns	brandwonden	**brant**wonden
carsickness	wagenziekte	**wah**ghenzeekte
a cold	verkoudheid	ver**kout**haiyt
coughing	hoest	hoost
diarrhoea	diarree	dee-yah-**ray**
earache	oorpijn	**oar**paiyn
fever	koorts	koarts
the flue	griep	ghreep
gastrointestinal disorders	maag- en darmstoornissen	mahgh ehn **darm**stoar-nis-en
a hangover	een kater	en **kah**ter
hay fever	hooikoorts	**hooy**koarts
headache	hoofdpijn	**hoaft**paiyn
insect bites	insectenbeten	in**sehk**tenbayten
a sore throat	keelpijn	**kayl**paiyn
sunburn	zonnebrand	**zon**-e-brant
wound infection	wondinfectie	**wont**infehksee

◄ **This is only available at the dispensing chemist's/on prescription**
Dat is alleen verkrijgbaar bij een apotheek/op recept
dat is a**layn** ver**kraiygh**bahr baiy en ahpoa**tayk**/op re**sehpt**

137

◀ **You'd better first consult a doctor**
U kunt beter eerst een arts raadplegen
ew kunt **bay**ter ayrst en arts **raht**playghen

◀ **This may not be sold to children**
Dit mag niet aan kinderen verkocht worden
dit magh neet ahn **kin**deren ver**koght wor**den

◀ **This medicine affects one's ability to drive**
Dit middel beïnvloedt de rijvaardigheid
dit **mid**-el be-**in**-vloot de raiy-**vahr**-degh-haiyt

◀ **This is toxic/inflammable/dangerous to children**
Dit is giftig/brandbaar/gevaarlijk voor kinderen
dit is **ghif**tegh/**brant**bahr/ghe**vahr**lek voar **kin**deren

aftershave (lotion)	after shave	'after shave'
brush	borstel	**bor**stel
clinical thermometer	koortsthermometer	**koarts**-tehr-moa-may-ter
comb	kam	kam
contraceptive	voorbehoedsmiddel	**voar**be-hoots-mid-el
cotton wool	watten	**wat**-en
cough drops	keelpastilles	**kayl**-pas-tee-yes
cough mixture	hoestdrank	**hoost**drank
deodorant	deodorant	day-yoa-doa-**rant**
disposable nappies	wegwerpluiers	**wehgh**wehrp-lœ-yers
dummy	(fop)speen	(**fop**)spayn
eardrops	oordruppels	**oar**drup-els
earplugs	oorwatjes	**oar**watyes
eau de Cologne	eau de cologne	oa de koa**lon**ye
elastic bandage	rekverband *n*	**rehk**verbant
eye shadow	oogschaduw	**oagh**-sghah-dew
feeding bottle	zuigfles	**zœgh**flehs
first-aid kit	verbandtrommel	ver**bant**-trom-el
gauze	verbandgaas *n*	ver**bant**ghahs
hairbrush	haarborstel	**hahr**borstel
healing ointment/salve	wondzalf	**wont**zalf
insect repellent (lotion/stick)	muggenolie/muggenstick	**mu**ghen-oalee/**mu**ghen-'stick'
iodine	jodium	**yoa**deeyum
laxative	laxeermiddel *n*	la-**xayr**-mid-el
lip balm	lippenzalf	**lip**-en-zalf
lipstick	lippenstift	**lip**-en-stift
nail brush	nagelborstel	**nah**ghel-borstel
nailfile	nagelvijl	**nah**ghel-vaiyl
nail polish/varnish	nagellak	**nah**ghel-lak
nose drops	neusdruppels	**nøs**drup-els

138

painkiller	pijnstiller	**paiyn**stil-er
perfume	parfum *n*	**par**fum
razor blades	scheermesjes	**sghayr**mehsyes
sanitary towels	maandverband *n*	**mahnt**verbant
scissors	schaar	sghahr
sedative	kalmeringsmiddel *n*	kal-**may**-rings-mid-el
shampoo	shampoo	**sham**poa
shaving brush	scheerkwast	**sghayr**kwast
shaving soap	scheerzeep	**sghayr**zayp
skin cream	huidcrème	**hœt**krehm
sleeping pills	slaaptabletten	**slahp**tahblehten
soap	zeep	zayp
sponge	spons	spons
spot/stain remover	vlekkenwater *n*	**vleh**kenwahter
sticking plaster	pleisters	**plaiys**ters
sun(tan) oil	zonnebrandolie	**zon**-e-brant-oa-lee
tampons	tampons	tam**pons**
tissues	papieren zakdoekjes	pah**pee**ren **zak**dookyes
toilet paper	toiletpapier *n*	twah**leht**pahpeer
tooth brush	tandenborstel	**tan**denborstel
tooth paste	tandpasta	**tant**pastah
vitamine pills	vitaminepillen	vee-tah-**mee**-ne-pil-en

CLOTHES AND SHOES

I prefer something ....
Ik heb het liefst iets in het ....
ik hehp heht leefst eets in heht ....

beige	beige	**beh**zhe
black	zwart	zwart
blue	blauw	blou
brown	bruin	brœn
green	groen	ghroon
grey	grijs	ghraiys
lilac	lila	**lee**lah
orange	oranje	oa**ran**ye
pink	roze	**ro**ze
red	rood	roat
white	wit	wit
yellow	geel	ghayl
multicoloured	bont	bont
deep/pale blue	donkerblauw/lichtblauw	**don**kerblou/**light**blou

I prefer ....
Ik geef de voorkeur aan ....
ik ghayf de **voar**kør ahn ....

a floral pattern	een bloemmotief	en **bloom**-moa-teef
unpatterned	effen	**eh**fen
checked	geruit	ghe**rœt**
large check	geblokt	ghe**blokt**
dotted	gestippeld	ghe-**stip**-elt
striped	gestreept	ghe**straypt**

Is this made of ....?
Is dit gemaakt van ....?
is dit ghe**mahkt** van ....?

corduroy	ribfluweel	**rip**flew-wayl
cotton	katoen	kah**toon**
felt	vilt	vilt
flannel	flanel	flah**nehl**
imitation leather	kunstleer	**kunst**layr
lace	kant	kant
leather (cowskin)	(rund)leer	(**runt**)layr
linnen	linnen	**lin**-en
new wool	scheerwol	**sghayr**wol
nylon	nylon	**naiy**lon
rayon	kunstzijde	**kunst**zaiyde
silk	zijde	**zaiy**de
synthetic fibre	kunstvezel	**kunst**vayzel
synthetic material	kunststof	**kunst**stof
velvet	fluweel	flew-**wayl**
worsted	kamgaren	**kam**ghahren

Can this be ironed/Is this machine-washable?
Kan dit worden gestreken/in de machine worden gewassen?
kan dit **wor**den ghe**stray**ken/in de mah**shee**ne **wor**den ghe**was**-en?

Is this colourfast/non-shrinkable?
Is dit kleurecht/krimpvrij?
is dit klør**ehght**/krimp**vraiy**?

I take (a) size ....
Mijn maat is....
maiyn maht is ....

This is too big/small for me
Dit is mij te groot/klein
dit is maiy te ghroat/klaiyn

It's too tight/loose
Hij valt te nauw/wijd
haiy valt te nou/waiyt

The shoes pinch here
De schoenen knellen hier
de **sghoo**nen **kneh**len heer

140

SHOPPING

Do you have a larger/smaller size?
Heeft u een maatje groter/kleiner?
hayft ew en **mah**tye **ghroa**ter/**klaiy**ner?

Can it be altered?
Kan het vermaakt worden?
kan heht ver**mahkt wor**den?

When will it be ready?
Wanneer is het klaar?
wa**nayr** is heht klahr?

May I try it on?
Mag ik het passen?
magh ik heht **pa**-sen?

Where is the fitting room?
Waar is de paskamer?
wahr is de **pas**kahmer?

Where can I find a mirror?
Waar is een spiegel?
wahr is en **spee**ghel?

Can these shoes/this shoe be repaired?
Kunnen deze schoenen/kan deze schoen worden gerepareerd?
kunen **day**ze **sghoo**nen/kan **day**ze sghoon **wor**den geraypah**rayrt**?

Where is the nearest cobbler's?
Waar is een schoenmaker?
wahr is en **sghoon**mahker?

I'd like to have new soles/heels
Ik wil nieuwe zolen/hakken
ik wil **neeoo**e **zoa**len/**hak**-en

belt (for men)	broekriem	**broek**reem
belt (for women)	ceintuur	saiyn**tewr**
blouse	blouse	bloos
boots	laarzen	**lahr**zen
brassiere, bra	beha	bay**hah**
buttons	knopen	**knoa**pen
cardigan	vest n	vehst
children's clothes	kinderkleding	**kin**derklayding
coat	mantel	**man**tel
denim jacket	spijkerjasje n	**spaiy**ker-yasye
dress	jurk	yurk
dressing gown, robe	kamerjas	**kah**meryas
fur coat	bontjas	**bont**yas
gloves	handschoenen	**hant**sghoonen
handkerchief	zakdoek	**zak**dook
hat	muts	muts
headscarf	hoofddoek	**hoaft**dook
jeans	spijkerbroek	**spaiy**kerbrook
knee socks	kniekousen	**knee**kousen
knitting wool	breiwol	**braiy**wol
ladies' cardigan	damesvest n	**dah**mesvehst
ladies' wear	damesconfectie	**dah**meskonfehksee
men's wear	herenconfectie	**hay**renkonfehksee

141

nightdress, nightgown	nachtpon	**naght**pon
(under)pants/panties	onderbroek, slipje *n*	**on**derbrook, **slip**ye
pyjamas	pyjama	pee**yah**mah
rain/trench coat	regenjas	ray**ghen**yas
sandals	sandalen	san**dah**len
shirt	overhemd *n*	**oa**verhehmt
shoehorn	schoenlepel	s**ghoon**laypel
shoe laces	schoenveters	s**ghoon**vayters
shoe polish	schoensmeer	s**ghoon**smayr
shoes	schoenen	s**ghoo**nen
shorts	short *n*	'short'
skirt	rok	rok
slippers	pantoffels, sloffen	pan**to**fels, **slo**fen
socks	sokken	**sok**en
sole	zool	zoal
sports wear	sportkleding	**sport**klayding
suit	kostuum *n*	kos**tewm**
sweater	trui	trœ
thread	garen	**ghah**ren
tie	das	das
tights	panty	**pehn**tee
tracksuit	trainingspak	'**trai**nings'-pak
trousers	pantalon, lange broek	**pan**tahlon, **lang**e brook
umbrella	paraplu	pahrah**plew**
underwear	ondergoed *n*	**on**derghoot
vest	(onder)hemd *n*	(**on**der)hehmt
waist slip	onderrok	**on**der-rok
women's suit	mantelpak *n*	**man**telpak
zip	ritssluiting	**rits**-slœting

PHOTO, FILM AND VIDEO EQUIPMENT

I'd like to have a ....
Ik wil graag een ....
ik wil ghrahgh en ....

colour film	kleurenfilm	**klœ**renfilm
black-and-white film	zwartwitfilm	zwart**wit**film
cassette, cartridge	filmcassette	**film**ka-seh-te
slide film	diafilm	**dee**yah-film
a 27 DIN/100 ASA film	een film van 27 DIN/100 ASA	en film van **zay**ven-ehn-twintegh din/**hon**dert **ah**sah

for 20/36 shots   voor 20/36 opnamen   voar **twin**tegh/
    zehs-ehn-dehrtegh **op**nahmen

for outdoors   voor daglicht   voar **dagh**light
for indoors   voor kunstlicht   voar **kunst**light

I'd like to have a 8 millimeter/super 8 cassette/video cassette
Ik wil graag een 8 mm/super 8 filmcassette/videofilmcassette
ik wil ghrahgh en aght **mee**leemayter/**sew**per aght ka**seh**te/**vee**deeyoa-film-ka-seh-te

I'd like to have this film developed and printed
Kunt u deze film voor mij ontwikkelen en afdrukken?
kunt ew **day**ze film voar maiy ont**wike**-len ehn **af**dru-ken?

mat   mat   mat
glossy   glanzend   **ghlan**zent
5 x 3 inches   negen bij dertien   **nay**ghen baiy **dehr**teen
    (centimeter)   (**sehn**teemayter)

I'd like to have these slides framed
Ik wil de dia's ingeraamd hebben
ik wil de **dee**yahs **in**gherahmt **heh**ben

When will they be ready?
Wanneer zijn ze klaar?
wa**nayr** zaiyn ze klahr?

Could you make 4 passport photos?
Kunt u vier pasfoto's maken?
kunt ew veer **pas**foatoas **mah**ken?

Can this camera be repaired?
Kan deze camera worden gerepareerd?
kan **day**ze **kah**merah **wor**den gheraypah**rayrt**?

The .... is broken   ◀ **The camera will have to be sent to the manufacturer**
Er is een defect aan de ....   U moet de camera naar de fabriek sturen
ehr is en de**fehkt** ahn de ....   ew moot de **kah**merah nahr de fah**breek stew**ren

◀ **It will be quite expensive**
Dit zal veel gaan kosten
dit zal vayl ghahn **kos**ten

battery	batterij	ba-te-**raiy**
camera	fototoestel *n*	**foa**toa-toostehl
cine film	smalfilm	**smal**film
enlargement	vergroting	ver**ghroa**ting
exposure counter	opnameteller	**op**nahme-tehler
exposure meter	belichtingsmeter	be**light**ings-mayter
film camera	filmcamera	**film**kah-me-rah
film transport mechanism	filmtransport *n*	**film**transport

filter screen	filter n	filter
colour filter	kleurenfilter n	klœrenfilter
sun filter	UV-filter	ew-vay filter
flashbulbs	flitslampjes	flitslampyes
flashcubes	flitsblokjes	flitsblokyes
flash gun, electronic flash	flitser	flitser
flashlight	flitslicht n	flitslight
high-speed film	snelle film	snehle film
lens	lens	lehns
lens cap	lenskap	lehnskap
lens hood	zonnekap	zon-e-kap
micro objective	micro-objectief n	meekroa-op-yehk-teef
negative	negatief n	nay-ghah-teef
objective, object glass	objectief n	opyehkteef
35 mm	vijfendertig millimeter	vaiyf-ehn-dehrtegh meeleemayter
70 mm	zeventig millimeter	zayventegh meeleemayter
135 mm	honderdvijfendertig millimeter	hondert-vaiyf-ehn-dehrtegh meeleemayter
rangefinder	afstandsmeter	afstantsmayter
shutter	sluiter	slœter
size	formaat n	formaht
slide	dia	deeyah
slide frames	diaraampjes	deeyah-rahmpyes
soundtrack	geluidsspoor n	ghelœts-spoar
tripod	statief n	stahteef
underwater camera	onderwatercamera	onderwahter-kahmerah
video camera	videocamera	vee-dee-yoa-kah-me-rah
video cassette	videocassette	vee-dee-yoa-ka-seh-te
video cassette recorder	videorecorder	vee-dee-yoa-'recorder'
viewfinder	zoeker	zooker
wide-angle lens	groothoeklens	ghroathooklens
zoom lens	zoomlens	zoomlehns

TRAVEL AND CAMPING EQUIPMENT

(see 'Sports and recreation' for bathing and sports equipment)

air mattress	luchtbed n	lughtbeht
attaché case	diplomatenkoffer	dee-ploa-mah-ten-ko-fer
awning	luifel	lœfel
bottle opener	flesopener	flehs-oapener
briefcase	aktentas	aktentas

144

bucket	emmer	**eh**mer
Calor Gas	butagas	**bew**tah-ghas
camping equipment	kampeeruitrusting	kam**payr**-œtrusting
candles	kaarsen	**kahr**sen
charcoal	houtskool	**houts**koal
clothes peg	wasknijper	**was**knaiyper
compass	kompas *n*	kom**pas**
cool box/bag	koelbox, koeltas	**kool**box, **kool**tas
corkscrew	kurketrekker	**kur**ke-trehker
cups	kopjes	**kop**yes
cutlery	bestek *n*	be**stehk**
deck chair	ligstoel	**ligh**stool
disposable cutlery	wegwerpbestek *n*	**wehgh**wehrp-bestehk
disposable plates	wegwerpborden	**wehgh**wehrp-borden
first-aid kit	verbandkist	ver**bant**kist
folding bed	opklapbed *n*	**op**klapbet
folding chair	klapstoel	**klap**stool
folding/drop-leaf table	klaptafel	**klap**tahfel
fork	vork	vork
gas burner/jet	gasbrander	**ghas**brander
groundsheet	grondzeil *n*	**ghront**zaiyl
hammer	hamer	**hah**mer
hammock	hangmat	**hang**mat
inflator	(lucht)pomp	(**lught**)pomp
iron casserole	braadpan	**braht**pan
kettle	fluitketel	**flœt**kaytel
knife	mes *n*	mehs
lamp	lamp	lamp
lantern	lantaarn	lan**tahrn**
matches	lucifers	**lew**seefehrs
mattress	matras *n*	mah**tras**
methylated spirits, meths	brandspiritus	**brant**speereetus
mugs	bekers	**bay**kers
pan, pot	pan	pan
plastic bag	plastic zak	'plastic' zak
plates	borden	**bor**den
pocketknife, penknife	zakmes *n*	**zak**mehs
Primus (stove)	primus	**pree**mus
rope	touw *n*	tou
rucksack	rugzak	**rugh**zak
saucer	schotel	**sghoa**tel
scissors	schaar	sghahr
screwdriver	schroevedraaier	**sghroo**-ve-drah-yer

145

shoulder bag	schoudertas	**sghou**der-tas
spit	braadspies	**braht**spees
spoon	lepel	**lay**pel
suitcase	koffer	**ko**-fer
sunshade	zonnescherm n	**zon**-e-sghehrm
tent	tent	tehnt
tent peg	tentharing	**tehnt**hahring
tent pole	tentstok	**tehnt**stok
Thermos (flask)	thermosfles	**tehr**mosflehs
tin opener	blikopener	**blik**oapener
torch	zaklantaarn	**zak**lantahrn
travelling case, valise	reistas	**raiys**tas
umbrella	paraplu	pahrah**plew**
washing powder	waspoeder n	**was**pooder

BOOKS, MAGAZINES, STATIONARY

Where do I find a bookshop/stationer/newsstand?
Waar is een boekhandel/kantoorboekhandel/kiosk?
wahr is en **book**handel/kan**toar**bookhandel/kee**yosk**?

Do you have any books in English on ....?
Heeft u boeken in het Engels over ....?
hayft ew **boo**ken in heht **ehng**els **oa**ver ....?

the Netherlands	Nederland	**nay**derlant
Belgium	België	**behl**-ghee-ye
this area	deze streek	**day**ze strayk
this town	deze stad	**day**ze stat
the scenery	het natuurschoon	heht nah**tewr**sghoan
history	geschiedenis	ghe**sghee**denis
monuments	monumenten	moanew**mehn**ten
bicycle tours	fietstochten	**feets**toghten
walks	wandelingen	**wan**delingen
with lots of pictures	met veel foto's	meht vayl **foa**toas

Do you also have translated Dutch/Flemish literature?
Heeft u vertaalde Nederlandse/Vlaamse literatuur?
hayft ew ver**tahl**de **nay**derlantse/**vlahm**se leeterah**tewr**?

Do you sell British/American newspapers/magazines?
Heeft u Engelse/Amerikaanse kranten/tijdschriften?
hayft ew **ehng**else/ahmayree**kahn**se **kran**ten/**taiyt**sghriften?

art books	kunstboeken	**kunst**booken
atlas	atlas	**at**las
ball pen	balpen	**bal**pehn
book	boek *n*	book
calculator	calculator	kalkew**lah**tor
children's books	kinderboeken	**kin**derbooken
cookbook	kookboek *n*	**koak**book
crayons	kleurpotloden	**klør**potloaden
crime novel	detectiveroman	'detective'-roaman
dictionary	woordenboek *n*	**woar**denbook
Dutch-English	Nederlands-Engels	**nay**derlants-**eng**els
English-Dutch	Engels-Nederlands	**eng**els-**nay**derlants
drawing pins	punaises	pew**nay**ses
envelopes	enveloppen	ehn-ve-**lop**-en
airmail	voor luchtpost	voar **lught**post
eraser	vlakgom *n*	**vlak**ghom
exercise book	schrift *n*	sghrift
felt-tip pen	viltstift	**vilt**stift
foreign newspapers	buitenlandse kranten	**bœ**tenlantse **kran**ten
fountain pen	vulpen	**vul**pehn
glue	lijm	laiym
ink (cartridges)	inkt(patronen)	inkt(pah**troa**nen)
literature	literatuur	leeterah**tewr**
magazine	tijdschrift *n*	**taiyt**sghrift
map	landkaart	**lant**kahrt
(city) map, street plan	plattegrond	plat-e-**ghront**
road map	wegenkaart	**way**ghen-kahrt
topographical map	topografische kaart	toa-poa-**ghrah**-fee-se kahrt
walking/hiking map	wandelkaart	**wand**el-kahrt
monthly	maandblad *n*	**mahnt**blat
(daily) newspaper	dagblad *n*	**dagh**blat
newspaper	krant	krant
notepad, writing pad	schrijfblok *n*	**sghraiyf**blok
paper	papier *n*	pah**peer**
paperbacks	pockets	'pockets'
paperclips	paperclips	'paperclips'
pencil	potlood *n*	**pot**loat
pencil sharpener	puntenslijper	**pun**tenslaiyper
playing cards	speelkaarten	**spayl**kahrten
postcards	ansichtkaarten	**an**sightkahrten
rubber bands	elastiekjes	aylas**teek**yes
ruler	lineaal	leenee**yahl**
sale	opruiming, uitverkoop	**op**rœming, **œt**verkoap

sellotape, Scotch tape	plakband *n*	**plak**bant
travel guide	reisgids	**raiys**ghits
art guide	kunstreisgids	**kunst**-raiys-ghits
hiking guide	wandelgids	**wan**del-ghits
typewriter ribbon	schrijfmachinelint *n*	**sghraiyf**-mah-shee-ne-lint
weekly	weekblad *n*	**wayk**blat
wrapping paper	pakpapier *n*	**pak**pahpeer

JEWELRY AND WATCHES

Can you fix this watch/bracelet/chain?
Kunt u dit horloge/deze armband/deze ketting repareren?
kunt ew dit hor**loa**zhe/**day**ze **arm**bant/**day**ze **keh**ting raypah**ray**ren?

Could you clean this?
Kunt u dit schoonmaken?
kunt ew dit **sghoan**mahken?

The watch is fast/slow
Het horloge loopt voor/achter
heht hor**loa**zhe loapt voar/**agh**ter

When will it be ready?
Wanneer is het klaar?
wanayr is heht klahr?

◄ **This cannot be repared**
Dit is onherstelbaar
dit is **on**hehrstehlbahr

◄ **The battery must be changed**
De batterij moet vervangen worden
de ba-te-**raiy** moot ver**vang**en **wor**den

How many carats is this?
Hoeveel karaat is dit?
hoovayl kah**raht** is dit?

◄ **14/18 carats**
14/18 karaat
vayrteen/**agh**teen kah**raht**

Can I have this name engraved in it?
Kan deze naam erin gegraveerd worden?
kan **day**ze nahm ehr**in** gheghrah**vayrt wor**den?

(travel) alarm clock	(reis)wekker	**(raiys)**wehker
amulet	amulet	ahmew**leht**
battery	batterij	ba-te-**raiy**
bracelet	armband	**arm**bant
brass	messing *n*	**meh**sing
brooch	broche	brosh
chain bracelet	schakelarmband	**sghah**kel-armbant
chrome	chroom *n*	ghroam
copper	(rood)koper *n*	(roat)**koa**per
crown	opwindknopje *n*	**op**wint-knopye
crystal	kristal *n*	kris**tal**
cut diamond, brilliant	briljant	bril**yant**
diamond	diamant	deeyah**mant**
earrings	oorbellen	**oar**behlen
emerald	smaragd	smah**ragt**
glass	glas *n*	ghlas

148

gold	goud n	ghout
gold leaf	bladgoud n	**blat**ghout
gold-plated	doublé	doo**blay**
jade	jade	**yah**de
jewel box/case	juwelenkistje n	yew-**way**-len-kis-ye
ladies' watch	dameshorloge n	**dah**mes-horloazhe
leather	leer n	layr
men's watch	herenhorloge n	**hay**ren-horloazhe
mother of pearl	parelmoer	**pahr**elmoor
necklace	halsketting	**hals**kehting
pearl necklace	parelsnoer n	**pahr**elsnoor
pewter	tin n	tin
pin	speld	spehlt
platinum	platina n	**plah**teenah
pocket watch	zakhorloge n	**zak**horloazhe
quartz watch	kwartshorloge n	**quarts**-horloazhe
ring	ring	ring
wedding ring	trouwring	**trou**ring
signet ring	zegelring	**zay**ghelring
ruby	robijn	roa**baiyn**
sapphire	saffier	sa**feer**
silver	zilver n	**zil**ver
silverware	tafelzilver n	**tah**felzilver
spring	veer	vayr
(stainless) steel	(roest)vrij staal n	**(roost)**vraiy stahl
tobacco box	tabaksdoos	tah**baks**doas
topaz	topaas	toa**pahs**
watch	horloge n	horloazhe
digital	digitaal	deeghee**tahl**
dial watch	... met wijzers	... meht **waiy**zers
watch chain	horlogeketting	horloazhe-kehting
watchstrap	horlogebandje n	horloazhe-bantye
white gold	witgoud n	**wit**ghout
wristwatch	polshorloge n	**pols**horloazhe

COINS AND STAMPS

annual collection	jaarcollectie	**yahr**-ko-lehk-see
block	blok n	blok
coin album	muntenalbum n	**mun**ten-album
commemorative coins	gelegenheidsmunten	ghe**lay**-ghenhaiyts-munten
commemorative stamps	gelegenheidspostzegels	ghe**lay**-ghenhaits-postzayghels

149

Souvenirs

Most souvenir shops offer the usual range of souvenirs, such as wooden shoes, clay pipes, toy windmills, dolls in Volendam costumes, etc. You can, however, buy really valuable (and therefore often quite expensive) souvenirs in department stores and quality shops. Try for instance the famous Dutch cigars, flower bulbs (carefully read the instructions for a good result), flowery earthenware from Makkum, Royal Delft blue pottery (look for the pottery marks to avoid fake articles), Leerdam glassware, cheese (not the pre-packed Edam 'cannon balls', but fresh cheese from the market), Schoonhoven silverware and - if your budget permits you to do so - Amsterdam diamonds (with or without the usual guided tour of the factory). When in Belgium, do not forget to taste the delicious chocolate. Flemish lace is of undisputed top quality and so are the cut and uncut diamonds of Antwerp.

Talking about wooden shoes: do the Dutch really wear them? Indeed, quite a few farmers do, but their *klompen* are unpainted (unlike the souvenir clogs). Wooden shoes are far more resistant to the soft and wet clay of the farmland below sea level. Nobody wears them, however, without a thin leather or rubber 'inside shoe' which keeps their feet dry and warm. When entering a farmhouse (always through the kitchen, never through the front door which is for weddings and funerals only), a farmer always takes off his wooden shoes. City folks sometimes buy painted clogs for decoration purposes; they hang them on the wall outside their houses as an alternative for the usual clay flower pots.

first day cover	eerste-dagenveloppe	ayrste-**dagh**-ehnvelop
gold coins	gouden munten	**ghou**den **mun**ten
loose-leaf	losbladig	los**blah**degh
mint proof, specimen coin	muntproef	**munt**proof
not perforated	ongetand	**on**ghetant
ordinary stamps	gewone zegels	ghe**woa**ne **zay**ghels
perforated	getand	ghe**tant**

postmarked	gestempeld	ghe**stehm**pelt
series	serie	**say**ree
sheet	vel *n*	vehl
silver coins	zilveren munten	**zil**veren **mun**ten
special postmark	gelegenheidsstempel	ghe**lay**ghenhaiyts-stempel
stamp	postzegel	**post**zayghel
stamp album	postzegelalbum *n*	**post**zayghel-album
very beautiful	zeer fraai	zayr frahy

IN OTHER SHOPS

Can these glasses be repaired?
Kan deze bril gerepareerd worden?
kan **day**ze bril gheraypah**rayrt wor**den?

Do you have a pair of sunglasses for me?
Heeft u voor mij een zonnebril?
hayft ew voar maiy en **zon**-e-bril?

| contact lenses, contacts | contactlenzen | kon**takt**lenzen |
| fluid for contact lenses | vloeistof voor contactlenzen | **vlooy**stof voar kon**takt**lehnzen |

Do you sell foreign cigars/cigarettes?
Heeft u buitenlandse sigaren/sigaretten?
hayft ew **bœ**tenlantse see**ghah**ren/seeghah**reh**ten?

filter-tipped cigarettes	filtersigaretten	**fil**ter-seeghahrehten
matches	lucifers	**lew**seefehrs
rolling tobacco	shag	shehk
tobacco	tabak	tah**bak**

LAUNDRETTE AND DRY-CLEANER'S

Where can I find a laundrette?
Waar is een wasserette?
wahr is en was-e-**reh**-te?

Where can I have my clothes cleaned?
Waar kan ik kleding laten reinigen?
wahr kan ik **klay**ding **lah**ten **raiy**neghen?

Could I have this cleaned/dry-cleaned?
Kan dit voor mij gereinigd/gestoomd worden?
kan dit voar maiy ghe**raiy**neght/ghe**stoamt wor**den?

◀ **This needs special treatment**
Dit vraagt een speciale behandeling
dit vrahght en spaysee**yah**le be**han**deling

◀ **This stain won't come out**
Deze vlek krijgen wij er niet uit
dayze vlehk **kraiy**ghen waiy ehr neet œt

151

crease-resistant	kreukvrij	krøk**vraiy**
detergent	zeeppoeder *n*	**zayp**-pooder
to dry-clean	stomen	**stoa**men
dry-cleaning	chemisch reinigen	**ghay**mees **raiy**neghen
dryer	droogtrommel	**droagh**trom-el
hand wash only	met de hand wassen	meht de hant **was**-en
to iron	strijken	**straiy**ken
main wash	hoofdwas	**hoaft**was
no ironing	niet strijken	neet **straiy**ken
prewash	voorwas	**voar**was
synthetic, artificial	synthetisch	sin**tay**tees
to wash	wassen	**was**-en
wash at 40 degrees	op 40 graden wassen	op **vayr**tegh **ghrah**den **was**-en
wash in lukewarm water	lauw wassen	lou **was**-en
washing machine	wasautomaat	**was**outoamaht
waterproof	waterdicht	**wah**terdight

AT THE HAIRDRESSER'S

| ladies' hairdresser | dameskapper | **dah**mes-kap-er |
| barber | herenkapper | **hay**ren-kap-er |

Can I make an appointment?
Kan ik een afspraak maken?
kan ik en **af**sprahk **mah**ken?

How long will it take?
Hoe lang kan het duren?
hoo lang kan heht **dew**ren?

Do you also cut children's hair?
Knipt u ook kinderen?
knipt ew oak **kin**deren?

A shave and a haircut, please
Knippen en scheren alstublieft
knip-en ehn **sghay**ren alstew**bleeft**

Not so short
Niet te kort
neet te kort

A little shorter ....
Iets korter ....
eets **kor**ter ....

on top	bovenop	boaven**op**
at the back of the neck	in de nek	in de nehk
at the back	aan de achterkant	ahn de **agh**terkant
on the sides	aan de zijkanten	ahn de **zaiy**kanten

Just a trim, please
Wilt u alleen de punten bijknippen?
wilt ew a**layn** de **pun**ten **baiy**knip-en?

Washing and styling, please
Wassen en watergolven alstublieft
was-en ehn **wah**tergholven alstew**bleeft**

beard	baard	bahrt
bleached streaks	coupe soleil	koop soa**laiy**
to blow-dry	föhnen	**fø**nen
braid, plait	vlecht	vlehght
brilliantine	brillantine	brilyan**tee**ne
colour rinse	kleurspoeling	**klør**spooling
comb	kam	kam
to comb	kammen	**kam**-en
to cut	knippen	**knip**-en
dandruff	roos	roas
dry hair	droog haar *n*	droagh hahr
to dye	verven	**vehr**ven
greasy hair	vet haar *n*	veht hahr
hairdo	kapsel *n*	**kap**sel
hair dryer	droogkap	**droagh**kap
hair gel	gel	'gel'
hair spray	haarlak	**hahr**lak
long hair	lang haar *n*	lang hahr
loss of hair	haaruitval	**hahr**œtval
lotion	lotion	loa**syon**
manicure	manicure	mahnee**kew**re
moustache	snor	snor
perm	permanent *n*	pehrmah**nehnt**
ponytail	paardestaart	**pahr**de-stahrt
punk hairstyle	punkkapsel *n*	**punk**-kapsel
rinse	spoeling	**spool**ing
setting-lotion	haarversteviger	**hahr**ver-stay-ve-ghing
shampoo	shampoo	**sham**poa
to style	opkammen	**op**kam-en
wave	watergolf	**wah**ter-gholf
to wave/curl/crimp	krullen	**krul**-en
whiskers	bakkebaard	**bak**-e-bahrt

IN THE BEAUTY PARLOUR

(see also the list under 'Toiletries and medicines')

Can I make an appointment?
Kan ik een afspraak maken?
kan ik en **af**sprahk **mah**ken?

How long will it take?
Hoe lang kan het duren?
hoo lang kan heht **dew**ren?

| beauty parlour | schoonheidssalon | **sghoan**-haiyts-sahlon |
| to depilate | ontharen | ont**hah**ren |

153

face pack	gezichtsmasker *n*	ghe**zights**masker
a facial	gezichtsverzorging	ghe**zights**verzorghing
full treatment	volledige behandeling	vo-**lay**-de-ghe be**han**deling
manicure	manicure	mahnee**kew**re
mudpack	modderbehandeling	**mo**derbehandeling
pedicure	pedicure	paydee**kew**re
to shave	scheren	**sghay**ren

SIGHTSEEING AND RELAXING

AT THE TOURIST INFORMATION OFFICE

Where is the tourist information?
Waar is het VVV-kantoor?
wahr is heht vay-vay-vay-kan**toar**?

Do you speak English?
Spreekt u Engels?
spraykt ew **ehng**els?

I'd like to have some information/a leaflet on ....
Ik wil graag inlichtingen/een folder hebben over ....
ik wil ghrahgh **in**ligh-ting-en/en **fol**der **heh**ben **oa**ver ....

bus services	busdiensten	**bus**deensten
camp sites	kampeerterreinen	kam**payr**teh-raiy-nen
car hire/rental	autoverhuur	**ou**toa-verhewr
city walks	stadswandelingen	**stats**wan-de-ling-en
.. day excursions	meerdaagse excursies	**mayr**dahgh-se ex**kur**sees
day trips	dagexcursies	**dagh**ehx-kur-sees
entertainment	uitgaansmogelijkheden	**œt**ghahns-moa-ghe-lek-hay-den
entertainment for children	amusement voor kinderen	ahmewse**mehnt** voar **kin**deren
events	evenementen	ayve-ne-**mehn**-ten
guest houses	pensions	pehn**syons**
holiday cottages/	vakantiehuisjes/	vah**kan**see-hœsyes/
** bungalows**	bungalows	'bungalows'
hotels	hotels	hoa**tehls**
monuments	monumenten	moanew**mehn**ten
museums	musea	mew-**say**-yah
public transport	openbaar vervoer	**oa**penbahr ver**voor**
rent-a-bike	fietsverhuur	**feets**verhewr
sightseeing cruises	rondvaarten	**ront**vahrten
trains	treinen	**traiy**nen
youth hostels	jeugdherbergen	**yøgt**hehr-behr-ghen
fishing	vissen	**vis**-en
walks, hikes	wandelingen	**wan**de-ling-en
water sports, aquatics	watersport	**wah**ter-sport

Do you have any leaflets in English?
Hebt u folders in het Engels?
hehbt ew **fol**ders in heht **ehng**els?

Do you have a map of the city/area?
Hebt u een stadsplattegrond/streekkaart?
hehpt ew en **stats**plat-e-ghront/**strayk**kahrt?

155

Do you have bicycle/hikers' maps?
Hebt u fietskaarten/wandelkaarten?
hehpt ew **feets**kahrten/**wan**delkahrten?

Could you draw the route?
Kunt u de route intekenen?
kunt ew de **roo**te **in**taykenen?

Which are the main sights?
Wat zijn de belangrijkste bezienswaardigheden?
wat zaiyn de be**lang**raiykste be-zeens-**wahr**-degh-hay-den?

Where do I find the ....?
Waar vind ik de/het ....?
wahr vint ik de/heht ....?

aquarium	aquarium *n*	ah-**quah**-ree-yum
botanical garden	botanische tuin	boa**tah**neese tœn
castle	kasteel *n*	kas**tayl**
cathedral	kathedraal, dom	kate**drahl**, dom
caves	grotten	**ghrot**-en
chapel	kapel	kah**pehl**
church	kerk	kehrk
fortress	vesting	**vehs**ting
houses of parliament	parlementsgebouw *n*	par-le-**mehnts**-ghe-bou
market, market place	markt, marktplein *n*	markt, **markt**plaiyn
monastery, convent	klooster *n*	**kloas**ter
museum	museum *n*	mew-**say**-yum
observation point	uitzichtpunt *n*	œtzights-punt
opera (house)	opera	**oa**perah
palace	paleis *n*	pah**laiys**
park	park *n*	park
ruins	ruïne	rew-**ee**-ne
theatre	schouwburg	**sghou**burgh
town/city hall	raadhuis *n*	**raht**hœs
zoo	dierentuin	**dee**rentœn

Could you point it out on the map?
Kunt u het op de plattegrond aanwijzen?
kunt ew heht op de plat-e-**ghront aan**waiyzen?

Is it open today?
Is het vandaag geopend?
is heht van**dahgh** ghe-**oa**-pent?

Do they charge an entrance fee?
Moet er entree betaald worden?
moot ehr ehn**tray** be**tahlt wor**den?

Do you also sell guides/maps/street plans?
Verkoopt u ook gidsen/kaarten/plattegronden?
ver**koapt** ew oak **ghit**sen/**kahr**ten/plat-e-**ghron**-den?

Where do the buses leave?
(Van)waar vertrekken de bussen?
(van)**wahr** ver**trehk**ken de **bus**-en?

◀ **You will be picked up at your hotel**
U wordt bij uw hotel afgehaald
ew wordt baiy eww hoa**tel af**ghe-hahlt

VISITING A MUSEUM

Where is the (museum of/for) ....?
Waar is het (museum van/voor) ....?
wahr is heht (mew-**say**-yum van/voar) ....?

agriculture	landbouw	**lant**bou
applied arts	toegepaste kunst	**too**ghe-pas-te kunst
archaeology	oudheidkunde	**out**haiyt-kunde
arts and crafts	kunstnijverheid	kunst**naiy**verhaiyt
carriages	rijtuigen	**raiy**tœghen
ceramics	keramiek	kayrah**meek**
ethnographical museum	volkenkundig museum	volken**kun**degh mew-**say**-yum
fishery	visserij	vis-e-**raiy**
folk art	volkskunst	**volks**kunst
geology	geologie	ghay-oa-loa-**ghee**
history	historisch museum	his**to**-rees mew-**say**-yum
literature	letterkunde	**leh**terkunde
maritime museum	scheepvaartmuseum	**sghayp**-vahrt-mew-say-yum
military museum	legermuseum	**lay**gher-mew-say-yum
municipal history	stadsgeschiedenis	**stats**-ghe-sghee-de-nis
musical history	muziekgeschiedenis	mew-**zeek**-ghe-sghee-de-nis
natural sciences	natuurwetenschappen	nah-**tewr**-way-ten-sghap-en
open-air museum	openluchtmuseum	oa-pen-**lught**-mew-say-yum
oriental art	oosterse kunst	**oas**terse kunst
postal museum	postmuseum	**post**-mew-say-yum
prehistory	prehistorie	**pray**histoaree
railway museum	spoorwegmuseum	**spoar**wehgh-mew-say-yum
regional history	streekgeschiedenis	**strayk**ghe-sghee-de-nis
sculpture	beeldhouwkunst	**baylt**-hou-kunst
stamps	postzegelmuseum	**post**zayghel-mew-say-yum
technique	techniek	tehgh**neek**
textile industry	textielnijverheid	tex**teel**naiy-ver-haiyt
visual arts	beeldende kunst	**bayl**dende kunst
zoology	zoölogie	zoa-oa-loa-**ghee**

Is the museum open to the public?
Is het museum vrij toegankelijk?
is heht mew-**say**-yum vraiy too**ghan**kelek?

◀ **No, you have to take a guided tour**
Nee, alleen met een rondleiding
nay, a**layn** meht en **ront**laiyding

How much is the entrance fee?
Hoeveel bedraagt de entree?
hoovayl be**drahgt** de ehn**tray**?

◀ **The entrance is free**
De toegang is vrij
de **too**ghang is vraiy

Two children's tickets
Twee kinderkaartjes
tway **kin**derkahrtyes

Two adult tickets
Twee kaartjes voor volwassenen
tway **kahr**tyes voar vol-**wa**-se-nen

Is there a special exhibition?
Is er een bijzondere tentoonstelling?
is ehr en bee**zon**dere tehn**toan**stehling?

Do you have a map/guide/catalogue?
Heeft u een plattegrond/gids/catalogus?
hayft ew en plat-e-**ghront**/ghits/kah**tah**loaghus?

Can I take pictures?
Mag ik fotograferen?
magh ik foatoa-ghrah**fay**ren?

◀ **You have to pay**
Alleen tegen betaling
a**layn tay**ghen be**tah**ling

◀ **Only without flash and without tripod**
Alleen zonder flitslicht en zonder statief
a**layn zon**der **flits**light ehn **zon**der stah**teef**

Is there a ..../Where is the ....?
Is er een ..../Waar is de/het ....?
is ehr en ..../wahr is de/heht ....?

attendant	suppoost	su**poast**
cafeteria	cafetaria	kah-fe-**tah**-ree-yah
cloakroom	garderobe	gharde**ro**be
coffee machine	koffieautomaat	**ko**fee-outoamaht
crèche	crèche	'crèche'
exit	uitgang	**œt**ghang
film showing	filmvoorstelling	**film**voarstehling
lecture	lezing	**lay**zing
museum shop	museumwinkel	mew-**say**-yum-win-kel
restaurant	restaurant *n*	rehstoa**rant**
toilet	toilet *n*	twah**leht**

VISITING CASTLES, CHURCHES ETC.

(for questions regarding entering see 'Visiting a museum')

When does the guided tour start?
Hoe laat begint de rondleiding?
hoo laht be**ghint** de **ront**laiyding?

Is there a tour in English?
Is er een rondleiding in het Engels?
is ehr en **ront**laiyding in heht **ehng**els?

May we look around on our own?
Mogen we hier vrij rondkijken?
moaghen we heer vraiy **ront**kaiyken?

fortress	vesting	**veh**sting
rampart	vestingwal	**veh**stingwal
bastion	bastion *n*	bastee**yon**
roundel	rondeel *n*	ron**dayl**

ammunition room	munitiekamer	mew**nee**tsee-kahmer
dungeon	kerker	**kehr**ker
manor, stately home	landhuis *n*	**lant**hœs
country estate	landgoed *n*	**lant**ghoot
castle	kasteel *n*	kas**tayl**
palace	paleis *n*	pah**laiys**
royal	koninklijk	**koa**-nin-klek
ducal	hertogelijk	hehr**toa**ghelek
earl's	grafelijk	**ghrah**felek
episcopal	bisschoppelijk	bis-**sghop**-e-lek
great hall	ridderzaal	**ri**-der-zahl
reception hall	ontvangsthal	ont**vangst**hal
ballroom	balzaal	**bal**zahl
monastery, convent	klooster *n*	**kloas**ter
abbey	abdij	ap**daiy**
cathedral	kathedraal, dom	kate**drahl**, dom
church	kerk	kehrk
synagogue	synagoge	seenah**ghoa**ghe
nave	schip *n*	sghip
choir	koor *n*	koar
altar	altaar *n*	**al**tahr
vault	gewelf *n*	ghe**wehlf**
treasure room	schatkamer	**sghat**kahmer
Benedictines	benedictijnen	bay-ne-dik-**taiy**-nen
Cistercians	cisterciënzers	sis-ter-see-**yehn**-sers
Dominicans	dominicanen	doa-mee-nee-**kah**-nen
Franciscans	franciscanen	fran-sis-**kah**-nen
prehistoric	prehistorisch	prayhis**toa**rees
Roman	Romeins	roa**maiyns**
Medieval	middeleeuws	mi-del-**ayoos**
Pre-Romanesque	preromaans	prayroa**mahns**
Romanesque	romaans	roa**mahns**
Gothic	gotisch	**ghoa**tees
Renaissance	renaissance	re-nay-**san**-se
Baroque	barok	bah**rok**
Rococo	rococo	ro-ko-**koa**
classicistic	classicistisch	klas-see-**sis**-tees
Neo-Gothic	neogotisch	nay-oa-**ghoa**tees
modernistic	modernistisch	moa-dehr-**nis**-tees
modern	modern	moa**dehrn**
Art Nouveau	Jugendstil (Neths. only)	**yoo**-gent-shteel
contemporary	eigentijds, hedendaags	aiy-ghen**taiyts**, **hay**den-dahghs
16th century	16de-eeuws	zehsteende-**ayoos**

Een gracht in Amsterdam

1	Oude koopmanshuizen
2	Pakhuizen met klokgevels
3	Een boogbrug
4	Een draaiorgel
5	De orgelman
6	Een kleine bijdrage
7	Roestige fietsen
8	Woonboten in de gracht

A canal in Amsterdam

Old merchants' houses
Gabled warehouses
An arched bridge
A street organ
The organ-grinder
A small contribution
Rusty bicycles
Houseboats in the canal

f = feminine, *m* = masculine, *n* = neuter, *pl* = plural (contrary to the English equivalent), *pop.* = popular speech, *sg* = singular (contrary to the English equivalent)

A road - autoweg
AA patrol - wegenwacht
able to, to be - kunnen
aboard - aan boord
above - over
abroad - in het buitenland
acceleration - versnelling
accept, to - aannemen
accident - ongeluk *n*
accompanied by - vergezeld van
accompany, to - vergezellen
accross - over
acid - zuur *n*
acquaintance (person) - kennis
acquaintance (act) - kennismaking
acquit, to - kwijtschelden
add, to - optellen
address - adres *n*
adhesive tape - plakband *n*
adjust, to - verstellen
aerial - antenne
afraid, to be - angstig/bang zijn
afternoon - middag
afterwards - daarna, later
again - weer, opnieuw
against - tegen
agent - agent *m*, agente *f*
agree, to - afspreken
agreement - overeenkomst
ahead - vooruit
ailment - kwaal
air - lucht
air, to - luchten
airmail, by - per luchtpost
air mattress - luchtbed *n*

airport - luchthaven, vliegveld *n*
airsick - luchtziek
alarm clock - wekker
aliens registration office -
  vreemdelingendienst
all - alles
all right! - in orde! OK! oké!
allow, to - toestaan
almost - bijna
alone - alleen
along - langs
also - ook
alteration - wijziging
always - altijd
ambulance - ambulance, ziekenauto
amount - bedrag *n*
animal - dier *n*, beest *n*
annexe - dependance, bijgebouw *n*
announcement - mededeling, aankondiging
annual - jaarlijks, elk jaar
answer - antwoord *n*
answer, to - antwoorden
ant - mier
antifreeze - antivries
antique dealer - antiquair
antiques - antiek *n/sg*
any - enige
apartment building - flat
apologies - excuses, verontschuldigingen
appeal - beroep *n*
apple - appel
apple juice - appelsap *n*
application form - aanvraagformulier *n*
apply, to - aanvragen
appointment - afspraak

161

approximately - ongeveer
aquatics - watersport
area - gebied *n*, streek, regio
arm - arm
armrest - armleuning
around - rond
arrange, to (a time/date) - afspreken
arrival (time) - aankomst(tijd)
arrive, to - aankomen
arrow - pijl
art - kunst
artificial (respiration) -
  kunstmatig(e ademhaling)
artist - kunstenaar
as (...) as - zo (...) als
ash - as
ash tray - asbak, asbakje *n*
ask, to - vragen
at - te, in
at night - 's avonds
at once - dadelijk
at the bottom of - onderin
attic - zolder
attract, to - aantrekken
audience - publiek *n*
authorization - machtiging
automatic - automatisch
autumn - herfst, najaar *n*
aviation - luchtvaart
award - prijs
awful - erg
awkward - lastig
axle - as
baby - baby
baby food - babyvoeding
baby-sitter - oppas
bachelor - vrijgezel
back (body) - rug
back (building, sheet) - achterkant
back (chair) - rugleuning
backwards - achteruit, terug
bacon - (ontbijt)spek *n*
bad - slecht

bad (food) - bedorven
bad luck - pech
bag - zak
baked beans - witte bonen in tomatensaus
bakery - bakker
balcony - balkon *n*
ball - bal
ball(point) pen - balpen
band - band
bandage, to - verbinden
bandage - verband(gaas) *n*
bank (fin.) - bank
bank (river) - oever, waterkant
bank notes - papiergeld *n/sg*, bankbiljetten
banknote - bankbiljet *n*, (pop.) briefje *n*
bannisters - leuning *sg*
barriers - spoorbomen
basement - kelder
basket - mand
bath (tub) - bad(kuip)
bath foam - badschuim *n*
bath room - badkamer
bath towel - badhanddoek
bathing trunks - zwembroek
battery (car) - accu
battery - batterij
bay - baai, inham
beach - strand *n*
beard - baard
beautiful - mooi
because - omdat, doordat
because of - door
bed and breakfast - logies en ontbijt
bed - bed *n*
bee - bij
beef - rundvlees *n*
beer - bier *n*
before - voor(dat)
begin, to - beginnen
behind - achter
Belgian (person) - Belg *m*, Belgische *f*
Belgian - Belgisch
Belgium - België *n*

bell - bel
belt - gordel, riem
bench - bank
bend - bocht
benzine - wasbenzine
berth - couchette
best before ... - houdbaar tot ..., uiterste verkoopdatum
best - best(e)
best wishes from ... - groeten uit ...
better (... than) - beter (... dan)
between - tussen
beyond - voorbij, achter
bicarbonate of soda - zuiveringszout *n*
bicycle - fiets, rijwiel *n*
bicycle repair man - fietsenmaker
bicycle route - fietsroute
bicycle tour - fietstocht
bicycle track - fietspad *n*
bile - gal
bill - nota
bird - vogel
birthday - verjaardag
birthday, today's my - ik ben vandaag jarig
biscuit - koekje *n*
bite - beet
bite, I've got a - (ik heb) beet!
bite, to - bijten
bitter - bitter
black ice - gladheid
black - zwart
blackboard - schoolbord *n*
blame, to - kwalijk nemen
bland - flauw
blanket - deken
blind (shade) - zonnescherm *n*
blind (adj.) - blind
blister - blaar
block(age) - verstopping
blocked - afgesloten, verstopt
blood - bloed *n*
blue - blauw
blunt - bot

blush, to - kleuren, blozen
board - plank
boat - boot, schip *n*
body - lichaam *n*
boil - steenpuist
boiled - gekookt
bone - bot *n*
bonnet - motorkap
book - boek *n*
book, to - bespreken, reserveren, boeken
booked - gereserveerd
bookshop - boekhandel, boek(en)winkel
boot (car) - bagageruimte
boot (shoe) - laars
border - grens
born - geboren
borrow, to - lenen van
both - beide(n)
bother, to - lastig vallen
bottle - fles
bottom - onderkant, bodem
boulder - rotsblok *n*
bowels - ingewanden
box - doos
boy - jongen
bracelet - armband
brake - rem
branch - tak
brass - (rood)koper *n*
bread - brood *n*
breadth - breedte
break - pauze
break, to - breken
breakdown - panne, pech
breakdown truck - sleepwagen
breakdown van - kraanwagen
breakfast - ontbijt *n*
breast - borst
breath - adem
breath, short of - benauwd
breathlessness - ademnood
bridge - brug
bridgemaster - brugwachter

163

bright - licht
bring, to - brengen
broken - gebroken
broken down - kapot
brother - broer
brother-in-law - zwager, (Flemish:) schoonbroer
brown - bruin
bruise - blauwe plek
brush - borstel
bucket - emmer
buckle - gesp
bud - knop
build, to - bouwen
building - gebouw n
bulb - (bloem)bol
bumper - bumper
burden - last
burn - brandwond
burn, to - verbranden
burnt - aangebrand
bus - (auto)bus
bus station - busstation n
bus stop - bushalte
bush - struik
busy, to be - het druk hebben
but I am/it is! - wèl
butcher - slager
butcher's - slagerij
butter - boter
butter, to - smeren
buttermilk - karnemelk
button - knoop
buy, to - kopen
buyer - koper
by - per, door
byroad - binnenweggetje n
cabbage - kool
cabin - hut
cable (telegram) - telegram
cable (rope) - kabel
cake - cake, koek, taart
calf - kuit

call, to (phone) - opbellen
call, to (yell) - roepen
camera - camera, fototoestel n
camp - kamp n
camp site shop - campingwinkel
camp, to - kamperen
campfire - kampvuur n
camping equipment - kampeeruitrusting
camping license - kampeervergunning
camping permit - kampkaart
camping site - kampeerterrein n, camping
can, to - kunnen
cancel, to - afzeggen, annuleren
candle - kaars
canoe - kano
can opener - blikopener
canned vegetables - blikgroente sg
canvas - zeildoek n
caption - onderschrift n, opschrift n
car - auto, wagen
car park (indoors) - parkeergarage
car park (outdoors) - parkeerplaats
caravan - caravan
carburettor - carburateur
cardigan - vest n
cards, to play - kaarten
careful, be - (wees) voorzichtig!
carrot - wortel, peen
carry, to - dragen, brengen
carsick - wagenziek
cart - kar
carton - slof
case - kist
cash register - kassa
castle - kasteel n, slot n
casualty (wounded) - gewonde
casualty (dead) - dode, slachtoffer n
cat - kat, poes
cathedral - kathedraal, dom
cattle - vee n
cattle breeder - veehouder
cattle market - veemarkt
cave - grot

164

cemetery - begraafplaats, kerkhof *n*
centimetre - centimeter
central - centraal
central heating - centrale verwarming
centre - centrum *n*
century - eeuw
chain (jewel/lock) - ketting
chair - stoel
chambermaid - kamermeisje *n*
chamois leather - zeem, zeemleer *n*
chance - kans
change, to (transport) - overstappen
change, to (goods in a shop) - ruilen
change, to (to transform) - veranderen
change, to (to alter) - wijzigen
change, to (money) - wisselen
channel - kanaal *n*
charcoal - houtskool
charter flight - chartervlucht
chassis - chassis *n*
cheap - goedkoop
cheat, to - oplichten, bedriegen
cheat, to (school) - spieken
check - controle
check, to - nakijken, controleren
cheek - wang
cheers! - proost! op uw gezondheid!
cheese - kaas
chess, to play - schaken
chew, to - kauwen
chewing gum - kauwgom
chicken - kip
chicken (meat) - kippevlees *n*
chief - chef, hoofd *n*, baas
child - kind *n*
chilly - fris, koel
chin - kin
chippings, loose - steenslag *n*
chocolate - chocolade
chocolate (drink) - chocolademelk
chocolate bar - (chocolade)reep
choose, to - kiezen
chop, to - hakken

church - kerk
churchyard - kerkhof *n*
cigarette - sigaret
cinema - bioscoop
city - stad
city council - gemeenteraad
city hall - gemeentehuis *n*, stadhuis *n*
civil servant - ambtenaar
class - klasse
class (school) - klas
clean - schoon
clean, to - opruimen, schoonmaken
clear - helder
cliff - klip
climate - klimaat *n*
cloakroom - garderobe
clock - klok, uurwerk *n*
clock tower - klokketoren
cloister - kloostergang
close, to - sluiten, dicht doen
closed - dicht, gesloten
closet - kast
closing time - sluitingstijd
cloth (canvas) - zeil(doek) *n*
cloth (fabric) - stof
cloth (rag) - doek
cloth, piece of - lap
clothes - kleding *sg*, kleren
clothes peg - wasknijper
clothesline - waslijn
cloudy - bewolkt
clutch - koppeling
coach (bus) - touringcar, toerbus
coach (carriage) - rijtuig *n*, koets
coachwork - carrosserie
coast guard - kustwacht
coast - kust
coat - jas
cobbler - schoenmaker
cockroach - kakkerlak
coffee - koffie
coffee bar - café *n*, koffiehuis *n*
coffee bean - koffieboon

coffee pot - koffiepot
coin - munt
coin collector - muntenverzamelaar
cold, common - verkoudheid
cold cuts - vleeswaren
cold - koud
cold, to have a - verkouden zijn
collar - kraag
collection (of letters) - lichting
collision - aanrijding, botsing
colour - kleur
comb - kam
come, to - komen
compartment - coupé
compass - kompas *n*
complain, to - klagen
complaint - klacht
complaints form - klachtenformulier *n*
complete (a form), to - invullen
complete - compleet, volledig, (ge)heel
compliment - compliment *n*
compulsory - verplicht
concerning - in verband met, met
  betrekking tot, betreffend(e)
concert - concert *n*
concussion - hersenschudding
condition (qualification) - voorwaarde
condition (circumstance) - omstandigheid
conditional - voorwaardelijk
condom - condoom *n*
confectionary - snoepgoed *n*
congratulate, to - feliciteren
congregation - gemeente
connect, to - verbinden
constable - (politie)agent *m*, agente *f*
contagious - besmettelijk
continually - steeds
continuous - voortdurend
contraceptive - voorbehoedsmiddel *n*
contract - contract *n*
convent - klooster *n*
cook - kok *m*, kokkin *f*
cook, to - koken

copper - koper *n*
cork - kurk
cork oak - kurkeik
corkscrew - kurketrekker
corner - hoek
correct - juist, goed, correct
correct, that's - dat/het klopt
correspond, to (letters) - corresponderen
correspond, to (comparison) -
  overeenkomen, corresponderen
corridor - gang, hal
cost, to - kosten
cosy - gezellig
cot - kinderbedje *n*
cotton - katoen
cotton wool - watten *pl*, watje *n*
couch - bank
cough, to - hoesten
counter (office) - loket *n*
counter (shop) - toonbank
country - land *n*
country, in the - op het platteland
country house - buitenverblijf *n*, buitenhuis *n*
countryside - platteland *n*
couple - paar *n*
(a) couple of - (een) paar
court - gerecht *n*, rechtbank
court of law - rechtbank
courtyard - binnenplaats
cousin - neef *m*, nicht *f*
crab - krab
crack - barst
crack, to - barsten
cradle - wieg
crash - aanrijding
crash helmet - valhelm
cream - room
crooked - scheef
cross, to - oversteken
cross - kruis *n*
crossing - kruising, kruispunt *n*
crossing - overtocht, oversteek
cry, to - huilen

cub - welp, jong *n*
cup - kop, kopje *n*
cupboard - kast
cupcake - taartje *n*, cakeje *n*
current (water/electricity) - stroming, stroom
current (adj.) - huidig, tegenwoordig
curtain - gordijn *n*
custom - gebruik *n*
customs - douane *sg*
customs (tax) - invoerrechten
cut down, to - kappen
cut - snee
cut, to - knippen
cutlery - bestek *n*
dam - dam
damage - beschadiging, schade
damage, to - beschadigen
damaged - beschadigd
damp - vochtig
dampproof - vochtwerend
dance, to - dansen
dandruff - roos
danger - gevaar *n*
dangerous - gevaarlijk
dare, to - durven, wagen
date (appointment) - afspraak
date (between lovers) - afspraakje *n*
date - datum
date of birth - geboortedatum
daughter - dochter
day - dag
day after tomorrow, the - overmorgen
day before yesterday, the - eergisteren
dazzle, to - verblinden
dead - dood, overleden
dead-end (street) - doodlopend(e straat)
deadly - dodelijk
deaf - doof
dear .... - beste ....
debt - schuld
decanter - karaf
deck chair - strandstoel, ligstoel
decoration - versiering

decrease, to - verminderen
deep - diep
deep-freeze - diepvries
degrees - graden
dehydrated milk - melkpoeder
delay - uitstel *n*
delay (timetable) - vertraging
deliver, to - bestellen, afleveren
dentist - tandarts
dentures - kunstgebit *n/sg*
depart, to - vertrekken
department - afdeling
department store - warenhuis *n*
departure - vertrek *n*
deposit (on bottles) - statiegeld *n*
depth - diepte
descend, to - afdalen
desire, to - wensen
desk (furniture) - bureau *n*
desk (information) - balie *n*
desolate - verlaten
dessert - dessert *n*, nagerecht *n*,toetje *n*
destination - bestemming
detain, to - vasthouden
detergent - wasmiddel *n*, waspoeder *n*
detour (road works) - omleiding,
  wegomlegging
detour (alternative route) - omweg
detour, to make a - omrijden
develop, to - ontwikkelen
deviate, to - afwijken
diabetes - suikerziekte
diarrhoea - diarree
diesel oil - dieselolie
diet - dieet *n*
diet food - dieetvoeding
difference - verschil *n*
different - anders, verschillend
difficult - moeilijk
dig, to - graven
digestion - spijsvertering
dimmer - parkeerlicht *n*
dinner - avondeten *n*, diner *n*

167

direct - direct, rechtstreeks
direction - richting, kant, koers
directions - gebruiksaanwijzing *sg*
dirty - vies, vuil, smerig
disabled - gehandicapt, invalide
discharge, to (unload) - lossen
discount - korting
discover, to - ontdekken
discuss, to - bespreken
dish (part of a meal) - gerecht *n*, schotel
dish (plate) - bord *n*
dishes, to do the - afwassen
dishonest - oneerlijk
disinfect, to - ontsmetten
disinfectant - ontsmettingsmiddel *n*
dispatch, with - met spoed
dispensing chemist's - apotheek
distance - afstand
distant - ver
distinguished - voornaam
distress - benauwdheid
district - wijk
ditch - sloot
dive, to - duiken
diversion - wegomlegging
diving board - duikplank
division - indeling
divorced - gescheiden
dizzyness - duizeligheid
do one's hair, to - kappen
do, to - doen
doctor - dokter
dog - hond
doll - pop
domestic - binnenlands
domestic animals - huisdieren
done - gaar
donkey - ezel
door (building) - deur
door (car) - portier *n*
door knob - deurknop
doorman - portier
double - dubbel

double bed - tweepersoonsbed *n*
double room - tweepersoonskamer
down - beneden, onderaan
downhill - bergafwaarts
draught - tapbier *n*, bier *n* van de tap
draught - tocht
draught, there's a - het tocht
draw, to - tekenen
draw, to (a line) - trekken
draw up the bill, to - de rekening opmaken
drawback - bezwaar *n*
dress - jurk
drink, to - drinken
drink to, to - toosten op
drinking water - drinkwater *n*
drive - rit
drive, to - rijden
drive into, to - inrijden
driving license - rijbewijs
drum - trommel
dry cleaner's - stomerij
dry - droog
dry, to - drogen
duration - duur
during the daytime - overdag
dust - stof *n*
dustbin - vuilnisbak
dustman - vuilnisman
Dutch - Nederlands
Dutchman - Nederlander
Dutchwoman - Nederlandse
each - elk(e), ieder(e)
ear - oor *n*
early - vroeg
earth - aarde
earthenware - aardewerk *n*
ease, to be at - op zijn gemak zijn
east - oosten *n*
east of - ten oosten van
easy - (ge)makkelijk, licht
eat, to - (op)eten
economical - zuinig
edge - kant, rand, hoek

edible - eetbaar
egg, hard-boiled - hardgekookt ei *n*
egg, soft-boiled - zachtgekookt ei *n*
eggs, fried - gebakken ei *n*
eggs, scrambled - roerei *n*
elbow - elleboog
electric - elektrisch
electric shaver - scheerapparaat *n*
elevator - lift
embark, to - inschepen
embassy - ambassade
emergency - spoedgeval *n*
emergency brake - noodrem
emergency exit - nooduitgang
emergency number - alarmnummer *n*
emergency treatment - spoedbehandeling
employee - werknemer
employer - werkgever
empty - leeg
encounter - ontmoeting
end - eind(e) *n*
engagement - verloving
engine - motor, machine
engine trouble - motorpech
England - Engeland
English - Engels
Englishman - Engelsman
Englishwoman - Engelse
enjoy, to - genieten (van)
enlargement - vergroting
enough - genoeg
enter, to - binnenkomen
entire - (ge)heel
entirely - helemaal
entrance - toegang, ingang
entrance gate - toegangshek *n*
entrance ticket - (toegangs)kaartje *n*
envelope - envelop
environment - omgeving
equal - gelijk
equip, to - uitrusten
equipment - uitrusting
era - tijdperk *n*

escalator - roltrap
escape - vlucht, ontsnapping
establish, to - vestigen
estate agent - makelaar
even (of a number) - even
even (intensifier) - zelfs
evening - avond
every - elk(e), ieder(e)
everyone - iedereen
exact money - gepast geld *n*
excellent - uitstekend, voortreffelijk
except - behalve, uitgezonderd
exchange office - wisselkantoor *n*
exchange rate - wisselkoers
exciting - spannend, opwindend
excursion - uitstapje *n*
excuse me! - neem mij niet kwalijk!
pardon! (pop.) sorry!
exhibition - tentoonstelling
exit - uitgang
exit (road) - afrit
expect, to - verwachten
expectation - verwachting
expenses - (on)kosten
expensive - duur
expire, to - verlopen
express - per expresse
express train - sneltrein
external - uitwendig
extinguish, to (fire) - blussen
extinguish, to (cigarette) - uitdoven
eye - oog *n*
fabric - doek *n*
face - gezicht *n*
face, to - uitzien op
facing - tegenover, uitziend op
factory - fabriek
faint - flauwte
faint, to - flauwvallen
fall, to - vallen
fall - val
family - familie, gezin *n*
family name - achternaam

famous - beroemd
fancy, to - zin hebben in
far - ver
far off - in de verte
farm - boerderij
farmer - boer
fast (firmly fixed) - vast, stevig
fast (quick) - vlug
fast, to - vasten
fat - dik, vet
father - vader
faulty - defect
favourable - gunstig
fear - angst
feather - veer
feel, to - voelen
feeling - gevoel *n*
felt-tip pen - viltstift
fence - hek *n*
ferry - pont, veerboot
fetch, to - halen
fever - koorts
few - weinig
(a) few - (een) paar
fiancé(e) - verloofde
field - gebied *n*
field (profession) - vakgebied *n*
field (sports) - veld *n*
fierce - fel
file (office) - dossier *n*
file (tool) - vijl
fill, to - vullen
fill up, to - tanken
filling station - tankstation *n*
film - film, filmrolletje *n*
film camera - filmcamera
filter - filter *n*
filter coffee - filterkoffie
filter-tipped cigarette - filtersigaret
find, to - vinden
fine (penalty) - boete
fine (delicate) - fijn
finish, to - opmaken, beëindigen

finished - afgesloten, voltooid, op, over
fire (accident) - brand
fire (flames) - vuur *n*
fire alarm - brandmelder
fire brigade - brandweer
fire extinguisher - brandblusser
fire works - vuurwerk *n/sg*
firm (firm) - hard, stevig
first - eerste
first-aid kit - verbandkist
first-aid dressing - noodverband *n*
fish - vis
fish bone - graat
fisherman - visser
fitting room - paskamer
fix, to - vastmaken
fixed - afgesproken, vast(gesteld)
fixed (firm) - vast
flag - vlag
flame - vlam
Flanders - Vlaanderen
flask - veldfles
flat - plat, vlak
flea - vlo
flea market - vlooienmarkt
Fleming - Vlaming *m*, Vlaamse *f*
Flemish - Vlaams
flight - vlucht
floor - grond, vloer
flour - bloem, meel *n*
flow, to - stromen, vloeien
flower - bloem
flue - griep
fly, to - vliegen
fly - vlieg
flyover - viaduct *n*
fog - mist
folk art - volkskunst
follow, to - volgen
food - eten *n*, etenswaar, voedsel *n*
food(stuffs) - levensmiddelen
foot - voet
football - voetbal

footpath - voetpad *n*
forehead - voorhoofd *n*
foreign - buitenlands
foreign country - buitenland *n*
foreigner - buitenlander *m*, buitenlandse *f*
forest - bos *n*
forest road - bosweg
forget, to - vergeten
fork (cutlery) - vork
fork (road) - wegsplitsing
fortress - vesting, fort *n*
found - gevonden
fountain - fontein
fountain pen - vulpen
fowl - gevogelte *n*
fracture - breuk
fragments - scherven
fragrant - geurig
frame (glasses) - montuur *n*
frame (metal) - frame *n*
frame (painting/picture) - lijst
frame of, within the - binnen het kader van
France - Frankrijk *n*
fraud - oplichting, fraude
free (no charge) - gratis
free - vrij
freedom - vrijheid
freezer - diepvriezer
French - Frans
Frenchman - Fransman
Frenchwoman - Française
fresh - fris, vers
freshwater - zoetwater
fried - gebakken
friend - vriend *m*, vriendin *f*
friendly - aardig, vriendelijk, vriendschappelijk
from - van, uit
front - voorkant
front (house) - gevel
front, in - vooraan
frost - vorst
frozen food - diepvriesmaaltijd

fruit - fruit *n*, vruchten *pl*
fruit juice - vruchtesap *n*
fruit stand - fruitstalletje *n*
fry, to - bakken
full of - vol (met)
fun - plezier
further - verder
fuse - stop, zekering
gain weight, to - aankomen
gait - gang
game (match) - wedstrijd, spel(letje) *n*
game (animals) - wild *n*
garage - garage
garden - tuin
garlic - knoflook
gas - gas *n*
gas cylinder - gasfles
gate(way) - poort
gear - versnelling
general - algemeen
general practitioner - huisarts
gentleman - heer
German - Duits
German - Duitser *m*, Duitse *f*
Germany - Duitsland *n*
get, to - krijgen, worden
get in/on, to - instappen
get lost, to - verdwalen
gift - geschenk *n*, cadeau *n*
gig - concert *n*
girl - meisje *n*
give, to - geven
give someone's regards to someone, to - de groeten doen aan
give up, to - opgeven
gladly - graag
glance - blik
glass - glas *n*
glasses - bril *sg*
glazed frost - ijzel
glue - lijm
glue, to - lijmen
go, to - gaan

go away! get lost! - ga weg!
go flat, to - leeglopen
go out, to - uitgaan
goat - geit
gold (noun) - goud n
gold (adj.) - gouden, van goud
gold-plated - verguld
gone - weg
good - goed
good night! - welterusten!
goodbye! - dag!
goose - gans
gorge - kloof
gradually - langzamerhand
granddaughter - kleindochter
grandson - kleinzoon
grass - gras n
gratitude - dank
graze - schaafwond
grease - vet n
grease, to - smeren
greasy - vet
Great Britain - Groot-Brittannië n
green - groen
greengrocer - groentehandelaar
greeting - groet
grey - grijs
grill, to - roosteren, grillen
grilled - geroosterd, gegrild
grocer - kruidenier
groceries - kruidenierswaren
ground floor - begane grond
ground floor, on the - gelijkvloers
ground sheet - grondzeil n
grounds - veld n/sg
group - groep
guarantee, certificate of - garantiebewijs n
guarantee - garantie
guard - bewaker, wacht
guarded - bewaakt
guest - gast
guesthouse - pension n
guide (book/person) - gids

guilty - schuldig
guy rope - scheerlijn
habit - gewoonte
hail - hagel
hair - haar n
hairdresser - kapper
hairpin bend - haarspeldbocht
hair spray - haarlak
half (adj.) - half
half (noun) - helft
hall (corridor) - hal
hall - zaal
hallo! - dag!
ham - ham
hammer - hamer
hand - hand
hand over, to - overhandigen
handbag - handtasje n
handbrake - handrem
handiwork - handwerk n
handkerchief - zakdoek
handlebars - stuur n/sg
hangover - kater
happiness - blijdschap
happy - blij
harbour - haven
hard of hearing - slechthorend
hardly - nauwelijks
haricot beans - witte bonen
harvest - oogst
hat - hoed
have, to - hebben
have to, to - moeten
have lost, to - kwijt zijn
head - hoofd n
head (animal) - kop
health - gezondheid
healthy - gezond
hear, to - horen
hear, to (understand) - verstaan
hearing - gehoor n
hearing aid - gehoorapparaat n
heart - hart n

heart patient - hartpatiënt
heartburn - maagzuur *n*
heat - warmte
heat (dense) - hitte
heating - verwarming
heaven - hemel
heavy - zwaar
heel (shoe) - hak
height - hoogte
helm - stuur *n*
help - hulp
helping - portie
herbs - kruiden
here - hier
here you are - alstublieft
hidden - verstopt
high - hoog
high tide - vloed, hoog water *n*
highchair - kinderstoel
hiking hut - trekkershut
hill - heuvel
hip - heup
hire, to - huren
hitchhike, to - liften
hitchhiker - lifter
hobby - liefhebberij, hobby
hold, to - (vast)houden
hole - gat *n*
holiday - feestdag, vrije dag
holidays - vakantie *sg*
home - thuis
homecoming - thuiskomst
homework - huiswerk *n*
honest - eerlijk
hook - haak
horns - horens
horse - paard *n*
horse power - paardekracht, p.k.
hose - slang
hospitable - gastvrij
hospital - ziekenhuis *n*
host - gastheer
hostess - gastvrouw

hot - heet
hot air balloon - (hete)luchtballon
hour - uur *n*
house - huis *n*
houseboat - woonboot
household appliances - huishoudelijke artikelen
housekeeping - huishouding
housewife - huisvrouw
how - hoe
how long - hoe lang
how much/many - hoeveel
hungry, to be - honger hebben
hunt(ing) - jacht
hurry - haast
hurry up, to - voortmaken, zich haasten
hurt, to - zeer/pijn doen
husband - man, echtgenoot
hypodermic needle - injectienaald
ice - ijs *n*
ice cream - ijsje *n*
ice cubes - ijsblokjes
ideal - ideaal
identification - identificatie
identification card - legitimatiebewijs *n*
identity card - identiteitsbewijs *n*
if - als, indien
ignition - ontsteking
ill - ziek
illness - ziekte
illuminate, to - verlichten
image - voorstelling, beeld *n*
imitation (modifier) - imitatie-, namaak-
imitation (noun) - imitatie, namaak
immediately - direct, onmiddellijk
impassable - onberijdbaar
impeccable - foutloos
implement, to - invoeren, uitvoeren
impolite - onbeleefd
import duty - invoerrechten *pl*
import, to - invoeren, importeren
important - belangrijk
impossible - onmogelijk

included - inbegrepen
increasingly - steeds meer
indeed - inderdaad
indicate, to - aanwijzen
indicator - knipperlicht *n*
indigenous - inheems
infection - infectie, besmetting
infectious - besmettelijk
inflammation - ontsteking
inflate, to - oppompen
inform, to - informeren, mededelen
information - informatie, inlichtingen *pl*
information office - informatiebureau *n*
informed - op de hoogte
injured - gewond
injury - verwonding, wond
ink - inkt
innocent - onschuldig
inoculate, to - inenten
inquire about, to - informeren naar
insect - insekt *n*
insect bite - insektebeet
inside - binnen
insist, to - staan op
insufficient - onvoldoende
insurance company -
    verzekeringsmaatschappij
insurance policy - verzekeringspolis
insurance - verzekering
insure, to - verzekeren
intend to, to - van plan zijn
intention - bedoeling
intercity - interlokaal
interesting - interessant
internal - inwendig
international - internationaal
interpreter - tolk
interrupt, to - onderbreken, storen
intestinal infection - darminfectie
intestine - darm
introduce, to - voorstellen
iodine - jodium
iron (metal) - ijzer *n*

iron (adj.) - ijzeren, van ijzer
iron (appliance) - strijkijzer *n*
iron, to - strijken
iron wire - ijzerdraad *n*
ironing board - strijkplank
island - eiland *n*
itch - jeuk
itch, to - jeuken
jack - krik
jacket - jasje *n*, colbert *n*
jam - jam
jar - pot
jaw - kaak
jellyfish - kwal
jetty - pier, havenhoofd *n*
jewel - juweel *n*, sieraad *n*
jewellery - juwelier
job - werk *n*, baan
journey - reis, tocht
judge - rechter
jug - kan
juice - sap *n*
jump, to - springen
just - net
justice - recht *n*
keep, to - houden
key - sleutel
key hole - sleutelgat *n*
kick - trap, schop
kidney beans - bruine bonen
kind (type) - soort *n*
kind - aardig, vriendelijk
king - koning
kiss - kus, zoen
kiss, to - kussen, zoenen
kitchen - keuken
knee - knie
kneecap - knieschijf
knickers - onderbroek
knife - mes *n*
knock, to - kloppen
knot - knoop
know, to - weten

knowledge - kennis
lace - kant
ladies - dames
ladies' (toilet) - damestoilet *n*
lake - meer *n*
lamb (animal) - lam *n*, lammetje *n*
lamb (meat) - lamsvlees *n*
lame - mank, kreupel
lamp - lamp
land - land *n*
land, to - landen
landing - landing
landscape - landschap *n*
lane - rijbaan
language - taal
large - groot
last - laatste
last, to - duren
last week - verleden/vorige week
late - laat
laugh, to - lachen
launder, to - wassen
laundry room - wasruimte
laundry - wasgoed *n*
lawn - grasveld *n*
lawyer - advocaat
layer - laag
lazy - lui
leaf - blad *n*
leak - lek *n*
lean - mager
lean on/against, to - leunen op/tegen
learn, to - leren
leasing company - verhuurbedrijf *n*
leather - leer *n*, leder *n*
leathery - taai
leave, to - verlaten, weggaan
left luggage office - bagagedepot *n*
left, to the - linksaf, naar links
leg - been *n*
leg (animal) - poot
lemon - citroen
lend (to), to - (uit)lenen (aan)

length - lengte
lengthy - langdurig
lens - lens
Lent - vastentijd
less - minder
less than - minder dan
let, to - verhuren
let - verhuurd
lethal - giftig, dodelijk
let's get moving! - vooruit! kom op!
letter - brief
letter box - brievenbus
lettuce - sla
level - vlak
level crossing - spoorwegovergang
lick, to - likken
lie (on sth.), to - liggen (op)
lie, to (to tell lies) - liegen
life - leven *n*
life jacket - reddingsvest *n*, zwemvest *n*
lifeboat - reddingsboot
lift - lift
lift, to - optillen
light (adj.) - licht
light (noun) - licht *n*
lighter - aansteker
lights - verlichting *sg*
like, to - houden van, leuk vinden
line - lijn, streep
linen - linnen *n*, linnengoed *n*
lip - lip
lipstick - lippenstift
liquid - vloeistof
listen, to - luisteren
litre - liter
little - weinig
little (bit), a - een beetje
live - levend
live, to (to be alive/live a life) - leven
live, to (to dwell) - wonen
living - levend
lobster - (zee)kreeft
local - plaatselijk

local dish - streekgerecht *n*
local wine - streekwijn
lock - slot *n*
lock (gate) - sluis
locker - bagagekluis
long - lang
long live ... - (lang) leve ...
look after, to - zorgen voor
look - blik
look, to - kijken
look for, to - zoeken (naar)
loose (garment) - wijd
lose, to - kwijtraken, verliezen
loss - verlies *n*
lost - verloren
loud - hard, luid
louse - luis
love - liefde
love, to - houden van
love, to make - vrijen
lovely - heerlijk
low - laag
low-salt - zoutarm
lower, to - strijken
lubricant - smeermiddel *n*
luggage - bagage
luggage rack - bagagerek *n*
lump - klontje *n*
lunch - lunch, middageten *n*
lung - long
madam - mevrouw
magazine - tijdschrift *n*, blad *n*
magnet - magneet
main road - hoofdweg
main street - hoofdstraat
make, to - maken
male nurse - broeder, verpleger
man (male person) - man
man (human being) - mens
management - management *n*, leiding
manager - manager, directeur
manual - handleiding
many - veel

map (general) - kaart
map (country/region) - landkaart
map (city) - plattegrond
marble - marmer *n*
marbles - knikkers
marine/sea fish - zeevis
marriage - huwelijk *n*
married (to) - getrouwd/gehuwd (met)
massif - massief *n*
mast - mast
match - lucifer
match (sports) - wedstrijd
matchbox - luciferdoosje *n*
maternity ward - kraamkliniek
mattress - matras *n*
maximum speed - maximumsnelheid
maybe - misschien
mayor - burgemeester
mean, to (intention) - bedoelen
mean, to (meaning) - betekenen
meaningless - zinloos
meat - vlees *n*
mechanic - monteur
medical insurance -
    ziektekostenverzekering
medicine - geneesmiddel *n*, medicijn *n*
meet, to - kennismaken, ontmoeten
meet, to (request/requirement) -
    tegemoetkomen, voldoen
melon - meloen
mend, to - herstellen, maken, repareren
message - boodschap, bericht *n*
methylated spirits - spiritus
middle - midden *n*
midnight - middernacht
milk - melk
mill - molen
minced meat - gehakt *n*
mirror - spiegel
mislaid, to be - zoekraken
miss - (modern) mevrouw, (old-fashioned)
    mejuffrouw
missing, to be - ontbreken

mistake - fout, vergissing
mistaken, to be - zich vergissen
misunderstanding - misverstand *n*
mixed - gemengd
moan, to - klagen
moisture - vocht *n*
molar - kies
moment - ogenblik *n*, moment *n*
monarch - vorst *m*, vorstin *f*
monastery - klooster *n*
monastery garden - kloostertuin
money - geld *n*
monk - monnik
month - maand
moped - bromfiets, (pop.) brommer
more - meer
more than - meer dan
morning, in the - 's morgens
morning - morgen, ochtend
mosquito - mug
mother - moeder
motorbike - motor(fiets)
motorboat - motorboot
motorway - autosnelweg
mountain - berg
mountain range - bergketen, gebergte *n*
mountain scenery - berglandschap *n*
mountaineering boot - bergschoen
mouse - muis
moustache - snor
mouth - mond
mouth (animal) - bek
move, to (motion) - bewegen
move, to (things) - verplaatsen
move, to (to a new home) - verhuizen
much - veel
much, too - te veel
mud - modder
municipality - gemeente
muscle - spier
museum - museum *n*
mushroom - champignon
music - muziek

mustard - mosterd
nail (tack) - spijker
nail (body) - nagel
nailfile - nagelvijltje *n*
nail polish/varnish - nagellak
nail scissors - nagelschaartje *n*
naked - bloot, naakt
name - naam
name, Christian - voornaam
name, family - achternaam
napkin - servetje *n*
nappy - luier
narrow - nauw, smal
narrow gauge - smalspoor *n*
national anthem - volkslied *n*
National Health Service - ziekenfonds *n*
nationality - nationaliteit
natural - natuurlijk
nature - natuur
near - bij, dicht bij, in de buurt van, vlakbij
nearby - dichtbij
necessary, to be - nodig zijn
neck - hals
need, to - nodig hebben
needle - naald
needlework - handwerk *n*
negative - negatief
neighbourhood - buurt
nephew - neef
net - net *n*
Netherlands - Nederland *n*
never - nooit
new - nieuw
news - nieuws *n*
newspaper (general) - krant
newspaper (daily) - dagblad *n*, krant
newsstand - kiosk, tijdschriftenwinkel
next to - naast
next - volgend
nice (pleasant) - fijn, leuk
nice (friendly) - aardig
niece - nicht
night (before midnight) - avond

night (after midnight) - nacht
night watch(man) - nachtwaker
no .. (on signs) - verboden te .., geen ..
no camping - kampeerverbod
no overtaking - inhaalverbod
no vacancies - vol
nobody - niemand
noise - lawaai n, geluidshinder
noisy - lawaaierig
north - noorden n
north of - ten noorden van
nose - neus
note - briefje n
note (music) - noot
note, to - noteren
notepaper - briefpapier n
nothing - niets
now - nu
number (order) - nummer n
number (figure) - cijfer n
number (quantity) - aantal n
numberplate - nummerplaat, nummerbord n
nun - non
nurse - zuster, verpleegster
nut - moer
nut - noot
oars - roeiriemen
objection - bezwaar n
objection, notice of - bezwaarschrift n
octopus - inktvis
odd - oneven
of course - natuurlijk
of - van
offer, to - (aan)bieden
office - bureau n, kantoor n
office supplies - kantoorbehoeften
officer - officier
officer (police) - agent
official - officieel
often - vaak, dikwijls
oil - olie
ointment - zalf
ointment for burns - brandwondenzalf

old - oud
olive - olijf
olive oil - olijfolie
one-way traffic - eenrichtingsverkeer n
oneself - zelf
oneself, to ... - zich ...
onion - ui, (Flemish:) ajuin
only - alleen (maar), slechts
open - open, geopend
open, to - openen
ophthalmologist - oogarts
opponent - tegenstander
opposite - tegenover
or - of
oral - mondeling
orange - sinaasappel
orange juice - sinaasappelsap n
orchard - boomgaard
order - bestelling
order (army) - bevel n
order, to - bestellen, bevelen
ordinary - gewoon, normaal
origin - oorsprong, origine
original - oorspronkelijk, origineel
other - ander(e)
other side - overkant
out of order - defect, (pop.) stuk
out - uit
outside - buiten
over - over
over here - hierheen
over there - daar
overlooking - met gezicht/uitzicht op
overpopulation - overbevolking
overtake, to - inhalen
owner - eigenaar
packed lunch - lunchpakket n
packet - pak n
pain - pijn
painkiller - pijnstiller
painless - pijnloos
painstaking - nauwkeurig, nauwgezet
paint - verf

paintbrush - verfkwast
painting - schilderij *n*
palace - paleis *n*
pale (face) - bleek
pale (colour) - flets, bleek
pancake - pannekoek
panties - slipje *n/sg*
paper - papier *n*
papers - papieren, documenten
parallel to - evenwijdig aan
paralysed - verlamd
parcel - postpakket *n*
parents - ouders
park - park *n*
park, to - parkeren
parking disc - parkeerschijf
parking meter - parkeermeter
part - deel *n*
part (piece) - gedeelte *n*, stuk *n*
part (component) - onderdeel *n*
partially sighted - slechtziend
parts, spare - reserve-onderdelen
party - feest(je) *n*
party, to - feestvieren
passport - paspoort *n*
passport photo - pasfoto
past - verleden *n*
past, in the - vroeger, in het verleden
past (prep.) - voorbij
pastry - gebakje *n*, taart, taartje *n*
path - pad *n*
patience - geduld *n*
pavement - stoep, trottoir *n*
pay, to (general) - betalen
pay, to (bill) - afrekenen, betalen
pay attention, to - oppassen, opletten
peaceful - rustig
pearl - parel
pedestrian - voetganger
pedestrian crossing - zebrapad *n*, zebra
peg - klerenhanger
pencil - potlood *n*
people (general) - mensen *pl*

people (nation) - volk *n*
pepper - peper
percent - procent
performance - voorstelling
perfume - parfum *n*
period, to have one's - ongesteld zijn
permission - toestemming
permit - vergunning
person - persoon
personal - persoonlijk
pet - huisdier *n*
pet food - dierenvoedsel *n*
petrol - benzine
petrol station - benzinestation *n*, tankstation *n*
petrol tank - benzinetank
phlegm - slijm *n*
phone, to - (op)bellen
photo - foto
photocopy - fotokopie
photographer - fotograaf
phrase book - taalgids
physical - lichamelijk
physical education - gymnastiek
pie (pastry) - taart
pie (meat) - pasteitje *n*
piece - stuk *n*
piece of land - lap/stuk *n* grond
pillar - pilaar, zuil
pillow - kussen *n*
pillow case - kussensloop *n*
pimple - puist, pukkel
(safety) pin - (veiligheids)speld
pipe - pijp
pipe tobacco - pijptabak
pit - kuil
pitcher - kruik
pity, it's a - het is jammer
place - plaats
plain - vlakte
plan - plan *n*
plane - vliegtuig *n*
plant - plant

plastic - plastic
plate - bord *n*
platform (railway station) - perron *n*
play, to - spelen
playground - speelplaats
playing card - (speel)kaart
pleasant - aangenaam
please - alstublieft
pleased to meet you! - aangenaam!
pleasure - genoegen *n*
plug (elec.) - stekker
plug (bath) - stop
PO box - postbus
pocket - zak
pocketknife - zakmes *n*
poem (lit.) - gedicht *n*
poem (rhyme) - versje *n*, gedichtje *n*
point, to - wijzen
poison - gif *n*
poisoning - vergiftiging
pole - paal, stok
police - politie
police station - politiebureau *n*
policemen/policewoman - agent(e)
policy - polis
polish, to - poetsen
poor (bad) - zwak
poor (not rich) - arm
population - bevolking
pork - varkensvlees *n*
port - haven
possible - mogelijk
post - post
postage - port(o) *n*
postbox - brievenbus
postcard - briefkaart
postcard, picture - ansichtkaart
poster - aanplakbiljet *n*, affiche *n*
postman - postbode
postmark, to - stempelen
post office - postkantoor *n*
pot - pan
potatoes - aardappels

poultry - gevogelte *n*
pour, to - inschenken
powder - poeder *n*
powder (ammunition) - kruit *n*
power - kracht, sterkte
practical - handig
pram - kinderwagen
precise - precies, nauwkeurig
prefer, to - de voorkeur geven aan
pregnancy - zwangerschap
pregnant - in verwachting, zwanger
prescription (med.) - recept *n*
present - cadeau *n*, geschenk *n*
presentation - demonstratie, presentatie
press, to - drukken
pressure - druk
price - prijs
price list - prijslijst
price tag - prijskaartje *n*
print (photo) - afdruk
print - plaat
print, to - (af)drukken
proceed, to - verdergaan, doorgaan
process, to (photos) - ontwikkelen
profession - beroep *n*
prohibition - verbod *n*
prominent - vooraanstaand
promise - belofte
promise, to - beloven
pronounce, to - uitspreken
pronunciation - uitspraak
proof - bewijs *n*
property - eigendom *n*
proposal - voorstel *n*
propose, to - voorstellen
protest march - demonstratie, protestmars
Protestant - protestant
protruding - uitstekend
pudding (dessert, made of milk) - pudding
pull, to - trekken
pump - pomp
punctured tyre - lekke band
pure - zuiver, puur

purgative - laxeermiddel *n*
purpose - doel *n*
purse - portemonnee
put down, to - (vert.) neerleggen, (hor.) neerzetten
pyjamas - pyjama *sg*
quality - kwaliteit
quarrel - ruzie
quarter - kwart *n*
quarter (time) - kwartier *n*
quay - kade
queen - koningin
question - vraag
quick - snel, vlug
quiet - stil
quiet please! - stilte!
rabies - hondsdolheid
rail(way) - spoorweg, spoorlijn
railway ticket - treinkaartje *n*
rain - regen
raincoat - regenjas
rampart - wal
rare - zeldzaam
rat - rat
rate - tarief *n*
rather - nogal, tamelijk, vrij
raw - rauw
raw vegetables - rauwkost *sg*
razor blade - scheermesje *n*
read, to - lezen
ready - klaar
ready-to-wear - confectiekleding
real - echt
rear - achterkant, achterzijde
reason - reden, grond
receipt - bewijsje *n*, kwitantie
receive, to - ontvangen, krijgen
recently - laatst, onlangs
recipe - recept *n*
recommend, to - aanbevelen
record - plaat
recover, to - beter worden, herstellen
recovered - genezen, hersteld, weer beter

red - rood
Red Cross post - Rode Kruis-post
reel - klosje *n*, spoel
refrigerated - gekoeld
refrigerator - koelkast
refugee - vluchteling
refund - vergoeding
refuse, to - weigeren
regional dish - streekgerecht *n*
regional wine - streekwijn
register - register *n*
register, to - inschrijven, registreren
registered - aangetekend
related to, to be - familie zijn van
relation - verband *n*
release, to - losmaken, loslaten
release, to (book/record) - uitbrengen
reliable - betrouwbaar
relief - verlichting, opluchting
relieve, to - verlichten
remote - achteraf gelegen
rent - huur
rent, to - huren
rented car - huurauto
repair - reparatie
repeat, to - herhalen
repetition - herhaling
replace, to - vervangen
report (legal) - proces-verbaal *n*
represent, to (picture) - voorstellen
represent, to (firm/person) - vertegenwoordigen
request, to - verzoeken, vragen
request - verzoek *n*
require, to - nodig hebben, vereisen
research - onderzoek *n*
residence - verblijfplaats
residence permit - verblijfsvergunning
responsible - verantwoordelijk
rest, to - (uit)rusten
result - gevolg *n*, resultaat *n*
result (game/examination) - uitslag
reticent - gereserveerd

retired - gepensioneerd
return (trip) - terugkeer, terugreis
return ticket - retourtje *n*
rib - rib
ribbon - lint *n*
rice - rijst
rich (food) - vet
rich (wealthy) - rijk
ride - rit
ride, to - rijden
ride, to (bicycle) - fietsen
ride, to (horse) - paardrijden
ride, to give a - lift geven
right, to the - rechtsaf, rechts
right, to be - gelijk hebben
right of way - voorrang
right of way, to give - voorrang verlenen
right-hand - rechts
ring - ring
ring road - rondweg
ring, to - bellen
ripe - rijp
rise, to (in the morning) - opstaan
rise, to (level) - stijgen
risk - risico *n*
risky - riskant
river - rivier
road - weg
roadblock - (weg)versperring
road map - wegenkaart
road sign - verkeersbord *n*
road surface - wegdek *n*
road works - opgebroken rijweg, werk in
  uitvoering
roast, to - braden
roasted - gebraden
rock - rots
rocky - rotsachtig
roll, filled - belegd broodje *n*
Roman Catholic - rooms-katholiek
roof rack - imperiaal
room - kamer, vertrek *n*
root - wortel

rope - lijn, touw *n*
rose - roos
rotten - rot
rough (surface) - ruw
rough (behaviour) - hardhandig, ruw
round - rond
routine - routine
row, to - roeien
rowing boat - roeiboot
rub, to - wrijven
rubber band - elastiekje *n*
rucksack - rugzak
rudder - roer *n*
run, to (operate) - lopen, werken,
  functioneren
running water - stromend water *n*
rural - landelijk
rust - roest
rust, to - roesten
saddle - zadel *n*
safe - veilig
safety - veiligheid
safety belt - veiligheidsgordel
safety pin - veiligheidsspeld
sail - zeil *n*
sail, to (general) - varen
sailing, to go - (gaan) zeilen
sailing - afvaart, vertrek *n*
sailing (sport) - zeilsport, zeilen *n*
salad - salade
salary - salaris *n*
sale - opruiming, uitverkoop
sale, for - te koop
salesman - verkoper
salt - zout *n*
salt-free - zoutloos
saltpan - zoutpan
same, the - hetzelfde
sand - zand *n*
sandwich - boterham
sanitary towel - maandverband *n*
satisfaction - genoegdoening
satisfied with - tevreden met

sauce - saus
sausage - worst
save, to - redden
savoury - hartig
say, to - zeggen
say goodbye, to - afscheid nemen
scarf - sjaal
school - school
scissors - schaar *sg*
scoop - schep, schop
screw - schroef
screw, to - schroeven
screwdriver - schroevedraaier
sea - zee
seasick - zeeziek
season - seizoen *n*
seat - (zit)plaats
seawater - zeewater *n*
second-hand - tweedehands
securely - zeker
security - bewaking
see, to - zien
see a person, to - iemand spreken/
bezoeken
see you later! - tot straks!
seed - zaad *n*
seldom - zelden
sell, to - verkopen
send, to - (ver)zenden
sender - afzender
sense (point) - zin
senses (faculties) - zintuigen
sensitive - gevoelig
sentence - zin
separate - gescheiden, afzonderlijk
serious - zwaar, ernstig
serve, to - bedienen
serve, to (a meal) - serveren, opdienen
service (church) - kerkdienst
service included - bediening inbegrepen
sew, to - naaien
sewer - rioolbuis
shack - hut

shadow - schaduw
shallow - ondiep
shape - vorm
shark - haai
sharp - scherp
shave, to - scheren
sheep - schaap *n*
sheet (paper) - blad *n*, vel *n*
sheet (bed) - laken *n*
shelf - plank
shell - schelp
ship - schip *n*
shipping - scheepvaart
shipping company - rederij
shirt - (over)hemd *n*
shirt (sport) - shirt *n*
shoe - schoen
shoehorn - schoenlepel
shoelace - schoenveter
shoe polish - schoensmeer
shoeshine boy - schoenpoetser
shop - winkel
shop, to - boodschappen doen, winkelen
shopping, to go -gaan winkelen
shopping centre - winkelcentrum *n*
shop window - etalage
short - kort
short circuit - kortsluiting
shorts - korte broek
shoulder - schouder
show, to - tonen, laten zien
shower - douche
sick, to be - misselijk zijn
side - zijde, kant
side street - zijstraat
sideways - zijdelings
sieve - zeef
sights - bezienswaardigheden
sign - bord, bordje *n*
sign - teken *n*
sign, to - (onder)tekenen
signature - handtekening
significant - zinvol

VOCABULARY

signpost - wegwijzer
silk - zijde
silver - zilver *n*
similar - zelfde
simple - eenvoudig
simultaneously - tegelijkertijd
since - vanaf, sinds
single (ticket) - enkele reis
single (alone) - alleen
single (not married) - ongehuwd
single room - eenpersoonskamer
sister - zuster
sit, to - zitten
situated, to be - liggen, zich bevinden
size - formaat *n*, grootte
size (clothes) - maat
skid, to - slippen
skilful - handig
skin - huid
skirt - rok
sky - lucht
slab - plaat
slack - slap
slaughter, to - slachten
sleep - slaap
sleeper - slaapwagen
sleeping bag - slaapzak
sleep well! - welterusten!
sleeve - mouw
slice (thick) - plak
slice (thin) - plakje *n*, sneetje *n*
slide - dia
slide projector - diaprojector
slightly - wat, enigszins, een beetje
slim (negative) - mager
slim (positive) - slank
slippery - glad
slope - helling
slow - langzaam
slow, to be - achterlopen
slow train - stoptrein
small - klein, gering
small change - kleingeld *n*

smell - geur, reuk
smell (unpleasant) - stank
smell, to (with the nose) - ruiken
smell, to (flower/perfume) - geuren, ruiken
smell, to (unpleasantly) - stinken
smoke, to - roken
smoked - gerookt
smoking compartment - rookcoupé
smooth - glad
snail - slak
snake - slang
sneeze, to - niezen
snorkel - snorkel
snow - sneeuw
so - zo
soap - zeep
soccer - voetbal *n*
soccer/football stadium - voetbalstadion *n*
sock - sok
socket - stopcontact *n*
soda water - sodawater *n*, spuitwater *n*
soft - zacht
soft drink - frisdrank
soil - bodem, grond
sole (only) - enige
sole (shoe) - zool
solid - massief
some - enige, sommige, enkele
someone - iemand
someone else - iemand anders
something - iets
somewhere - ergens
somewhere else - ergens anders
son - zoon
soon - gauw, spoedig, straks, dadelijk
sore muscles - spierpijn *sg*
sore throat - keelpijn
sorry, to be - spijten
sound - geluid *n*
sound (healthy) - gezond
soup - soep
south - zuiden *n*
south of - ten zuiden van

souvenir (tourism) - souvenir *n*
souvenir (memory) - herinnering, aandenken *n*
spare parts - reserve-onderdelen
spare tyre - reservewiel *n*
spark - vonk
special - bijzonder, speciaal
special offer - aanbieding
specialist - specialist
speed - snelheid
spell, to - spellen
spider - spin
spit, to - spuwen, (pop.) spugen
splendid - prachtig, schitterend
splinter - splinter
sponge - spons
spoon - lepel
spoonful - schep, lepel
sports - sport *sg*
sports field - sportterrein *n*, sportveld *n*
spray, to - sproeien
spring (season) - lente, voorjaar *n*
spring (device) - veer
springboard - springplank
square (open area) - plein *n*
square (geom.) - vierkant *n*
squid - inktvis
stable - stal
stage - toneel *n*
stain - vlek
stain remover - vlekkenmiddel *n*
stairs, flight of - trap
stamp (post) - postzegel
stamp (pad) - stempel(kussen) *n*
stamp, to - frankeren
stand (market) - kraampje *n*, stalletje *n*
stand (stadium) - tribune
stand, to - staan
start - begin *n*
start, to - starten
station - station *n*
statue - standbeeld *n*
stay, to (position/condition) - blijven

stay, to (as a guest) - logeren, overnachten
steady, to go - verkering hebben
steel - staal *n*
steep - steil
steering wheel - stuur *n*
stem, to - stelpen
stick - stok
stick, to - plakken
sticking plaster - pleister
stiff - stijf
still - nog (steeds)
stockings - kousen
stomach - buik
stomachache - maagpijn, buikpijn
stone - steen
stop, to - stoppen, ophouden (met)
stop, to (someone) - tegenhouden
stop! - stop!
stopover - oponthoud *n*
store, to - stallen
storm - storm
storm lantern - stormlamp
stove - kachel
straight on - rechtdoor, rechtuit
straight - recht
strange - vreemd
stranger - vreemdeling
street - straat
streetlamp - straatlantaarn
string - snoer *n*
striped - gestreept
strong - sterk
student - student *m*, studente *f*
studies - studie *sg*
study, to - studeren
stuffed - gevuld
stuffy - benauwd
subtitles - ondertitels
suddenly - ineens, plotseling
suffering from, to be - last hebben van, lijden aan
sugar - suiker
sugar bowl - suikerpot

suit - kostuum *n*, (pop.) pak *n*
suitcase - koffer
summer (time) - zomer
summer holidays - zomervakantie
summer time (daylight saving time) -
  zomertijd
summit - top
sun - zon
sunbathe, to - zonnebaden, zonnen
sunburn - zonnebrand
sunglasses - zonnebril
sunshade - parasol
sunstroke - zonnesteek
suntan lotion/cream - zonnebrandcrème
suntan oil - zonnebrandolie
superficial - vluchtig, oppervlakkig
supermarket - supermarkt
supper - avondeten *n*
suppose, to - aannemen, veronderstellen
surcharge - toeslag
sure - zeker
sure?, are you - weet u het zeker?
surgery hours - spreekuur *n/sg*
surgery - spreekkamer
surname - achternaam
surprise - verbazing, verrassing
surprised - verbaasd, verrast
surrender, to - overgeven
suspense - spanning
swamp - moeras *n*
sway, to - slingeren
sweat - zweet *n*
sweater - trui
sweep, to - vegen
sweet (dear) - lief
sweet (taste) - zoet
sweet-and-sour - zoetzuur
sweetener - zoetjes *pl*
sweets - snoepjes
swerve, to - uitwijken
swim, to - zwemmen
swimming pool - zwembad *n*
swimsuit - badpak *n*

switch - knop, schakelaar
switch, to - schakelen
switch on, to (light/tv) - aandoen, aanzetten
table - tafel
table cloth - tafelkleed(je) *n*
tablet - pil, tabletje *n*
tailback - file
take, to (to ...) - (weg)brengen (naar ...)
take, to (action) - nemen
take, to (medicine) - innemen
take a bath, to - een bad nemen
take a seat, to - plaatsnemen
take care of, to - oppassen, zorgen voor
tall (person) - lang
tall (thing) - hoog
tame - tam
tampon - tampon
tank - tank
tanned - bruin
tap - kraan
taste, to (active) - proeven
taste, to (passive) - smaken
tasty - lekker
taut - strak
taxi rank - taxistandplaats
teach, to - leren, onderwijzen
teacher - leraar, onderwijzer, docent
tear - scheur
tear, to - scheuren
teaspoon - lepeltje *n*
telephone - telefoon
telephone, to - telefoneren, bellen
telephone booth/box - telefooncel
telephone directory - telefoonboek *n*
telephone number - telefoonnummer *n*
television - televisie
television network - televisienet *n*
temperature - temperatuur
temple - tempel
temporary - tijdelijk
tennis, to play - tennissen
tennis court - tennisbaan
tent - tent

tent peg/pin - tentharing
tepid - lauw
terminus - eindpunt *n*
terrace (outdoor café) - terras *n*
test - proef, test
thank, to - bedanken
that - dat, die
the other way around - andersom
theatre - schouwburg, theater *n*
theatrical performance - toneelvoorstelling
theft - diefstal
therefore - daarom
thermometer - thermometer
thermos flask - thermoskan
these - deze
thick - dik
thief - dief
thin - dun
thing - ding
think, to - denken
think, to (opinion) - vinden
thirsty, to be - dorst hebben
this - deze, dit
those - die
thought - gedachte
thread - draad, garen *n*
throat - keel
through - door
thumb - duim
thunderstorm - onweer *n*
ticket (fine) - bekeuring
ticket (theater/sports/transport) - kaartje
ticket collector - conducteur
tidal wave - vloedgolf
tide - getij *n*
tidy - net(jes)
tie (relation) - band
tie (clothes) - das
tight - strak
tights - panty *sg*
tile - tegel
time - tijd
timetable (railway) - spoorboekje *n*

timetable (busses, etc.) - dienstregeling
tin (can) - blik *n*
tin opener - blikopener
tin plate - blik *n*
tinned vegetables - blikgroente
tip - fooi
tired - moe
to (destination) - voor, aan
to (distance) - tot
to (direction) - naar
toadstool - paddestoel
tobacco - tabak
tobacconist - sigarenwinkelier
today - vandaag, heden
today (at present) - tegenwoordig
today's special - dagschotel
toe - teen
together - samen
toilet - toilet *n*, w.c.
toilet paper - toiletpapier *n*
toilet-trained - zindelijk
tomato - tomaat
tomorrow - morgen
tongs - tang *sg*
tongue - tong
too (to an excessive degree) - te
too (also) - ook
tools - gereedschap *n/sg*
tooth - tand
toothache - kiespijn
tooth brush - tandenborstel
tooth paste - tandpasta
top - dop, dopje *n*
top of, on - bovenop
torch - zaklantaarn
total - geheel *n*, totaal *n*
touch - gevoel *n*
tough - taai
tour - rondrit
tow, to - slepen
towel - handdoek
tower - toren
towline - sleepkabel

town - stad, plaats
toxic - giftig
toys - speelgoed *n/sg*
trade - handel
traditional dress/costume - klederdracht
traffic - verkeer *n*
traffic jam - file, opstopping
traffic lights - stoplichten
traffic sign - verkeersbord *n*
trailer - aanhangwagen, aanhanger
train - trein
translate, to - vertalen
translation - vertaling
trap - val
travel agency - reisbureau *n*
travel around, to - (rond)trekken
travel guide - reisgids
treatment - behandeling
tree - boom
trip - reis
tripod - statief *n*
trolley (supermarket) - winkelwagentje *n*
trouble, to - lastigvallen
trousers - (lange) broek
true - waar
true, it's - het is waar
trunk (tel.) - interlokaal
truth - waarheid
try, to - proberen
try on, to - passen
tune, to - stemmen
tunnel - tunnel
turn, to - draaien
turn into, to - veranderen in
twins - tweeling *sg*
tyre - band
ugly - lelijk
ulcer - zweer
umbrella - paraplu
unattended - onbewaakt
unconscious - bewusteloos
under - onder
underground (adj.) - ondergronds

underground (metro) - metro
underpants - onderbroek *sg*
understand, to (the sense) - begrijpen
understand, to (the words) - verstaan
unfair - oneerlijk
unfavourable - ongunstig
unhappy - ongelukkig
United Kingdom - Verenigd Koninkrijk *n*
untied - los
up(stairs) - boven
uprising - opstand
urgent - dringend
use - gebruik *n*
use, to - gebruiken
valley - dal *n*
value - waarde
valve - klep
vase - vaas
veal - kalfsvlees *n*
vegetable (noun) - groente
vegetable (adj.) - plantaardig
vegetarian - vegetarisch
verdict - uitspraak
verge - berm
vermin - ongedierte *n*
vertigo - hoogtevrees
very - zeer, erg, heel
vessel - vaartuig *n*
vest - hemd *n*
view of - uitzicht *n* op
view on - zicht *n* op
village - dorp *n*
vinegar - azijn
vineyard - wijngaard
visibility - zicht *n*
visible - zichtbaar
visit - bezoek *n*
visit, to (a person/shop) - bezoeken
visit, to (sightseeing) - bezichtigen,
  bezoeken
visiting card - visitekaartje *n*
voice - stem
vomit, to - braken, (pop.) overgeven

vote, to - kiezen, stemmen
voucher - tegoedbon, voucher
vulcano - vulkaan
wait, to - wachten
waiter - ober, kelner
waiting room - wachtkamer
waitress - serveerster
wake, to - wekken
walk, to - lopen, wandelen
walk - wandeling
wall - muur
wallet - portefeuille
want, to (to wish) - willen
want, to (to require) - nodig hebben
wardrobe - klerenkast
warm - warm
warn, to - waarschuwen
warning - waarschuwing
wash, to - wassen
wash, to have a - zich wassen
washing facilities - wasruimte
washing machine - wasmachine
washing soda - soda
washstand - wastafel
wasp - wesp
waste - afval *n*
watch - horloge *n*
watch out, to - uitkijken
water - water *n*
waterfall - waterval
waterskiing - waterskiën
way (manner) - manier
way (travel) - route, weg
way through - doorgang
weak - zwak
wear, to - dragen
weather - weer *n*
weather forecast - weerbericht *n*
wedding - bruiloft
week - week
weekend - weekeinde *n*
weigh, to - wegen
weight - gewicht *n*

weights and measures - maten en gewichten
welcome - welkom *n*
welcome! - welkom!
weld, to - lassen
well (adj.) - goed
well-known - bekend
west - westen *n*
west of - ten westen van
wet - nat
what - wat
wheel - wiel *n*
wheelchair - rolstoel
when - wanneer
where - waar(heen)
which (rel. pr.) - die, wat
which (inter. pr.) - welk(e)
while, a little - even(tjes)
whipped cream - slagroom
whistle, to - fluiten
who (rel. pr.) - die
who (inter. pron.) - welk(e), wie
wholemeal bread - volkorenbrood *n*
why - waarom
wide - breed
width - breedte
wife - vrouw, echtgenote
wild - wild
wind - wind
windbreak - windscherm *n*
windbreaker - zeiljack *n*
wind force - windkracht
wind vane - windvaan
winding - bochtig
windmill - (wind)molen
window - raam *n*
wine - wijn
wine cellar - wijnkelder
wine grower - wijnboer
wine list - wijnkaart
wing - vleugel
winter - winter
wire (elec.) - kabel

VOCABULARY

189

wish - wens
wish, to - wensen
within - binnen
witness - getuige
woman - vrouw
wood - hout
wool - wol
word - woord *n*
work, to - werken
work - werk *n*
works - fabriek *sg*
world - wereld
worn out - versleten
worried - ongerust, bezorgd

worthless - waardeloos
wrist - pols
wrong - fout, verkeerd
wrong, to be - ongelijk hebben,
  zich vergissen
yacht - (zeil)jacht *n*
year - jaar *n*
yellow - geel
yoghurt - yoghurt
young - jong
youth hostel - jeugdherberg
zip - ritssluiting
zoo - dierentuin

SOME DUTCH GEOGRAPHICAL NAMES

Amerika	America
(Verenigde Staten)	(United States)
Antwerpen	Antwerp
Australië	Australia
België	Belgium
Berlijn	Berlin
Brugge	Bruges
Brussel	Brussels
Denemarken	Denmark
Duitsland	Germany
Den Haag	The Hague
('s-Gravenhage*)	
Engeland	England
Frankrijk	France
Gent	Ghent
Griekenland	Greece
Groot-Brittannië	Great Britain
Hoek van Holland	Hook of Holland
Hongarije	Hongary
Ierland	Ireland
Italië	Italy
Keulen	Cologne
Londen	London

Luik	Liège
Luxemburg	Luxembourg
Maas	River Meuse
Middellandse Zee	Mediterranean
Nederland	Netherlands
Nieuw-Zeeland	New Zealand
Noordzee	North Sea
Noorwegen	Norway
Oostenrijk	Austria
Oostzee	Baltic (Sea)
Parijs	Paris
Rijn	River Rhine
Schelde	River Scheldt
Schotland	Scotland
Spanje	Spain
Vlaanderen	Flanders
Vlissingen	Flushing
Wenen	Vienna
Zweden	Sweden

* The name 's-Gravenhage is now
  obsolete and will only be used for
  ceremonial purposes.

COMMON DUTCH ABBREVIATIONS

afd.	afdeling	department
afz.	afzender	sent by
ANWB	---	Dutch automobile association affiliated with the AA/AAA
a.s.	aanstaande	next
a.u.b.	alstublieft	please
B, BG, P	begane grond, parterre	ground floor (Am.: first floor)
betr.	betreft, betreffend	concerning
B.Fr.	Belgische franken	Belgian francs
b.g.g.	bij geen gehoor	if there's no reply
blz., pag.	blad(zijde), pagina	page
BRT	Belgische Radio en Televisie	Belgian broadcasting corporation (Dutch language)
BTW	Belasting Toegevoegde Waarde	Value Added Tax
b.v., bijv.	bijvoorbeeld	for example
b.v.	besloten vennootschap	private limited company
ct.	cent	cent, smallest Dutch coin
dhr.	de heer	Mr.
dr.	doctor	Doctor (highest academic title)
drs.	doctorandus	academic title comparable to a Master's degree
ds.	dominee	minister, vicar
d.w.z.	dat wil zeggen	id est, that is
EG	Europese Gemeenschap	European Community
EHBO	Eerste Hulp bij Ongelukken	first-aid organization
ENFB	Eerste Nederlandse Fietsersbond	(First) Dutch cyclists' association
enz.	enzovoort	etcetera
excl.	exclusief	excluding
f, fl.	(originally: florijn)	Dutch guilders
fa.	firma	company
ing.	ingenieur	engineer (having finished higher vocational education)
inz.	inzake	concerning
i.p.v.	in plaats van	instead of
ir.	ingenieur	engineer (an academic title)
jl.	jongstleden	last
k	kelder	basement
KLM	Koninklijke Luchtvaart Maatschappij	Royal Dutch Airlines
km/u	kilometer per uur	kilometre per hour
KNAC	Koninklijke Nederlandse Automobiel Club	Royal Dutch Automobile Association

m.a.w.	met andere woorden	in other words
mevr.	mevrouw	Mrs.
m.i.v.	met ingang van	effective from
mr.	meester	academic degree, Master of Law
m.u.v.	met uitzondering van	with the exception of
NBT	Nederlands Bureau voor Toerisme	Dutch tourism office
nl.	namelijk	namely
NMBS	Nationale Maatschappij der Belgische Spoorwegen	Belgian national railways
NOS	Nederlandse Omroep Stichting	Dutch Broadcasting Foundation*
NS	Nederlandse Spoorwegen	Dutch railways
n.v.	naamloze vennootschap	limited liability company
n.v.t.	niet van toepassing	not applicable
o.a., o.m.	onder andere(n), onder meer	among other things/persons
p/a	per adres	care of
s.v.p.	s'il vous plaît (French!)	please
t.a.v.	ter attentie van	for the personal attention of
t.a.v.	ten aanzien van	regarding
TCB	Touring Club van België	Belgian touring club
t/m	tot en met	up to and including
t.o.	tegenover	opposite
v.a.	vanaf	from
v. Chr.	vóór Christus	Before Christ
VN	Verenigde Naties	United Nations
VS	Verenigde Staten	United States
VTB	Vlaamse Toeristenbond	Flemisch tourist association
VVV	Vereniging voor Vreemdelingenverkeer	Dutch tourist information office
zog., zgn.	zogenaamd	so-called
z.o.z.	zie ommezijde	please turn over
2e, 2de	tweede	second

* The Netherlands doesn't have a public broadcasting organisation comparable with Britain's BBC. Licences are granted to associations that represent particular groups in society, such as the liberally-inclined *AVRO*, the leftist *VARA*, the Protestant *EO* and *NCRV*, the Roman Catholic *KRO*, or bodies with a more general philosophy such as *TROS* and *Veronica*. The general public can become members of these organisations, and the more members they have the more airtime they are allocated. There are also various local stations. News bulletins and sports reports are provided by the Dutch Broadcasting Foundation (*NOS*), which is not open to public membership. There are commercial channels both in Holland (*RTL-4*) and Belgium (*VTM*). Most people have cable TV and can receive a hatful of channels - including BBC, CNN, and Super Channel. Both Dutch TV and BRT (Belgium) are heavily dominated by American - and to some extent British and Australian - imports. Mercifully, the Dutch and the Flemish prefer subtitles to voice-overs.